Provincial Furniture Design and Construction

Simple Colonial Furniture

Wood Carving and Whittling

How to Design Period Furniture

Design for the Craftsman

You Can Whittle and Carve, With Amanda W. Hellum

Making Useful Things of Wood

Woodwork for the Beginner

Craftwork in Metal, Wood, Leather and Plastics

Heirloom Furniture

Wood Carving and Whittling Made Easy

Furniture of Pine, Poplar, and Maple

How to Make Colonial Furniture

Reproducing Antique Furniture

Wood Carving and Whittling for Everyone

Masterpiece Furniture Making

FRANKLIN H. GOTTSHALL

Provincial Furniture Design and Construction

Crown Publishers, Inc., New York

Published by Crown Publishers, Inc., One Park Avenue, New York, New York 10016, and simultaneously in Canada by General Publishing Company Limited

Manufactured in the United States of America

Library of Congress Cataloging in Publication Data
Gottshall, Franklin H.
    Provincial furniture design and construction.
    Includes index.
    1. Furniture design.   2. Furniture making.
I. Title.
TT196.G67 1983   749′.1′0287   82-14879
ISBN: 0-517-54930-1

10 9 8 7 6 5 4 3 2 1

First Edition

Contents

Acknowledgments

The author wishes to give credit to the following for material help in making this work possible:

To my son, Bruce H. Gottshall, for taking and processing all the photographs in the book except those in Chapter One, which I took myself.

To the editors and publishers of *Early American Life* magazine for permission to include the pieces shown in Chapters Four, Twelve, Fifteen, and Sixteen, previously published by them.

To Paul W. Weller, local cabinetmaker, who built the pieces of furniture shown in Chapters Five, Six, Seven, Eight, Ten, Eleven, Thirteen, Fourteen, Fifteen, Sixteen, Twenty-one, Twenty-two, Twenty-three, Twenty-four, Twenty-five and Twenty-seven, and who repaired and restored the sideboard in Chapter Nine and the chair in Chapter Twenty-eight.

To my sister, Mrs. Estella Harlacher, who inherited our grandmother's walnut chest described in Chapter Eighteen.

To former students of mine at Berry College, in Georgia, who made the table shown in Chapter Twelve, which unfortunately did not survive a dormitory fire.

Preface

The pieces of furniture shown in this book were built by provincial cabinetmakers, skilled in the technicalities of their craft but not always as sensitive to some of the finer principles of design as the more thoroughly schooled artisans. This is borne out in a number of instances by poorly designed moldings, decorative elements not always in keeping with design characteristics one usually associates with the items on which they appear, and some lack of sensitivity to better proportions. All things considered, however, and despite such shortcomings, the pieces shown and described in the following pages have enough merit to warrant the consideration devoted to making them available for reproduction or emulation.

Much of the charm found in these pieces is in their provincial character. A number of the pieces shown have achieved an age that puts them in the antique category, while the more up-to-date pieces were built in school and home workshops. One owner of the antiques included in the book lived to see other pieces he owned in two of my earlier publications, but, much as I regret to mention this, has not survived to see those included here. He stipulated anonymity as a condition for letting the collection be sketched and photographed for publication, and in order to honor his wishes I am unable to reveal his identity, or that of his heirs, much as I regret not being able to do so.

I am, however, greatly pleased to be able to give credit to a friend of long-standing, Paul W. Weller, for giving me permission to include sixteen fine pieces he built and one he repaired and owns. No longer able to continue working at his trade because of advancing years, he has disposed of his tools and home workshop equipment, but continues to take justifiable pride in the adulation of many friends and customers he has served in the course of eighty-five fruitful years.

Several other pieces described in the book are family heirlooms or were made by former students whom I taught. Small private collections of furniture, like the pieces shown and described here, are of museum quality, and I consider them worthy of presentation for purposes of emulation or exact reproduction. It is with the hope and expectation that those who have profited by following the directions in my earlier publications will find this, my latest effort, equally useful and enjoyable.

Franklin H. Gottshall

Boyertown, Pennsylvania

ONE

Glove Box

SMALL BOXES, IN MANY SHAPES AND SIZES, AND made to serve a wide variety of uses, lend themselves beautifully to various forms of ornament. Decorating a box by coloring a design with paint, or by inlaying, or by carving parts of it, as has been done on the box shown in Fig. 1, is a pleasant task.

I made this glove box quite a few years ago, and while we no longer use it to hold gloves, we still keep it in a prominent place to hold stamps and envelopes. So, just in case someone planning to make a box like the one shown in Figs. 1 and 3 wishes to use it for some other purpose, the word "gloves" can be omitted and that area left without ornament, or another name or design can be put in its place.

Several applications of floor wax, briskly rubbed to preserve and polish the surface, were all that was used as a finish, and has sufficed to keep the box in good condition.

To make the box, cut two blocks of wood 3 inches thick, 4⅞ inches wide, and 3 inches long. Carefully sandpaper both sides, top, and bottom of the blocks to make the flat surfaces needed to glue sides (B), bottom (C), and top (D) to them, as shown in Fig. 4. Fig. 6 shows sides and ends after they have been glued together, while Figs. 7 and 8 show the setups for doing it.

Cut ¼-inch-deep recesses on both sides of blocks

FIG. 1

1

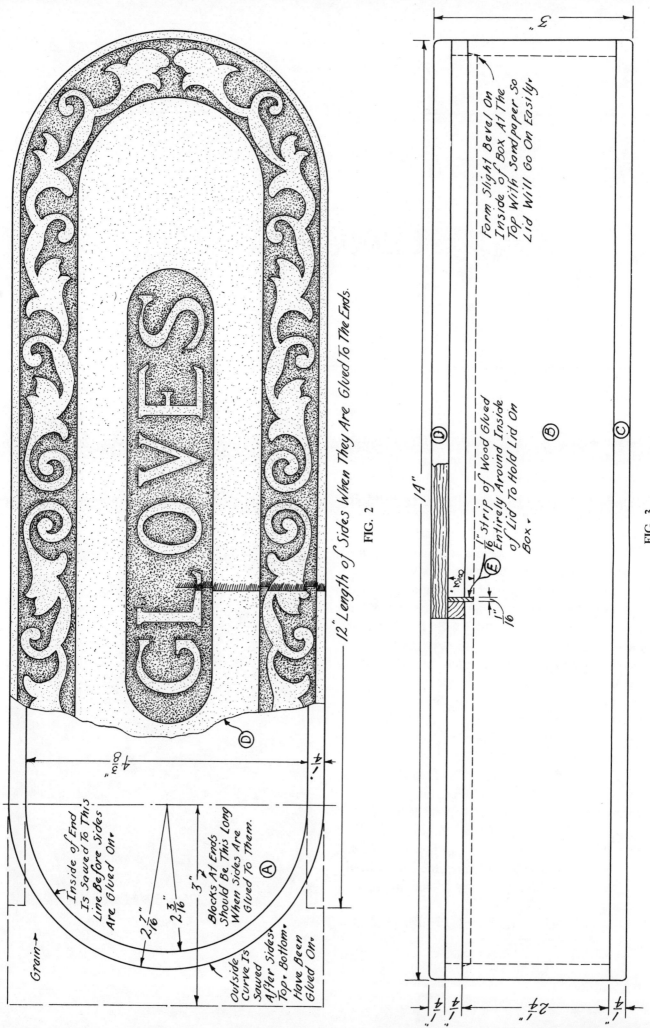

GLOVES

Grain →

$4\frac{3}{8}''$

$\frac{1}{4}''$

Inside of End
Is Sawed To This
Line Before Sides
Are Glued On.

$2\frac{1}{16}''$
$2\frac{3}{16}''$
$3''$

Blocks At Ends
Should Be This Long
When Sides Are
Glued To Them.

Outside
Curve Is
Sawed
After Sides,
Top, Bottom,
Have Been
Glued On.

Ⓐ

Ⓓ

12" Length of Sides When They Are Glued To The Ends.

FIG. 2

3"

Ⓓ

14"

$\frac{1}{16}''$

Ⓑ

Ⓒ

Ⓔ

$\frac{1}{16}''$

Form Slight Bevel On
Inside of Box At The
Top With Sandpaper So
Lid Will Go On Easily.

$\frac{1}{16}''$ Strip of Wood Glued
Entirely Around Inside
of Lid To Hold Lid On
Box.

$2\frac{1}{4}''$
$\frac{1}{4}''$
$\frac{1}{4}''$
$\frac{1}{4}''$

FIG. 3

FIG. 4

FIG. 6

caution I recommend to prevent fracturing of the joints should too much pressure be applied when tightening the hand screws. Fig. 5 also shows that I glued two pieces of wood together to make the blocks 3 inches thick.

When sides and ends have been glued together, as shown in Fig. 6, you will be ready to glue bottom (C) and top (D) to the assembled sides and ends. How to do this is shown in Fig. 4. Use enough clamps and hand screws to make tight joints. After gluing, the protruding wood on both sides of (C) and (D) may be planed down and sanded to make them flush with the sides. Carefully lay out the curves on both ends of the box to round the ends on the bandsaw, staying just far enough away from the convex curves drawn there to sand them smooth afterward.

(A) to glue sides (B) to them; then carefully draw the arcs shown in Fig. 7 on both tops and bottoms of (A) to enable you to hollow and smooth the inside curves, using the bandsaw, before the sides are glued on.

Fig. 7 shows a spacing block placed between the sides when they are being glued to block (A), a pre-

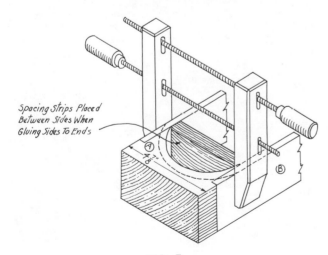

Spacing Strips Placed
Between Sides When
Gluing Sides To Ends

FIG. 7

FIG. 8

You now have a box glued together on all sides. This was done so that when lid and box are sawed apart, their sides and ends will line up exactly on both the inside and the outside. Carefully saw the lid and box apart. Sides may be sawn close to the lines, on the table saw, and the ends can then be separated more easily on the bandsaw. Then carefully smooth the adjoining surfaces with plane, files, and sandpaper.

When the lid and box fit together smoothly, draw the design on the lid to carve it. A full-sized pattern is provided in Fig. 9 for you to trace and use.

Fig. 10 shows the lid being carved. Usually, when doing this kind of carving, the design is outlined with carving chisels and gouges to a depth of about 1/16 inch, by driving the cutting edges straight down into the wood with a mallet. However, I use this method for only parts of the outline, and outline other parts

FIG. 10

FIG. 9

GLOVES

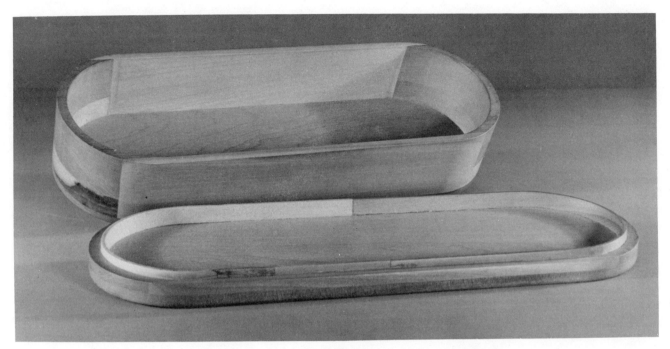

FIG. 5

with a narrow **V**-tool, and still other parts with the point of a sharp skew knife. In cutting the outline, I first stay just a little distance outside the lines, and then after lowering the background to the depth wanted (in this case about $\frac{1}{16}$ inch), I trim the edges carefully to the exact outline, smoothing the background as carefully as possible while doing this.

When the carving has been done, the strips constituting the lip to hold the top in place should be made and glued around the inside edges of the lid. Make these strips of wood $\frac{1}{16}$ inch thick and $\frac{3}{8}$ inch wide. While tulip poplar is not an ideally suited material to be bent around sharp curves, I find that it can be done quite easily on thin strips like this by soaking them in water overnight and then clamping them to dry around a form cut to the shape needed to make them fit the inside of the lid. Please note that this form must be reduced in size all around its edges by $\frac{1}{16}$ inch, which is the thickness of the strips of wood, or a bit more. Fig. 11 shows the forming of these strips. When dry, they should be glued fast to the inside of the rim of the lid, as shown in Fig. 5, and carefully sanded smooth.

FIG. 11

BILL OF MATERIAL

Yellow Poplar

2 Ends (A) 3″ x 4⅞″ x 3″ *
2 Sides (B) ¼″ x 3″ x 12″
1 Bottom (C) ¼″ x 5⅜″ x 14½″ †
1 Top (D) ¼″ x 5⅜″ x 14½″
Strips of wood (E) ¹⁄₁₆″ x ⅜″ to be glued around inside
   of lid rim

* The extra ½-inch thickness of these pieces will be enough to saw the lid and box apart, and flatten the joint where they come together.

† The extra ½-inch width and length of (C) and (D) should be provided to allow enough to trim the ends after the bottom and top have been glued to sides and ends.

TWO

Small Wall Cabinet

THIS QUAINT-LOOKING SMALL WALL CABINET, so definitely provincial in appearance, is of a type found in Pennsylvania homes in Colonial times. Poplar is the wood used here, but others were made of black walnut. What these small wall cabinets were used for is anybody's guess, and the design of some was changed so they could be hung in a corner of the room. One interesting feature is that this small cupboard, because of the arrangement of the two principal areas, would be equally useful if turned bottom end up, though the manner of hanging shown in Fig. 1, I've been told, is the customary way.

The unusual but attractive wrought-iron hinges were most likely forged by a local blacksmith and fastened with hand-forged iron nails. Iron butterfly hinges, **H**-hinges, or **H-L**-hinges could be substituted, a suggestion I'm making because such hinges are to be found in hardware stores, while those in Fig. 6 would probably have to be specially made.

I have reduced the thickness of stock from that used on the cupboard shown in Fig. 1, which is a full 1 inch thick, this being an indication of its ancient vintage. Reducing the thickness of stock will improve its proportions. Methods of joinery, such as that found where rails (H) and (I) are joined to stiles (G), are somewhat unusual, and may be held in

FIG. 1

place with only a short tongue-and-groove, rather than with the deeper and stronger mortise-and-tenon joints shown in my drawings.

To build the cupboard, make the two ends (A) first. Rabbet the back edges to join back (B) to it. This may be fastened to the ends with nails from the back. Cut grooves across ends (A) on the inside to hold shelf (E) and (F), if you intend to include shelf

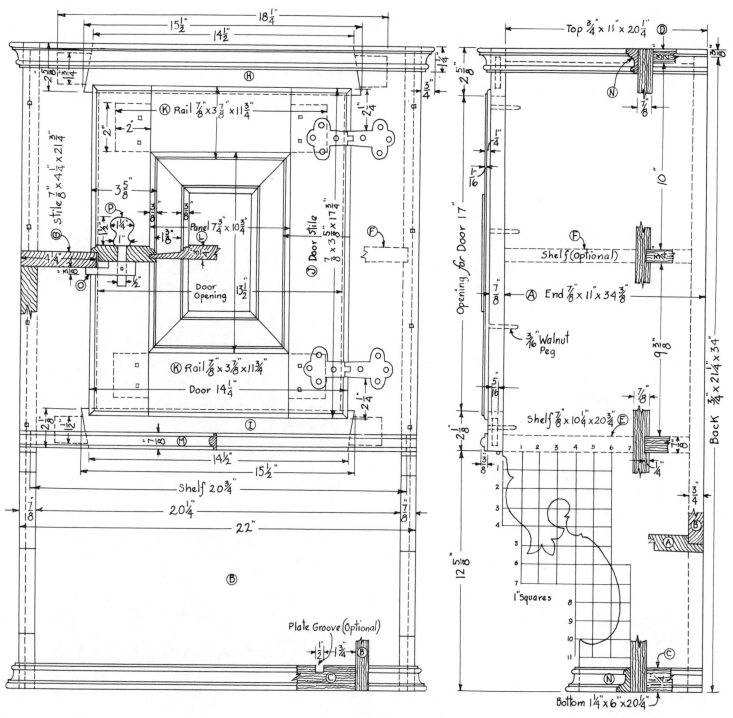

FIG. 2   FIG. 3

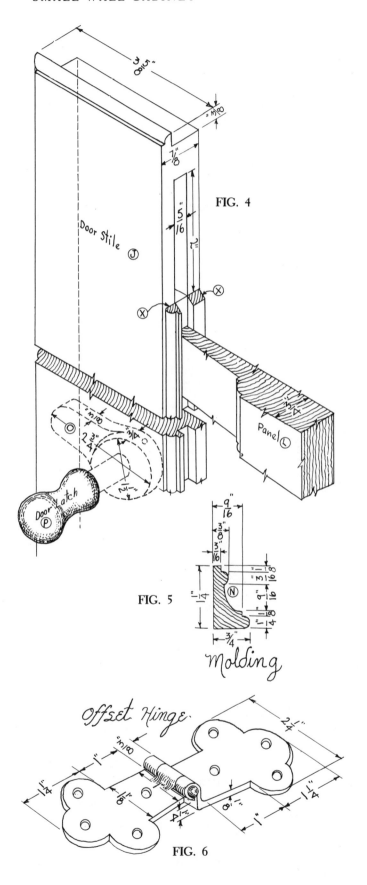

FIG. 4

Door Stile Ⓙ

Panel Ⓛ

Door latch Ⓟ

FIG. 5

Ⓝ

Molding

Offset Hinge

FIG. 6

(F). Then bandsaw the lower area to the shape shown in Fig. 3, after first making a full-sized pattern from the graph squares in Fig. 3; and file and sandpaper these edges smooth. Bottom (C) and top (D) can be nailed to the ends and back, since these nail heads can be hidden under molding (N). Moldings (M) and (N) can be glued to the front, spotted with glue, and bradded to the ends. If plates are to be displayed on the lower shelf, as in Fig. 1, it is a good idea to cut a plate groove 1¾ inches from the back, as shown in the cross section in Fig. 2.

When shelves (F) and (E) have been fitted to the grooves in both ends, they can be held in place with glue, though this is not absolutely necessary, because when bottom (C) and top (D) have been nailed to the ends and back, these shelves will be held in place without glue.

Make stiles (G), and rails (H) and (I), and cut and fit the mortise-and-tenon joints. Glue up this frame, and fit it to the front of the cupboard section. Glue the frame to the front edges of both ends; then drill 3/16-inch holes and drive 3/16-inch-square walnut pegs into these holes to help hold the frame in place. Besides strengthening these joints, the pegs add "flavor" to the appearance.

Make and fit the door. Cross-section details in Fig. 2, and the enlarged details shown in Fig. 4, will show how door parts are shaped and put together. Do not glue panel (L) to stiles (J), or to rails (K). Shape the molding on all of these; then cut mortises on stiles, tenons on rails, and miter the inside molding on stiles and rails where they come together at the inside corners of the door frame. See detail (X) in Fig. 4. Fit the panel to the grooves and glue the mortise-and-tenon joints. Drill 3/16-inch holes through these joints, and drive walnut pegs into them to strengthen the joints.

Figs. 2 and 4 show how the wooden door latch is made. Fit this loosely enough into the hole in the door stile so the knob can be turned to latch or unlatch the door. Then fasten the offset hinges, which, as I have indicated, may be done with more easily found substitutions if those shown in Fig. 6 cannot be duplicated.

BILL OF MATERIAL

Poplar or Walnut

2 Ends (A) ⅞″ x 11″ x 34⅜″
1 Back (B) ¾″ x 21¼″ x 34″
1 Bottom (C) 1¼″ x 6″ x 20¼″
1 Top (D) ¾″ x 11″ x 20¼″
1 Shelf (E) ⅞″ x 10¼″ x 20¾″
1 Shelf (F) ¾″ x 10¼″ x 20¾″
2 Stiles (G) ⅞″ x 4¼″ x 21¾″
1 Rail above door (H) ⅞″ x 2⅝″ x 18¼″

1 Rail below door (I) ⅞″ x 2⅛″ x 18¼″
2 Door stiles (J) ⅞″ x 3⅝″ x 17¾″
2 Door rails (K) ⅞″ x 3⅞″ x 11¾″
1 Door panel (L) ¾″ x 7¾″ x 10¾″
Molding below door (M) ⅜″ x ⅞″ x 22″
Molding for top and bottom (N) ¾″ x 1¼″ x 80″
  (approx.)
Latch (O) ¾″ x 1½″ x 2¾″
Door latch knob (P) 1¼″ diam. x 3½″

THREE

Small Wall Cupboard

LIKE THE SMALL WALL CABINET IN THE PREVI-ous chapter, this example of provincial Pennsylvania craftsmanship is quite worthy of being reproduced. The wood used here is black walnut.

As seems evident from examination of the photograph, Fig. 1, somewhere along the line an owner decided to install a lock on the drawer on the right and made a rather curious and not too wise a choice in his manner of going about it. His mismatched escutcheon plate is no help in pulling out the drawer, though inserting a key into the lock may help. The purpose would have been better served by keeping the original drawer pull and adding a smaller escutcheon plate like the one on the door. Except for this incongruous substitution, the rest of the brasses appear to be original.

To build the cupboard, make both ends (A) first. The upper ends of these are routed out to a depth of ⅜ inch to better seat and fasten the top, which can be nailed to both ends, back, and rail (C). The bottom (G), when it is put on, can also be nailed to the ends, back, and fastened with glue to rail (E).

Rabbet the back edges of ends (A). This will provide a place to fasten the back with finishing nails from the back. Grooves ¼ inch deep, cut across both ends, will hold the two shelves, and the shelves may be glued to the ends.

FIG. 1

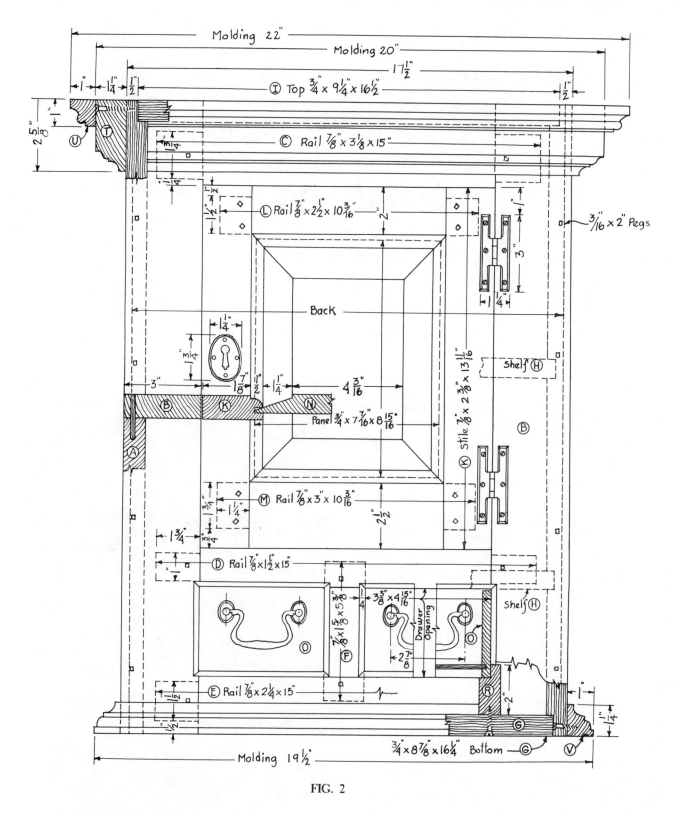

FIG. 2

Make the frame for the front, consisting of stiles (B), rails (C), (D), (E), and short stile (F). Mortise-and-tenon joints, glued and pinned, as shown in Fig. 2, hold this frame together. When assembled the frame is glued to front edges of ends (A) and top (I),

and also with the ³⁄₁₆-inch-square walnut pegs. These are driven into ³⁄₁₆-inch drilled holes.

Make the molding for the top and bottom. Molding (T) in front at the top may be glued on, but the two short return moldings should not be glued to the

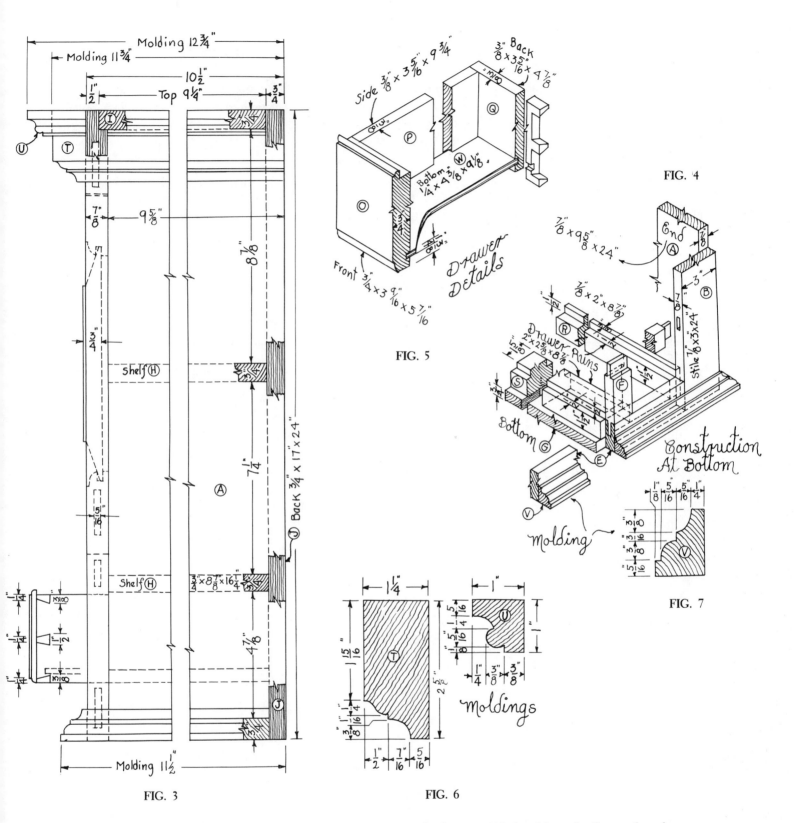

FIG. 3

FIG. 4

FIG. 5

FIG. 6

FIG. 7

ends because grain going in opposite directions may loosen the glue joint or cause other problems, so wood screws, or even finishing nails, are better here. Molding (U), however, may be glued to molding (T) on all three sides.

The bottom (G) should not be fastened to the cupboard until molding (V) has been put on the ends and front with wood screws from the inside, as shown in Fig. 2. By waiting to do it until then you need not nail the molding from the outside, thus making it unnecessary to disfigure molding surfaces with unsightly nail holes, like the ones you see in Fig. 1. Drawer runs (R) and (S) should also be fastened with wood screws to bottom (G) before nailing the bottom to the cupboard.

Make the door next. Rails and stiles are held together with mortise-and-tenon joints, though the molding cut on inside edges of these is mitered at the corners, and has grooves cut into these edges to hold the handsomely figured raised panel. When put together, the cabinet lock, and **H**-hinges should be fastened to the door, and the door fitted to the frame opening.

Make the two small drawers. Details for making these are shown in Figs. 3 and 5. Brass drawer pulls (see Fig. 2), when put on, will complete the job.

BILL OF MATERIAL

Walnut

2 Ends (A) ⅞″ x 9⅝″ x 24″
2 Stiles (B) ⅞″ x 3″ x 24″
1 Top rail (C) ⅞″ x 3⅛″ x 15″
1 Rail under door (D) ⅞″ x 1½″ x 15″
1 Rail under drawers (E) ⅞″ x 2¼″ x 15″
1 Short stile between drawers (F) ⅞″ x 1⅝″ x 5⅜″
1 Bottom (G) ¾″ x 8⅞″ x 16¼″
2 Shelves (H) ¾″ x 8⅞″ x 16¼″
1 Top (I) ¾″ x 9¼″ x 16½″
1 Back (J) ¾″ x 17″ x 24″
2 Door stiles (K) ⅞″ x 2⅜″ x 13¹¹⁄₁₆″
1 Door rail (L) ⅞″ x 2½″ x 10³⁄₁₆″

1 Door rail (M) ⅞″ x 3″ x 10³⁄₁₆″
1 Door panel (N) ¾″ x 7⁷⁄₁₆″ x 8¹⁵⁄₁₆″
2 Drawer fronts (O) ¾″ x 3⁹⁄₁₆″ x 5⁷⁄₁₆″
4 Drawer sides (P) ⅜″ x 3⁵⁄₁₆″ x 9¾″
2 Drawer backs (Q) ⅜″ x 3⁵⁄₁₆″ x 4⅞″
2 Drawer runs (R) ⅞″ x 2″ x 8⅞″
1 Drawer run (S) 2″ x 2⅝″ x 8⅞″
Molding (T) 1¼″ x 2⅝″ x 44″ (approx.)
Molding (U) 1″ x 1″ x 48″ (approx.)
Molding (V) 1″ x 1¼″ x 44″ (approx.)

Birch Plywood

2 Drawer bottoms (W) ¼″ x 4⅜″ x 9⅛″

FOUR

Cradle

ALL MY BROTHERS AND SISTERS AND I WERE rocked in a cradle very similar to the one shown here, and unfortunately, after it came into my possession, I let it be sold—a decision I've regretted ever since. The owner of a local antiques shop, in whose store window I saw this one displayed, gave his permission for me to photograph it and take the measurements from which these drawings are made.

The brass knobs on both sides of the cradle are original and were used to button down the coverlet.* (See Fig. 12.) The canopy rack atop the head end shaded the baby's eyes from the glare of lights or sun, and also supported netting spread over the cradle in order to ward off insects. It can be dropped behind the headboard when not in use, as shown in Fig. 4.

To build the cradle, plane and sand lumber to thicknesses of ½ inch for sides and ends. A pattern for the two sides may be made from Figs. 4 and 8. Pin members of dovetailing at the ends of both sides are narrow, and may be made by removing most of the waste between them on the bandsaw, and then finishing their shaping with a chisel to get the proper angles. If your bandsaw table can be tilted to the exact angle, once the lines have been laid out, little if any trimming with a chisel will be necessary.

*Brass knobs may be purchased from Ball and Ball Brasses, Exton, Pennsylvania 19341 (Catalog # G-17).

FIG. 1

FIG. 2

FIG. 3

Shape the foot and head ends of the cradle, and then lay out the tail members of the dovetail joints on both sides of these by placing the pin members over them to mark places where waste is to be sawed out to properly join the two members.

My cradle had a solid board for its bottom, but this bottom is made of three narrow strips of wood, shown in Figs. 1, 4, and 5, and these are nailed to the tops of both rockers.

A full-sized pattern of the rockers can be made from Fig. 11. These rockers are fastened to both sides of the cradle, as in Fig. 9, with wood screws. A strip of wood (E), gained and glued into the upper edges of both rockers, holds them firmly in position once they have been fastened to both sides of the cradle.

The octagon-shaped pieces fastened to the top of both sides are rabbeted along their entire length to join them flush with the inside of the cradle, as shown in Fig. 9.

Vertical members of the canopy rack are mortised into the octagon-shaped bearing rod, which, when joined to the two brackets shown in Figs. 4 and 5, permits the canopy to be placed either over the head of the cradle, as shown in Fig. 2, or back behind the headboard, as shown in Fig. 4.

FIG. 12

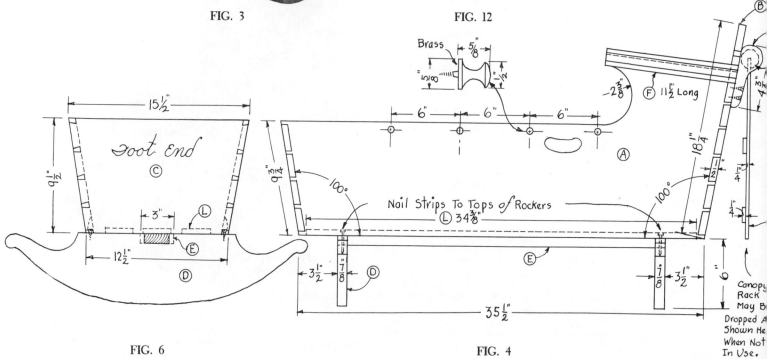

FIG. 6

FIG. 4

FIG. 10

FIG. 11

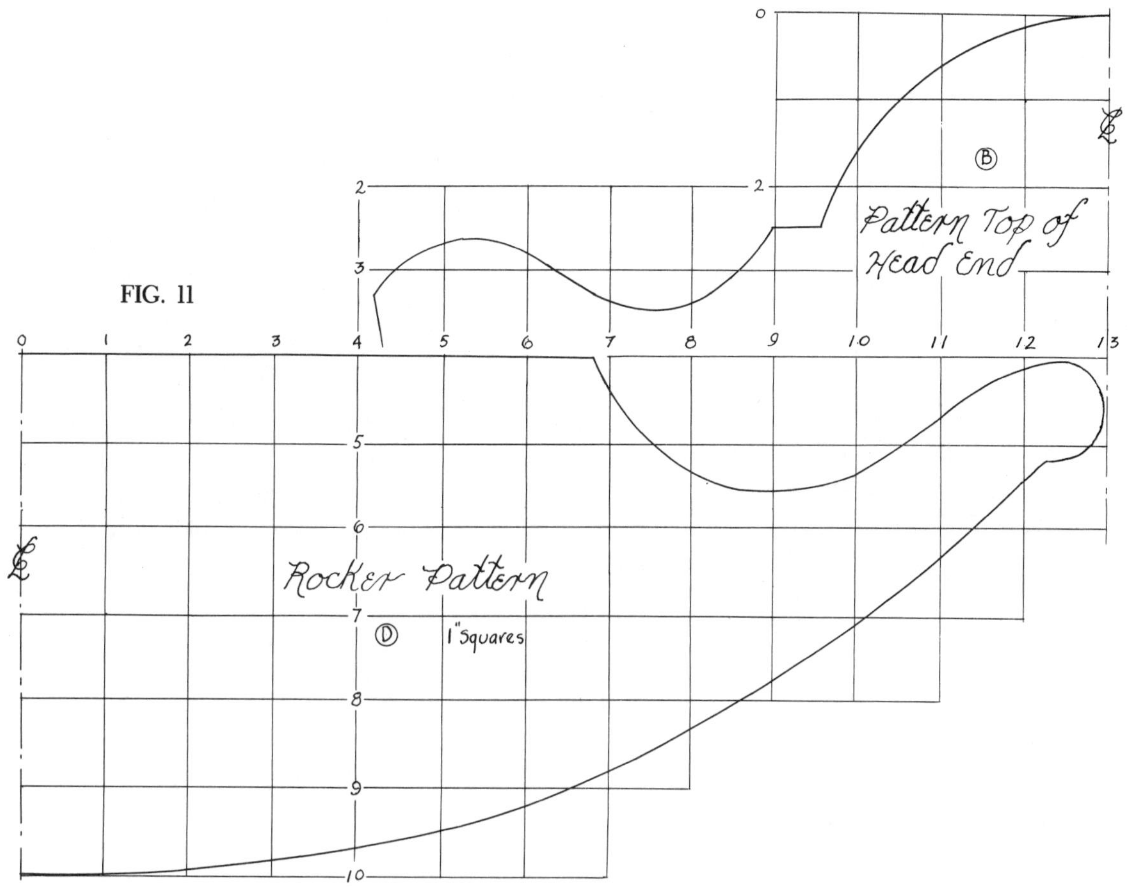

Pattern Top of Head End
Rocker Pattern
1" Squares

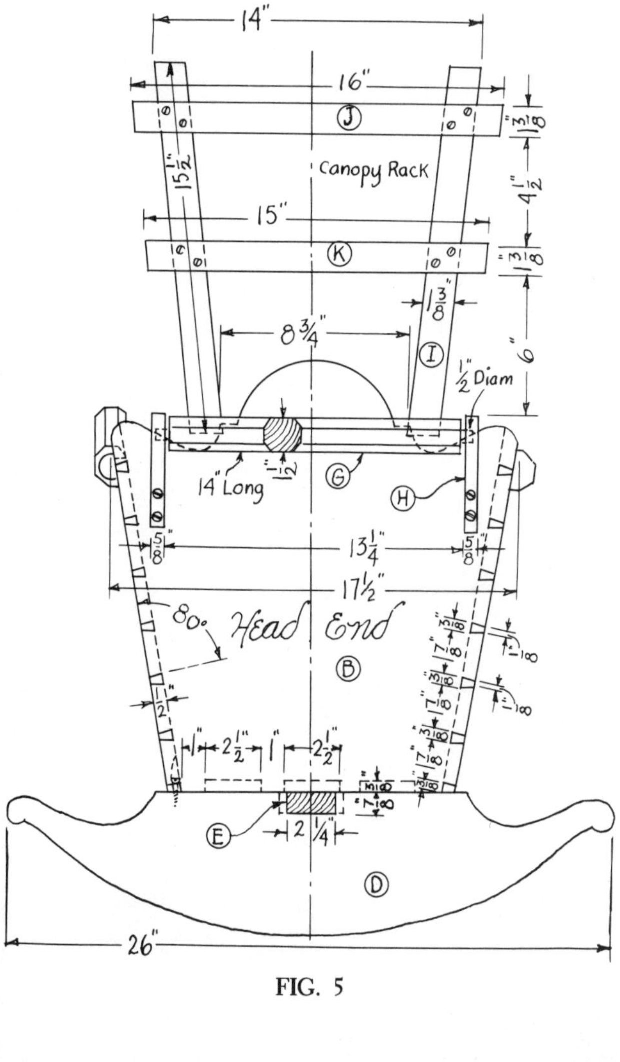

14"
16"
Canopy Rack
15"
8 3/4"
1/2" Diam
14" Long
13 1/4"
17 1/2"
Head End
26"

FIG. 5

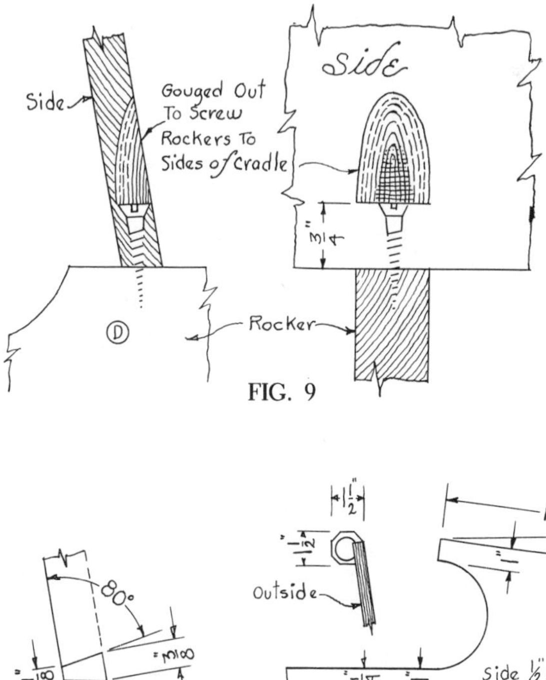

Side
Gouged Out To Screw Rockers To Sides of Cradle
Side
Rocker

FIG. 9

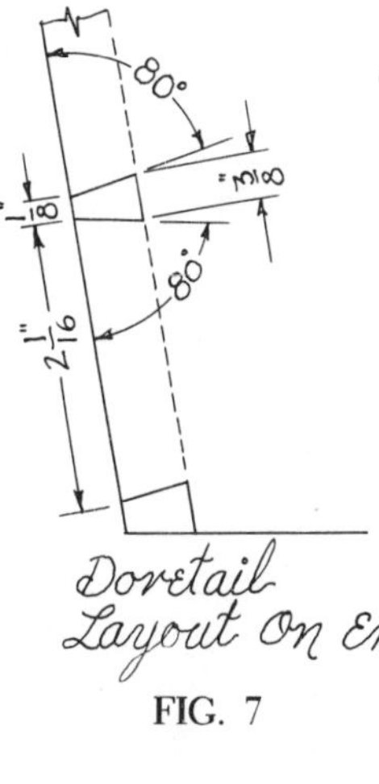

80°
80°
Dovetail Layout On Ends

FIG. 7

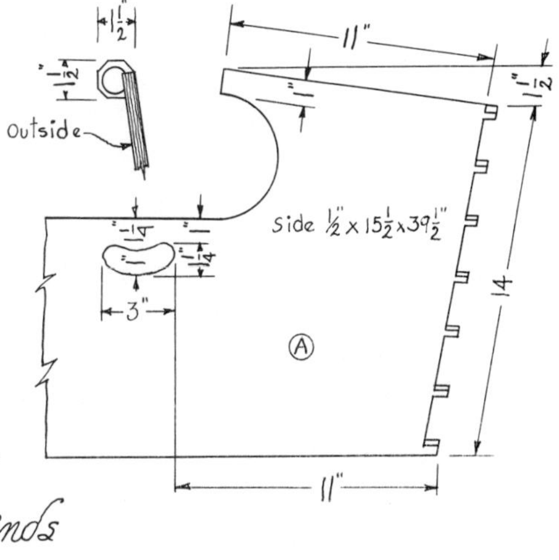

Outside
11"
Side 1/2 x 15 1/2 x 39 1/2"
3"
14
11"

FIG. 8

BILL OF MATERIAL

Cherry, Walnut, or Mahogany

2 Sides (A) ½″ x 15½″ x 39½″
1 Head end (B) ½″ x 18¼″ x 17½″
1 Foot end (C) ½″ x 9¾″ x 15½″
2 Rockers (D) ⅞″ x 6″ x 26″
1 Strip joining rockers (E) ⅞″ x 3″ x 28½″
2 Octagon rods, fastened to sides (F)
  1½″ x 1½″ x 11½″

1 Octagon-shaped bearing rod (G) 1½″ x 1½″ x 14″
2 Brackets to hold bearing rod (H) ⅝″ x 1¾″ x 4¾″
2 Vertical strips in canopy rack (I) ¼″ x 1⅜″ x 15½″
1 Horizontal strip in canopy rack (J) ¼″ x 1⅜″ x 16″
1 Horizontal strip in canopy rack (K) ¼″ x 1⅜″ x 15″
3 Strips in bottom of cradle (L) ⅜″ x 2½″ x 34⅜″

FIVE

Small Cabinet or Nightstand

MANY USES CAN BE FOUND FOR A SMALL CABInet like this one. It may be used as a bedside nightstand, as a side table by an easy chair, or any number of other uses. The nightstand shown in Fig. 1 is made of cherry. Walnut, mahogany, maple, or other hardwoods can be substituted.

In the working drawings (Figs. 2 and 3), I have substituted a more appropriate molding on the edges around the top than the kind shown in Fig. 1. I have also joined the front edges of ends (A) to stiles (B) with a tongue-and-groove joint, thus making it possible to dispense with nails to fasten the ends and the front frame together. Glue may be used instead, resulting in a worthwhile improvement.

Strips supporting the drawer are thick for so small a piece of furniture, but the reason for this becomes obvious when examining Fig. 4. Backing strip (O) behind rail (D) serves as a doorstop at the top of the door, while the front edge of the floor serves the same purpose there.

To build the cabinet, glue up boards to make ends (A). Cut grooves ¼ inch deep across the inside to hold the floor in place, and also for the shelf if one is to be included. Also rabbet the back edges of (A) to fasten the plywood back.

Make stiles (B), and make the tongue-and-groove joints to fasten (A) to (B), but do not glue these to-

FIG. 1

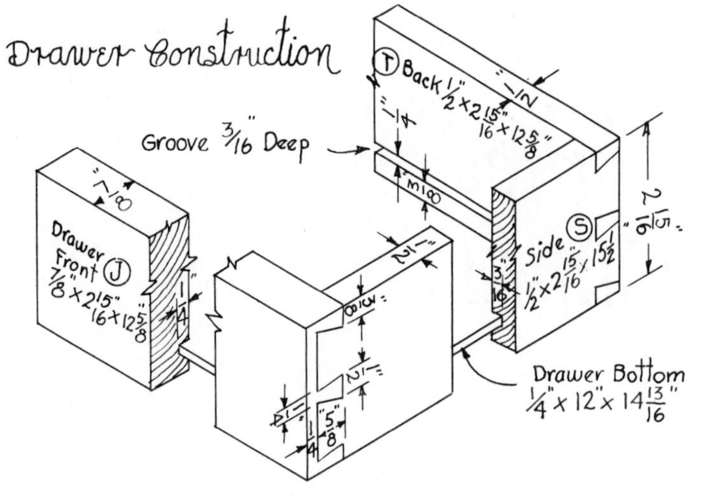
Drawer Construction
Back 1/2" × 2 15/16" × 12 5/8"
Groove 3/16 Deep
Drawer Front 7/8" × 2 15/16" × 12 5/8"
Side 1/2" × 2 15/16" × 15 1/2"
2 15/16"
Drawer Bottom 1/4" × 12" × 14 13/16"

FIG. 5

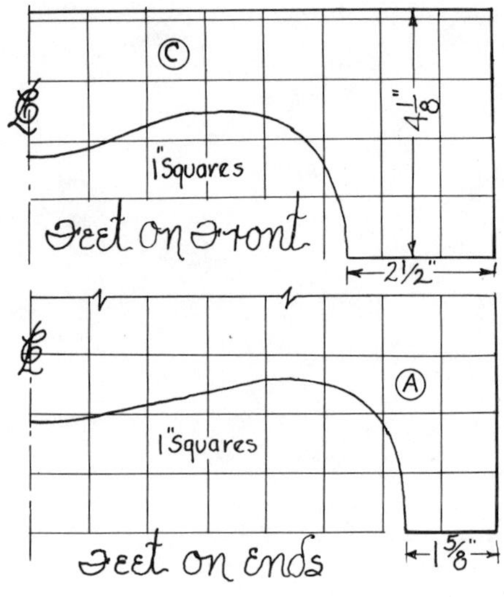
C
4 1/8"
1" Squares
Feet on Front
2 1/2"
A
1" Squares
Feet on Ends
1 5/8"

FIG. 6

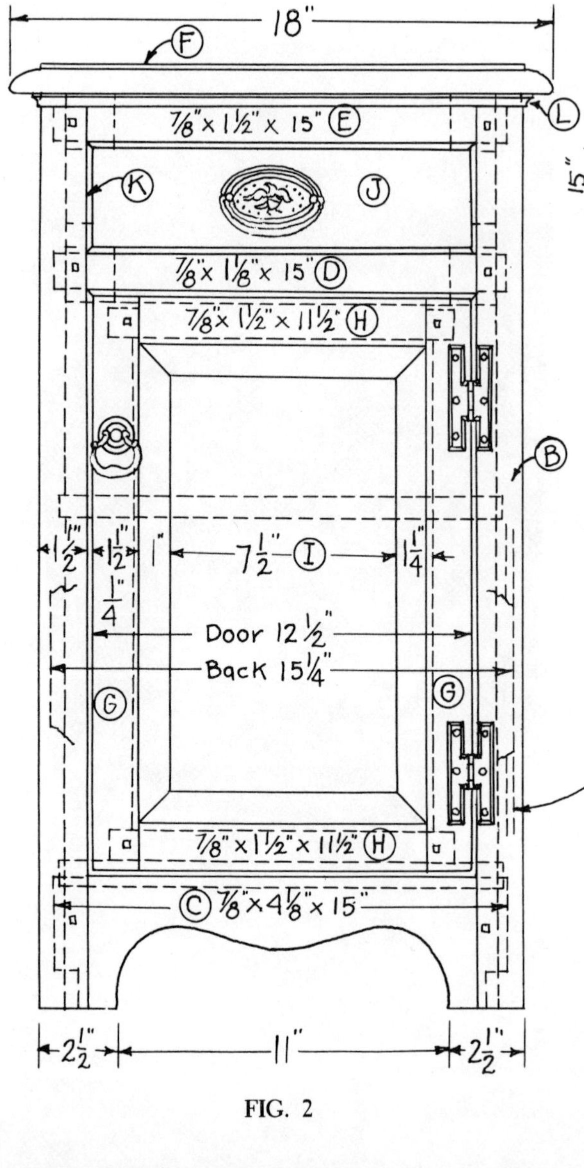
18"
F
L
7/8" × 1 1/2" × 15" E
K
J
7/8" × 1 1/8" × 15" D
7/8" × 1 1/2" × 11 1/2" H
B
1 1/2"
1 1/2"
1"
7 1/2" I
1 1/4"
1/4"
Door 12 1/2"
Back 15 1/4"
G
G
7/8" × 1 1/2" × 11 1/2" H
C 7/8" × 4 1/8" × 15"
2 1/2"
11"
2 1/2"

FIG. 2

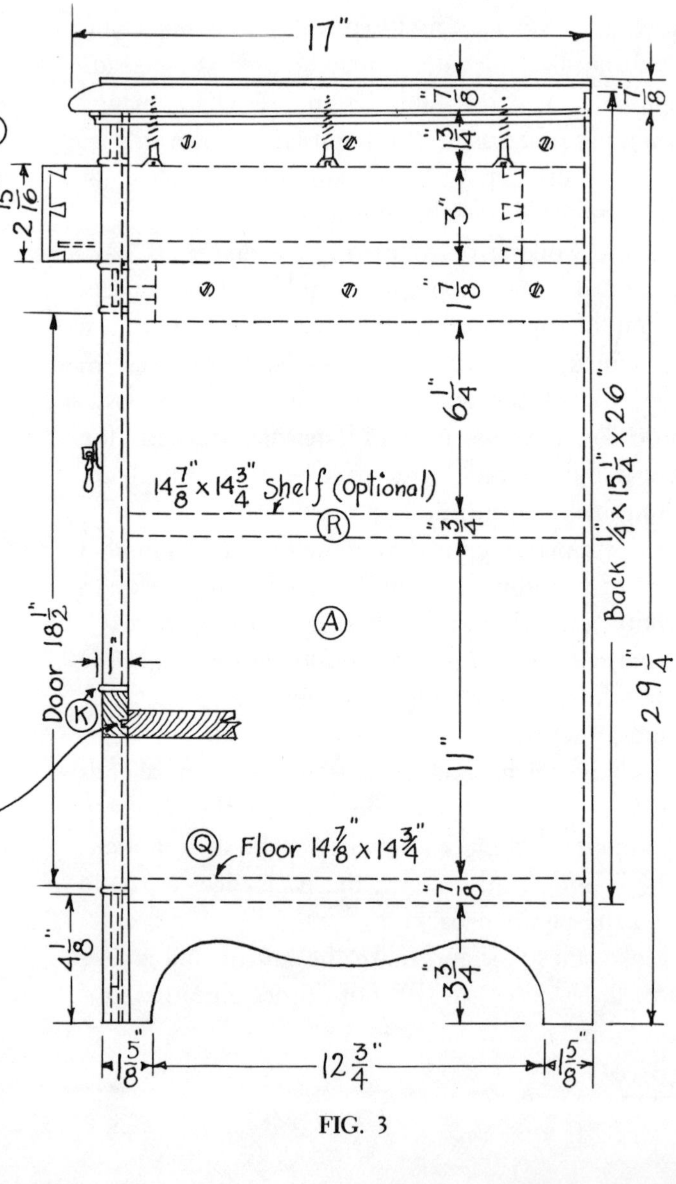
17"
7/8"
3/4"
2 15/16"
3"
7/8"
6 1/4"
14 7/8" × 14 3/4" Shelf (Optional)
R
3/4"
A
Back 1/4" × 15 1/4" × 26"
29 1/4"
Door 18 1/2"
K
11"
Q Floor 14 7/8" × 14 3/4"
7/8"
4 1/8"
3 3/4"
1 5/8"
12 3/4"
1 5/8"

FIG. 3

gether until the frame, consisting of (B), (C), (D), and (E), has been made. On the bandsaw, shape the feet on ends (A). Full-sized patterns of these may be made from Fig. 6.

Make strips (M), (N), and (P), and drill and countersink holes for the wood screws. Dado the front ends of (N) for the slip-joint used here to fasten strip (O), and make and glue these joints. Fasten drawer guides (P) to drawer runs (N). Then glue the floor and shelf to ends (A). Fasten strips (M) to ends (A) with wood screws.

Make top (F) and fasten it with wood screws to strips (M) before you fasten strips (N) to ends (A). Otherwise you might have difficulty doing this. Drawer guides (P) should be in place before you do this. One or more wood screws through (O) into (D) will hold these together.

You should now be ready to make the front frame. Make foot rail (C) and rails (D) and (E), and the mortise-and-tenon joints. Make these joints before bandsawing the bottom rail to form the feet. Careful fitting is required when making these joints, so the

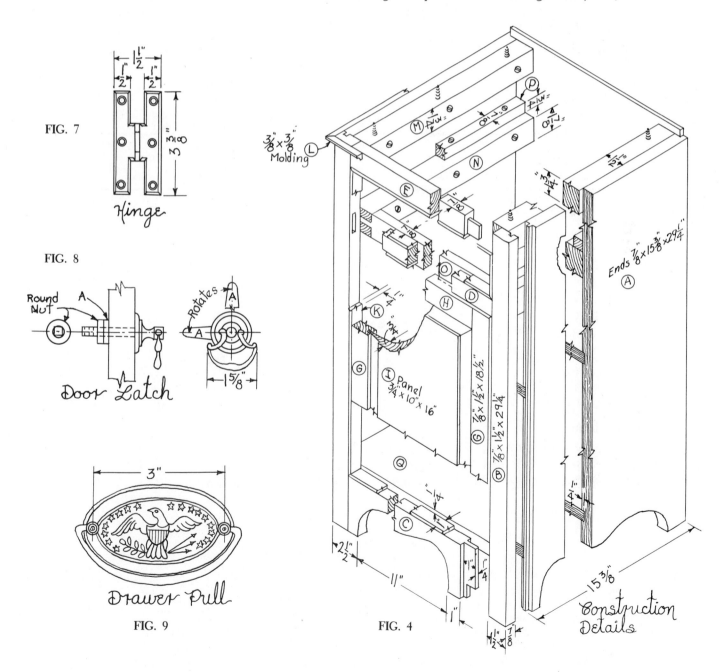

FIG. 7

Hinge

FIG. 8

Round Nut

Door Latch

Drawer Pull

FIG. 9

3/8" × 3/8" Molding

Ends 7/8 × 15 3/8 × 29 1/4

I Panel 3/4 × 10" × 16"

FIG. 4

Construction Details

tongue-and-groove joints will line up properly to fasten stiles (B) to ends (A), once the frame has been glued together.

Make and fit the drawer before nailing the plywood to the back. Details for making the drawer are shown in Fig. 5.

Make the door. Cut stiles and rails for the door frame, and make the mortise-and-tenon joints; then cut grooves on inside edges to hold the panel. Panel-raising may be done on the table saw. To do this elevate the saw teeth about 1/16 inch, or a little more, above the saw table, to cut kerfs to this depth paralleling all four edges of the panel. Do this on the face side of the panel. This forms the 1¼-inch border around the panel face. Depending on whether the

angle for cutting the bevel on these panel edges is done by tilting the saw blade or by tilting the saw table on your table saw, make the required setup to saw the beveled edges. To do this the saw extends above the saw table 1¼ inches, and with the panel back against the ripping fence, it is pushed through the saw to shape the beveled edges. (Panel-raising procedures are illustrated in Chapter Twenty-seven, Fig. 16.) This sawn beveled edge is smoothed down with a scraper blade and sandpaper. Panels like this should not be glued to rails or stiles, but left free to expand or contract with change of seasons.

Fit the door so it will not bind. Fasten the latch, hinges, and drawer pull.

BILL OF MATERIAL

Cherry

2 Ends (A) ⅞" x 15⅜" x 29¼"
2 Stiles (B) ⅞" x 1½" x 29¼"
Foot rail (C) ⅞" x 4⅛" x 15"
1 Rail under drawer (D) ⅞" x 1⅛" x 15"
1 Rail above drawer (E) ⅞" x 1½" x 15"
1 Top (F) ⅞" x 17" x 18"
2 Door stiles (G) ⅞" x 1½" x 18½"
2 Door rails (H) ⅞" x 1½" x 11½"
1 Door panel (I) ¾" x 10" x 16"
1 Drawer front (J) ⅞" x 2¹⁵⁄₁₆" x 12⅝"
Strips with front edge rounded to outline door and drawer openings (K) ¼" x 1" x 95"
Molding under top (L) ⅜" x ⅜" x 50" (approx.)

Poplar

2 Strips to fasten top to ends (M) 1½" x 1¾" x 14⅞"
2 Strips to support drawer (N) 1½" x 1⅞" x 14⅞"
1 Backing strip (O) for rail (D) ⅞" x 1⅞" x 14¼". This also acts as a doorstop.
2 Drawer guides (P) ¾" x ⅞" x 14⅞"
1 Floor (Q) ⅞" x 14⅞" x 14¾"
1 Shelf (R) ⅞" x 14⅞" x 14¾"
2 Drawer sides (S) ½" x 2¹⁵⁄₁₆" x 15½"
1 Drawer back (T) ½" x 2¹⁵⁄₁₆" x 12⅝"

Birch Plywood

1 Drawer bottom ¼" x 12" x 14¹³⁄₁₆"
1 Back of cabinet ¼" x 15¼" x 26"

SIX

Display Table

A SMALL TABLE, LIKE THE ONE IN FIG. 1, WILL be found useful to display a collection of treasures of one kind or another and to keep it free from daily dusting and constant care. The table serves a double purpose as a tea table.

In Figs. 2 and 3, on my drawings, I changed the shape and the manner of shaping the feet, which improves both their proportion and appearance. The feet on the table in Fig. 1 are formed by gluing thin pieces of wood to each side of the leg.

FIG. 1

23

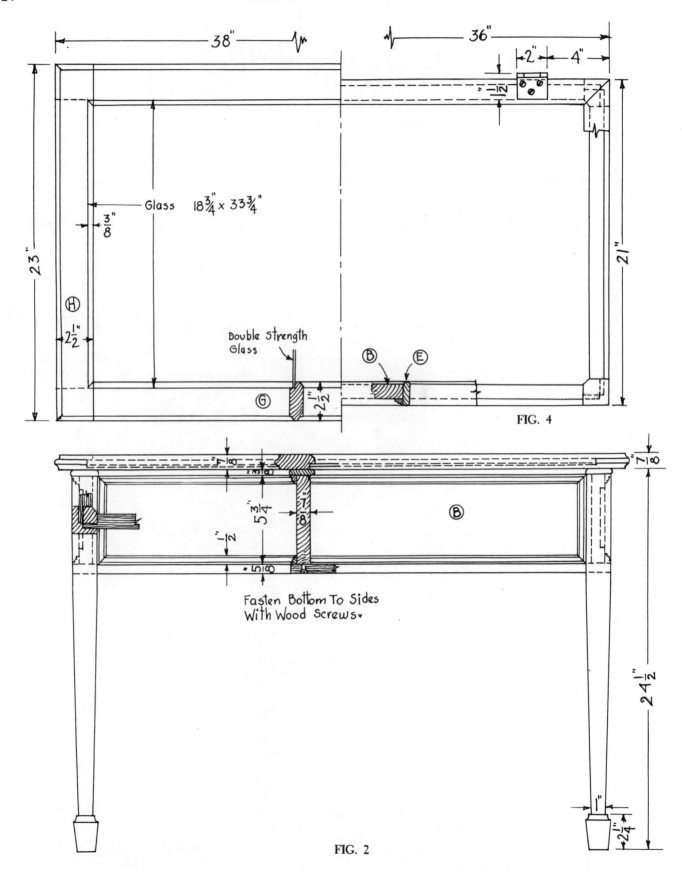

Glass $18\frac{3}{4}" \times 33\frac{3}{4}"$

Double Strength Glass

FIG. 4

Fasten Bottom To Sides
With Wood Screws.

FIG. 2

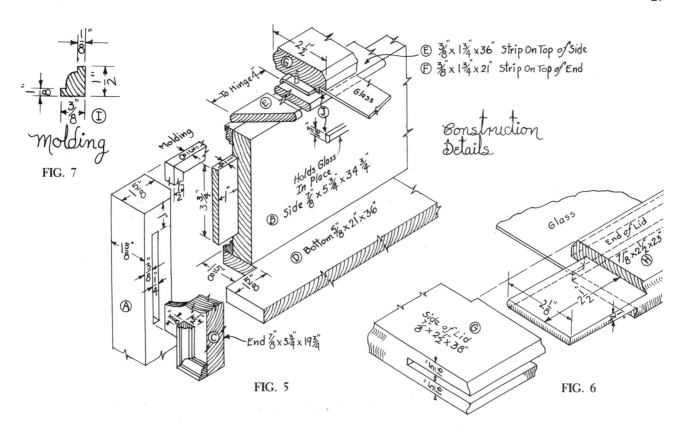

FIG. 7

molding

Ⓔ ⅜" x 1¾" x 36" Strip On Top of Side
Ⓕ ⅜" x 1¾" x 21" Strip On Top of End

Construction Details

Glass

Holds Glass In Place
Ⓑ Side ⅞ x 5¾" x 34¾"

Ⓓ Bottom ⅝ x 21" x 36"

End ⅞ x 5¾ x 19¾"

FIG. 5

End of Lid
⅞" x 2½" x 23"

Glass

Side of Lid
Ⓖ ⅞ x 2½" x 36"

FIG. 6

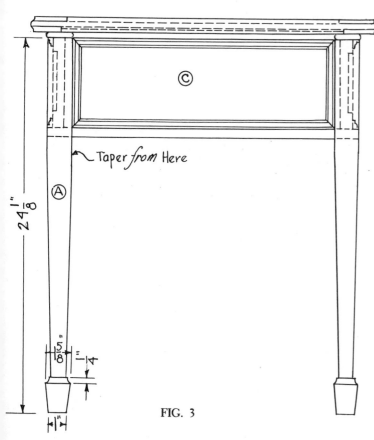

Taper from Here

24⅛"

FIG. 3

To build the table, make four legs, and square all four sides to one another. Lay out and cut mortises to hold tenons found on sides and ends of the table. By making these tenons so they are flush with the outsides of (B) and (C), they can be made longer, thus improving the strength of the joints.

After fitting all members of these joints, taper and shape legs and feet. Much of this can be done on the bandsaw, but sides must be smoothed with hand plane, wood scraper, files, and sandpaper. Carefully square all four sides of the legs to one another when tapering legs and forming feet.

Before gluing sides and ends to legs, make and fit the bottom (D). It can be fastened with wood screws to bottom edges of (B) and (C) after gluing the mortise-and-tenon joints.

Make the molding needed to go around the face sides of (B) and (C). Saw the miter joints and glue the molding to all four sides of the table. The extra thickness this provides along the upper edges of (B) and (C) is needed to provide a wider base for strips (E) and (F). These should also be glued fast to the top of the table frame. The hinges holding the lid are recessed into the lid and into strip (E) below it to come flush with the wood around them so the lid will lie flat on top of the table frame, as shown in Fig. 5.

Once the table frame is assembled and glued together, make the frame which holds the glass. Ends of (G) and (H) are joined together with open-ended mortise-and-tenon joints, shown in Fig. 6. Inside edges should be rabbeted to hold the glass, and beveled before gluing the joints, but it is better to shape the outside edges after gluing up the frame. Coats of stain, and other materials used for the finish, should all be applied before putting in the glass.

The glass is held in place with a very thin molding that I show in Fig. 5. This is better than fastening it to the frame with glazier points and putty because, should the glass ever break, the molding could easily be removed to replace the broken glass.

BILL OF MATERIAL

Cherry

4 Legs (A) 1⅝″ x 1⅝″ x 24⅛″
2 Sides (B) ⅞″ x 5¾″ x 34¾″
2 Ends (C) ⅞″ x 5¾″ x 19¾″
1 Bottom (D) ⅝″ x 21″ x 36″
2 Strips to go on top of sides (E) ⅜″ x 1¾″ x 36″

2 Strips to go on top of ends (F) ⅜″ x 1¾″ x 21″
2 Lid sides (G) ⅞″ x 2½″ x 38″
2 Lid ends (H) ⅞″ x 2½″ x 23″
Molding for sides and ends (I) ⅜″ x ½″ x 270″
   (approx.)
Molding to fasten glass in frame (J) ⅛″ x 3⁄16″ x 114″
   (approx.)

SEVEN

Child's Stretcher Table

THIS DIMINUTIVE STRETCHER TABLE MAY BE used not only by children but also by grownups. It is large enough to seat several children for a meal, playing games, or when engaged in other activities.

Full-sized tables similar to this one were found in kitchens in Colonial days and used as serviceable worktables. Many were made of walnut and poplar, but cherry was used to build this one.

FIG. 1

Construction Details

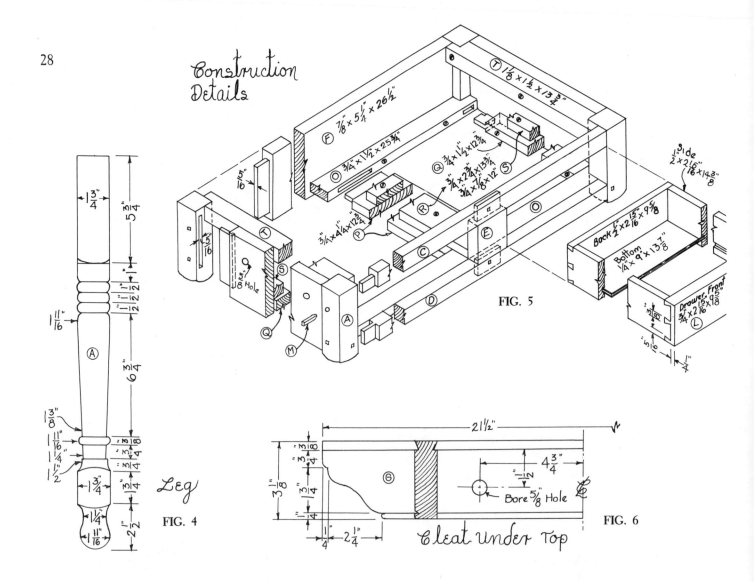

FIG. 5

FIG. 4

Leg

FIG. 6

Cleat under Top

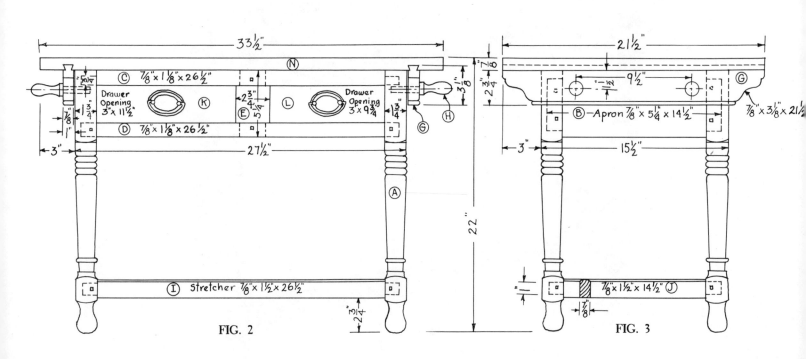

FIG. 2

FIG. 3

I have altered the construction in my drawings shown in the photograph (Fig. 1) slightly, both to improve the appearance and to strengthen the frame, by making the aprons and stretchers come flush with the outside of all four legs where they are joined together with mortise-and-tenon joints. Substituting flush joints for the offset ones found in Fig. 1 emulates the better type of joinery found in the best work of earlier times. It permits making stronger joints because tenons on rails can be lengthened and mortises in legs cut deeper. The appearance of the joints is also better.

To build the table, first turn the legs as shown in Fig. 4. Make layouts on the legs to cut mortises. When mortises have been cut, make aprons (B) and (F) and rails (C) and (D). Cut mortises into (C) and (D) where stile (E) is joined to them. Make stretchers (I) and (J), and then cut and fit tenons to all mortises. When these joints have been made, you are ready to glue up the table frame, consisting of legs, aprons, rails, stretchers, and stile (E). Take note of the fact that I have added square hardwood pegs to reinforce all mortise-and-tenon joints. These pegs, which should be about ³⁄₁₆ inch square, and 1½ inches long, are driven into ³⁄₁₆-inch-round holes. The holes can be drilled and pegs driven after clamps, pulling glue joints together, have been removed.

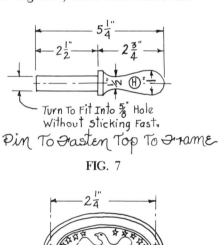

Turn To Fit Into ⅝" Hole
Without Sticking Fast.

Pin To Fasten Top To Frame

FIG. 7

Eagle Pull

FIG. 8

After gluing up the table frame, get out stock to make the frame to support the drawers. Poplar is used for this. Rails (O), (P), (Q) are put together with mortise-and-tenon joints, as shown in Fig. 5. Then drawer guides (R) and (S) are screwed to the upper side before the frame is fastened to the table with wood screws. Rail (O), just inside the drawer openings, may be glued to rail (D) to further reinforce this area. Rails (T), inside both ends of the table, serve to keep the drawers from angling down when being pulled out. Once these are in place, you are ready to make the drawers.

The two drawers on this table are not alike in width, and this was frequently the case with full-sized tables of this kind. Should you prefer them to be alike, the changeover would present no great difficulty. Details for making the smaller of the two drawers are shown in Fig. 5.

If there was a good reason for fastening tabletops to these tables in the manner shown, I am not cognizant of it, but it may be a holdover characteristic of earlier trestle tables of the English Gothic style, when much larger trestle tables were made with heavy removable rectangular tops of oak. Thus it may have been conformity to custom rather than requirements of utility on smaller tables of later date that influenced this feature. In the present instance it lends the kind of distinction to the design that makes it justifiable.

The running dovetail used to join the cleats to the top prevents warping on tops of this kind which were often made of single wide boards. This joint should be snugly fitted so no glue need be used to hold the cleats in place. Gluing the cleat to the top would probably cause the top to split, since it would not permit changes in width due to seasonal conditions.

The four pins used to fasten the top to the ends of the table should be turned so the dowel end is slightly smaller in diameter than the ⅝-inch holes bored into aprons (B) and cleats (G); but the reduction in diameter should not be enough to prevent them from staying in place.

The oval Eagle pulls should be fitted to the drawer fronts, but must be removed to apply the finish.

BILL OF MATERIAL

Cherry

4 Legs (A) 1¾" x 1¾" x 21⅛"
2 End aprons (B) ⅞" x 5¼" x 14½"
1 Rail above drawers (C) ⅞" x 1⅛" x 26½"
1 Rail below drawers (D) ⅞" x 1⅛" x 26½"
1 Stile between drawers (E) ⅞" x 2¾" x 5¼"
1 Back apron (F) ⅞" x 5¼" x 26½"
2 Cleats (G) ⅞" x 3⅛" x 21½"
4 Pins to fasten top to frame (H) 1" diam. x 5¼"
2 Stretchers (I) ⅞" x 1½" x 26½"
2 Stretchers (J) ⅞" x 1½" x 14½"
1 Front for drawer on left (K) ¾" x 2¹⁵⁄₁₆" x 11⅜"
1 Front for drawer on right (L) ¾" x 2¹⁵⁄₁₆" x 9⅝"
Pegs to reinforce mortise-and-tenon joints (M)
   ³⁄₁₆" x ³⁄₁₆"
1 Tabletop (N) ⅞" x 21½" x 33½"

Poplar

2 Rails in frame to support drawers (O) ¾" x 1½" x
   25¾"

1 Rail in frame to support drawers (P) ¾" x 4¼" x
   12¾"
2 Rails in frame to support drawers (Q) ¾" x 1½" x
   12¾"
1 Drawer guide between drawers (R) ¾" x 2¾" x
   13¾"
2 Drawer guides (S) ¾" x ⅞" x 12"
2 Pieces to keep drawers level when pulled out (T)
   1⅛" x 1½" x 13¾"
4 Drawer sides ½" x 2¹⁵⁄₁₆" x 14⅜"
1 Drawer back, right-hand drawer ½" x 2¹⁵⁄₁₆" x 9⅝"
1 Drawer back, left-hand drawer ½" x 2¹⁵⁄₁₆" x 11⅜"

Birch Plywood

1 Drawer bottom, right-hand drawer ¼" x 9" x 13⅞"
1 Drawer bottom, left-hand drawer ¼" x 10¾" x
   13⅞"

EIGHT

High-Back Settle Table

T HIS CHAIR-TABLE, OR PERHAPS IT SHOULD BE called a high-back settle table, can be made to serve as both table and seat. With the top down it is a good table, especially for the kitchen. With the top upright, as in Figs. 2 and 5, it becomes a comfortable seat, especially if a cushion is made to go on top of the seat to make it still more comfortable. The back, in its upright position, slants back enough to make it an easy seat in which to relax.

The wide tabletop, and perhaps even the shelf and the ends, should be glued up from narrower, well-seasoned boards.

FIG. 1

When all boards have been glued up, planed, and sanded, make patterns from Figs. 6, 7, 8, and 9, to saw them to shape. Edges should be carefully smoothed and trued up where bandsawing has been done to cut them to shape.

The cleats (F), under the top, with which the top is held in place over ends (C), are fastened with wood screws to the top. In Fig. 11 I show a better way of fastening these cleats to the top by cutting running

dovetail grooves clear across the underside of the tabletop, and sliding the running dovetails into these. If cleats (F) are joined to the top in this manner, and if the joints are properly fitted, the reinforcing strips (B) can be dispensed with. One or two wood screws in the middle of (F) would hold the cleat where it belongs, and this method of joining (F) to (A) would greatly reduce the likelihood of causing the wide top to warp or split.

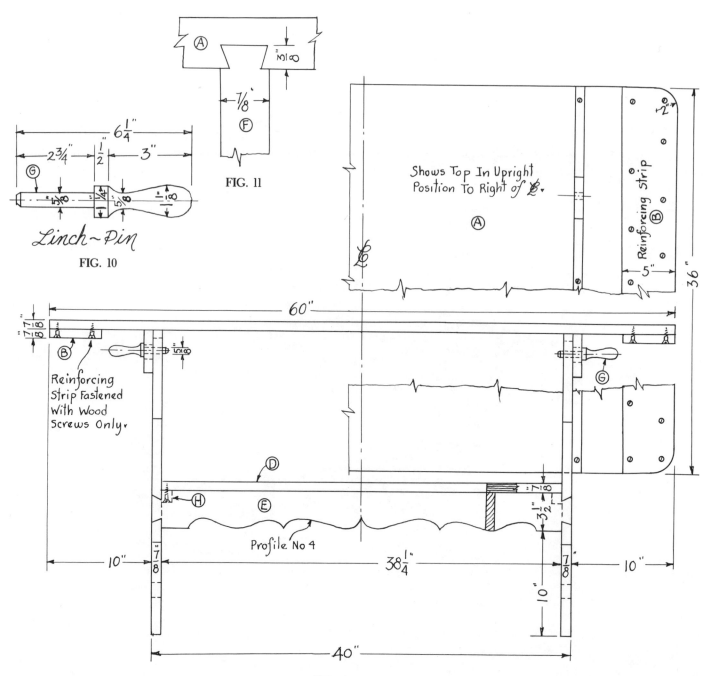

FIG. 11

Linch~Pin

FIG. 10

Shows Top In Upright Position To Right of ℄.

Reinforcing Strip

Reinforcing Strip Fastened With Wood Screws Only.

Profile No 4

FIG. 3

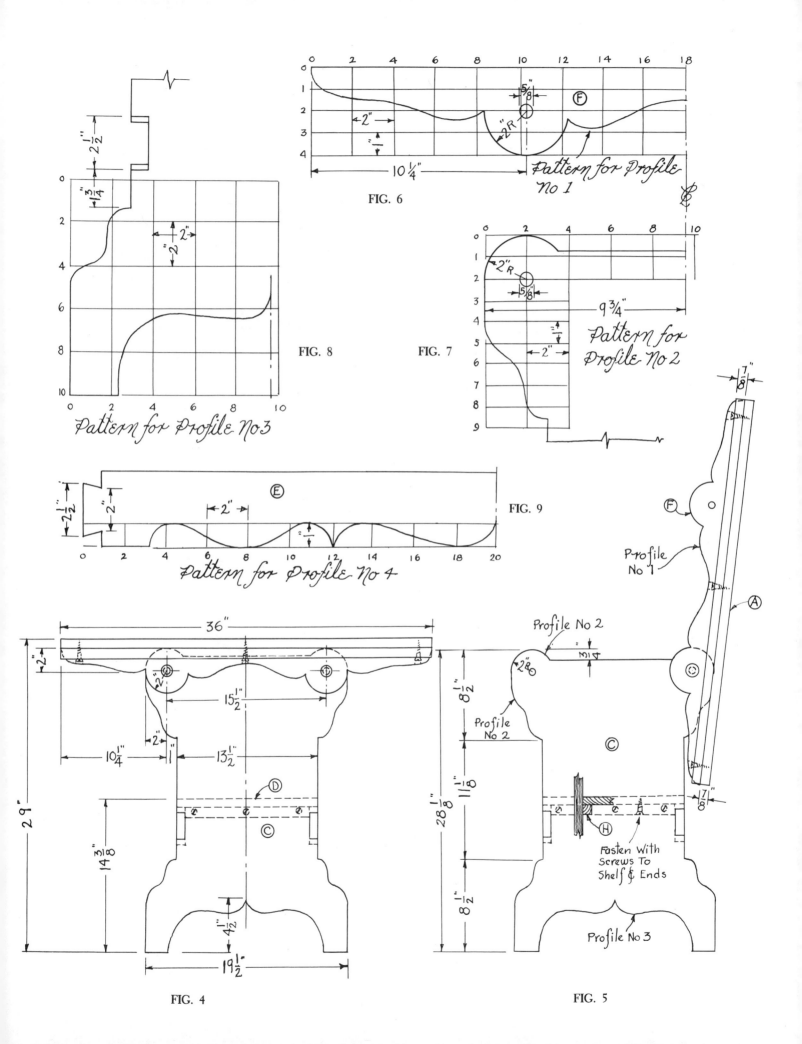

FIG. 6

Pattern for Profile No 1

FIG. 7

Pattern for Profile No 2

FIG. 8

Pattern for Profile No 3

FIG. 9

Pattern for Profile No 4

Profile No 1

Profile No 2

Profile No 2

Profile No 3

Fasten With Screws To Shelf & Ends

FIG. 4

FIG. 5

The top of the table shown in Figs. 1 and 2 is made as I show it in Figs. 3 and 4, from well-seasoned cherry boards, and it has been in constant use for more than ten years without splitting or warping. With reasonably controlled room temperatures, it should remain in good condition indefinitely, especially if enough coats of varnish are applied to both sides of the top to prevent moisture—or the lack of it—from unduly expanding or contracting the width during change of seasons.

Cherry, a fairly hardwood, used to build the table, is also durable enough to use for the linchpins. If you were to make the table of a softer wood, a hardwood should be used to turn all four of these.

FIG. 2

BILL OF MATERIAL

Cherry

1 Tabletop (A) ⅞″ x 36″ x 60″
2 Reinforcing strips for tabletop (B) ⅞″ x 5″ x 36″
2 Ends (C) ⅞″ x 19½″ x 28⅛″

1 Shelf (D) ⅞″ x 13½″ x 38¼″
2 Rails (E) ⅞″ x 3½″ x 40″
2 Cleats (see profile 1) (F) ⅞″ x 4″ x 36″
4 Linchpins (G) 1¼″ diam. x 6¼″
2 Strips to support shelf (H) ⅞″ x ⅞″ x 11¾″

NINE

Country Kitchen Sideboard

TALL COUNTRY-MADE SIDEBOARDS LIKE THIS one are still fairly plentiful in southeastern Pennsylvania. I own one made of poplar. Mine is painted and grained to simulate curly maple wood.

The cupboard shown in Fig. 1 is pine and it was refinished with several coats of varnish without stain to color it in order to show the aged natural wood grain. Spots over nail heads, formerly hidden under several coats of paint, show in the refinished piece. This objectionable defect can be minimized considerably by supporting shelves and frames in grooves cut into the ends of the sideboard, and by holding them in place with supporting strips (U) and (V). Few nails then need to be used. Box nails with heads, through the back, will adequately support shelves and frames there.

Vitreous-handled iron cupboard door catches, and drawer knobs like those found on the sideboard shown in Fig. 1, may be hard to find, so it may be necessary to make substitutions here. Brass door catches, like the one in Fig. 6, can be bought, and are suitable substitutes on a sideboard like this one.* Turned wooden drawer knobs may also be substituted for the kind used on the old model.

*Brass door catches may be purchased from Ball and Ball Brasses, Exton, Pennsylvania 19341. (Catalog number shown on Fig. 6.)

FIG. 1

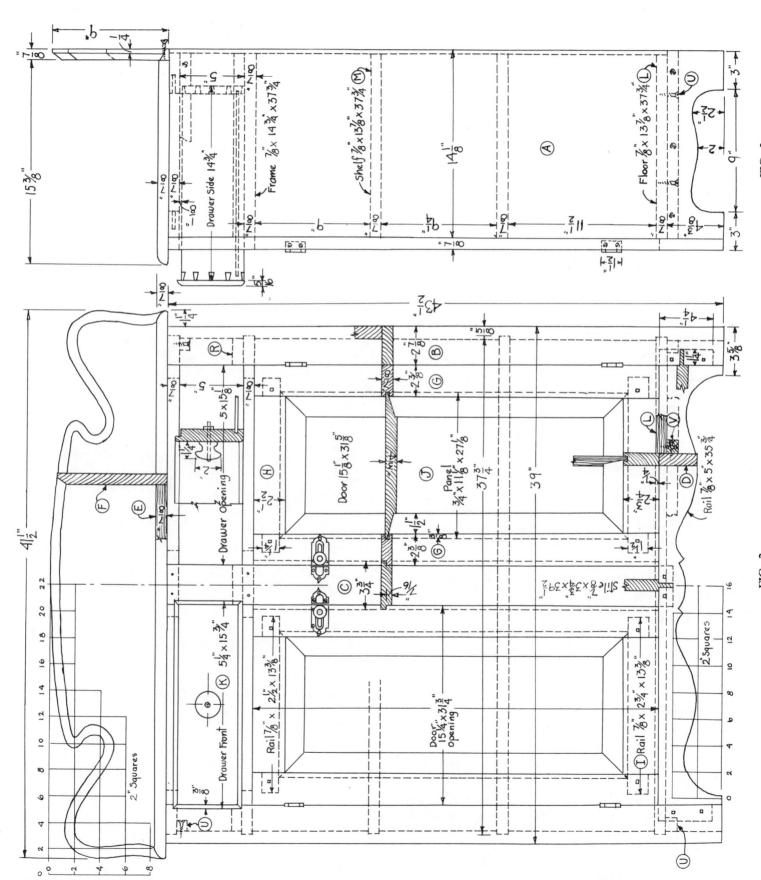

FIG. 3

FIG. 2

Building the cupboard should be fairly easy as there are no very difficult features. First make the two ends (A). Cut grooves to hold shelves and frames and rabbet the back edges to fasten the plywood back.

Make and fit floor (L), shelves (M), and the two frames at the top which holds the drawers. The frames are made with mortise-and-tenon joints.

Make the top (E) and fasten the upper frame to it with wood screws before gluing the shelves and the floor to the ends. Drill holes for wood screws into strips (U), and fasten the strips to the bottom of the upper frame. Make drawer guides (Q) and (R) and fasten them with wood screws to the top of the bottom frame.

Make a trial assembly of the ends, shelves, and frames, before gluing the shelves and floor to ends (A). Do not glue the frames to ends (A) because this might cause the ends of the sideboard to split if you do. Details shown in Fig. 4 help clarify construction of this upper part.

Make the frame for the front, consisting of stiles (B) and (C) and rail (D). Stile (C) is rabbeted on both edges where the rabbeted door stiles are lapped over it. The overlapping of these three members helps keep dust out of the cupboard, and also acts as a doorstop.

Join rail (D) to stiles (B) and (C) with mortise-and-tenon joints. Then bandsaw rail (D) to shape, and smooth the edges. Fit stile (C) to the places sawed out of the front rails (N), and when everything fits as it should, glue stiles (B) to ends (A), and stile (C) to front rails of both frames. Fasten strips (U) and (V) to floor (L), ends (A), and rail (D), with wood screws.

Make the drawers next, and fit them to their openings. Construction details for drawers are shown in Fig. 5.

Make the doors. Make door stiles (G) and rails (H) and (I). Cut mortise-and-tenon joints to fasten these together. Then groove inside edges to hold the panels, as shown in Fig. 2. Rabbet the stiles (G) where the door laps over stile (C). Make and fit the panels. (Panel-raising is described in Chapter Twenty-seven, Fig. 16.) Do not glue panels to rails or stiles, for these are held in place without glue. Fit doors to openings with enough clearance so they will open

and shut easily. Fit and fasten hinges, door catches, and drawer knobs.

Make the backboard (F) and fasten it with wood screws to the back edge of the top. Then make, and nail fast, the plywood back.

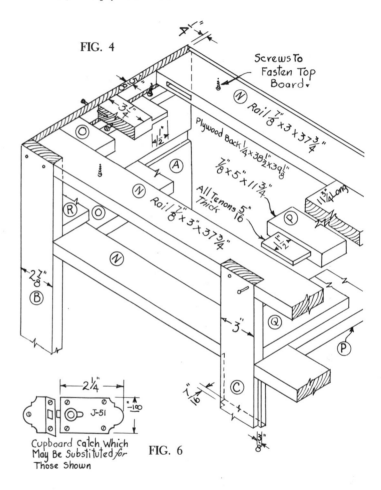

FIG. 4

Screws To Fasten Top Board.

Rail $\frac{7}{8}$" x 3 x 37$\frac{3}{4}$"

Plywood Back $\frac{1}{4}$ x 38$\frac{1}{2}$ x 39$\frac{1}{8}$"

$\frac{7}{8}$" x 5" x 11$\frac{3}{4}$"

All Tenons $\frac{5}{16}$" Thick

Rail $\frac{7}{8}$" x 3 x 37$\frac{3}{4}$"

Cupboard Catch Which May Be Substituted for Those Shown

J-51

2$\frac{1}{4}$

FIG. 6

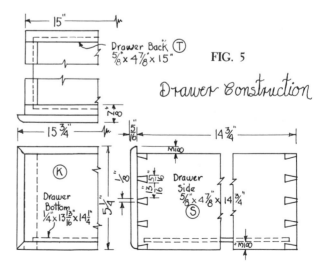

15"

Drawer Back (T) $\frac{5}{8}$" x 4$\frac{7}{8}$" x 15"

FIG. 5

Drawer Construction

15$\frac{3}{4}$"

(K)

Drawer Bottom $\frac{1}{4}$ x 13$\frac{13}{16}$ x 14$\frac{1}{4}$"

14$\frac{3}{4}$"

Drawer Side $\frac{5}{8}$" x 4$\frac{7}{8}$ x 14$\frac{3}{4}$

(S)

BILL OF MATERIAL

Pine

2 Ends (A) ⅞" x 14⅛" x 43½"
2 Stiles (B) ⅞" x 2⅞" x 43½"
1 Stile (C) ⅞" x 3¾" x 39½"
1 Bottom rail (D) ⅞" x 5" x 35¾"
1 Top (E) ⅞" x 15⅜" x 41½"
1 Backboard (F) ⅞" x 9" x 41½"
4 Door stiles (G) ⅞" x 2⅜" x 31⅝"
2 Door rails (H) ⅞" x 2½" x 13⅜"
2 Door rails (I) ⅞" x 2¾" x 13⅜"
2 Door panels (J) ¾" x 11⅛" x 27⅛"
2 Drawer fronts (K) ⅞" x 5¼" x 15¾"
1 Floor (L) ⅞" x 13⅞" x 37¾"
2 Shelves (M) ⅞" x 13⅞" x 37¾"
4 Rails in frames above and below drawers (N)
   ⅞" x 3" x 37¾"

4 Rails in frames (O) ⅞" x 3¼" x 11¾"
2 Rails in frames (P) ⅞" x 5" x 11¾"
1 Drawer guide (Q) ⅞" x 3" x 13⅞"
2 Drawer guides (R) ⅞" x 2" x 13⅞"
4 Drawer sides (S) ⅝" x 4⅞" x 14¾"
2 Drawer backs (T) ⅝" x 4⅞" x 15"
4 Strips to fasten floor and top frame to ends (U) ⅞" x
   ⅞" x 14⅞"
1 Strip to support front of floor (V) ⅞" x ⅞" x 35½"

Birch Plywood

1 Back ¼" x 38½" x 39⅛"
2 Drawer bottoms ¼" x 13¹³⁄₁₆" x 14¼"

TEN

Dry Sink Hutch

BEFORE INDOOR PLUMBING BROUGHT RUNNING water into houses, dry sinks like this hutch were in common use in many homes, or at least this was so in my section of Pennsylvania in my early youth. The tray held a dishpan filled with water, and usually a drying rack of sorts, in which to stack dishes until dry, when they could be stored elsewhere until they were needed again.

The item has been resurrected, though it is now put to a different use—usually as a kitchen sideboard, as is the one shown here, and also the one shown in Chapter Eleven. Cherry was used to build both, but the original models more often were made of pine, poplar, and sometimes walnut.

The construction presents no great difficulties for even amateur woodworkers, if instructions given in the drawings are adhered to.

First, plane and sand the lumber to sizes given in the Bill of Material. Saw both ends (A) to shape, as shown in Fig. 3. I do wish to call attention to the dovetail joints where the front (J) is joined to ends (A). It is not good practice to dovetail this front, the grain of which runs horizontally, to another board on which the grain runs vertically, as it does here. In this instance it is done for purposes of display rather than to achieve good construction, and considerable care is required when sawing, fitting, and assembling these two joints to avoid breaking off the pins formed on ends (A). These joints could (and should) be strengthened, by inserting a piece about 2 inches wide, like the one I show at (Z) in Fig. 10. The short piece is half-lapped, and glued to the inside of (A), thus strengthening this area so the dovetail joint can be made with little likelihood that the pins will split off.

Back edges of (A) should be rabbeted so the back may be nailed to them. Then make the dovetail joints to fasten the front (J) to both ends (A).

Make the frame which goes around the drawer fronts at the top, consisting of pieces (I), (G), (H), (F); and the frame to which the doors are fastened at the bottom, consisting of pieces (K), (L), and (M). Glue (J) to ends (A).

Make shelf (C), back (D), and brackets (E). Make the dovetail joints and glue the brackets to the back. Fasten (E) and (D) to shelf (C) with wood screws. Screw strips (U) to the underside of shelf (C) to keep the drawers level when pulled out; then fasten shelf (C) to ends (A) with ¾"-x-¾" strips of wood, fastened inside to both. These strips must first be fastened with wood screws to the shelf, then to the ends, before the back of the hutch can be put in place.

Make shelf (T), and glue the upper frame to its front edge. Make and fasten drawer guides (V) to shelf (T); then fasten these to ends (A).

The table board (B), and the floor (S), should now

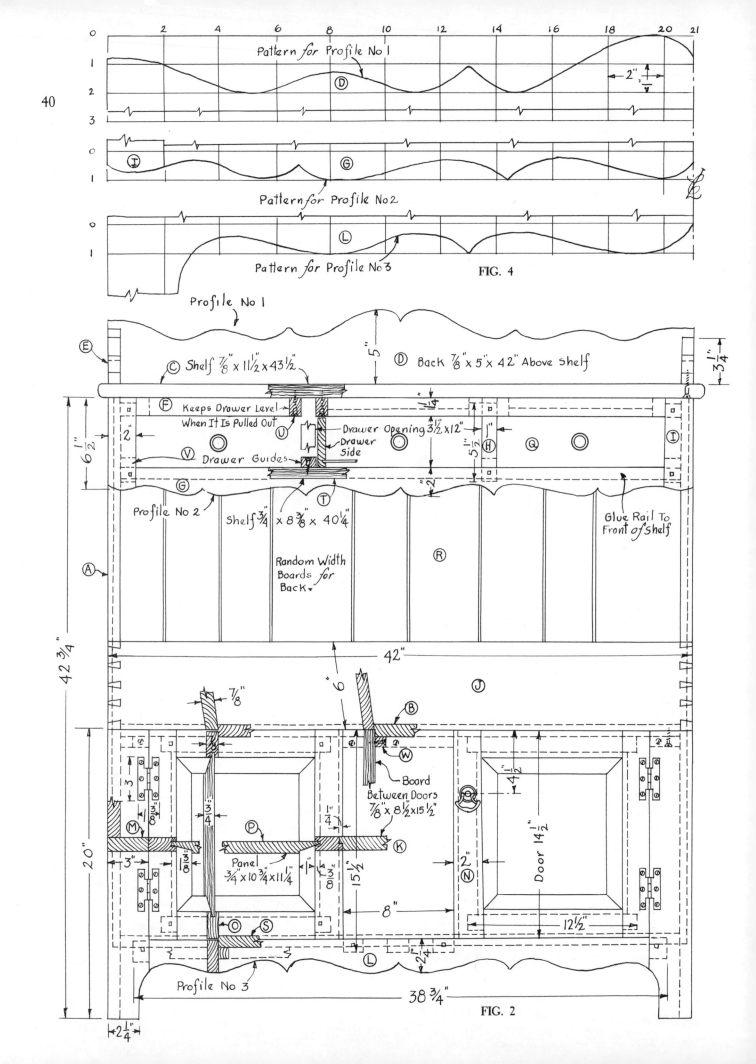

Pattern for Profile No 1

Ⓓ

2"

Ⓘ Ⓖ

Pattern for Profile No 2

Ⓛ

Pattern for Profile No 3

FIG. 4

Profile No 1

Ⓔ

5"

3¼"

Ⓒ Shelf ⅞" x 11½" x 43½"

Ⓓ Back ⅞" x 5" x 42" Above Shelf

Ⓕ Keeps Drawer Level
When It Is Pulled Out

Drawer Opening 3½"x12"

6½"

2"

1¼"

5½"

1"

Ⓤ

Drawer
Side

Ⓗ

Ⓘ

Ⓥ Drawer Guides

Ⓠ

Ⓖ

2"

Ⓣ

Profile No 2

Shelf ¾" x 8⅜" x 40¼"

Glue Rail To
Front of Shelf

Random Width
Boards for
Back

Ⓡ

Ⓐ

42"

6"

Ⓙ

⅞"

Ⓑ

Ⓦ

Board
Between Doors
⅞" x 8½" x 15½"

3

Ⓜ

¾

¼

Ⓟ

14½"

Ⓚ

Panel
¾" x 10¾" x 11¼"

15½

2"

Ⓝ

Door 14½"

8"

20

3"

12½"

Ⓞ Ⓢ

Ⓛ

2¼"

Profile No 3

38¾"

FIG. 2

42¾"

2¼"

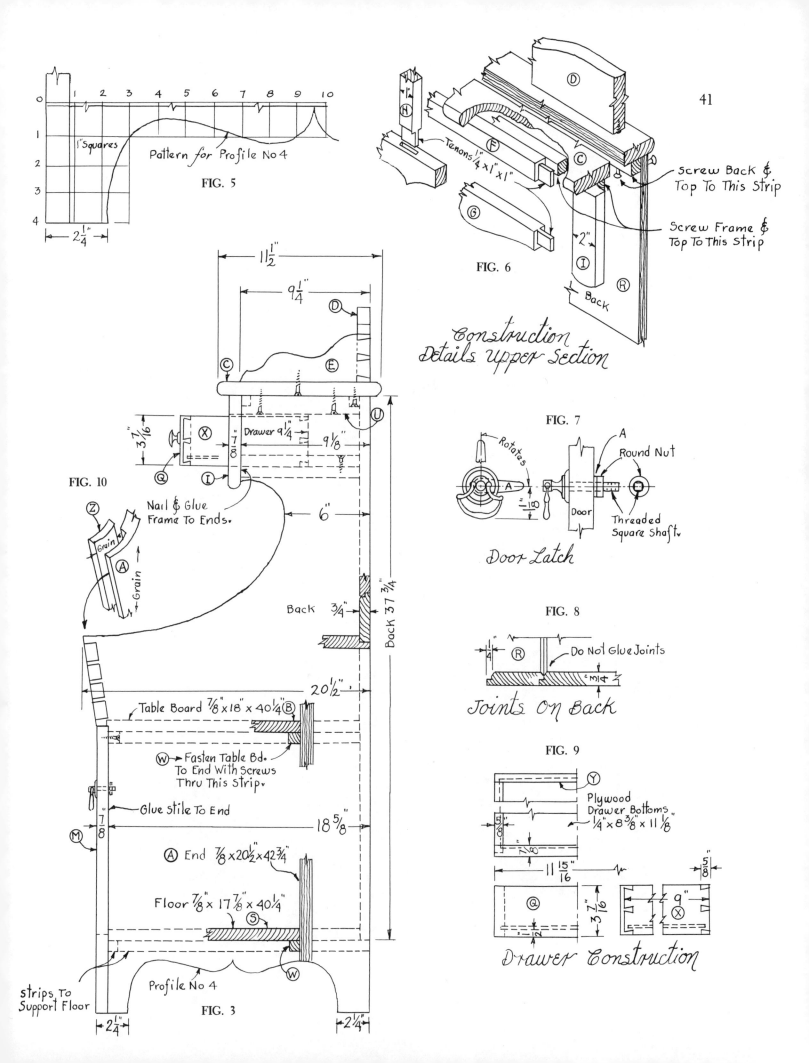

41

Pattern for Profile No.4

1" Squares

2¼"

FIG. 5

Tenons ¼"×1"×1"

Screw Back & Top To This Strip

Screw Frame & Top To This Strip

2"

Back

FIG. 6

Construction Details upper Section

FIG. 7

Rotates

A

Round Nut

Door

Threaded Square Shaft.

Door Latch

FIG. 8

R

¼"

Do Not Glue Joints

¾"

Joints On Back

FIG. 9

Y

Plywood Drawer Bottoms ¼"×8⅜"×11⅛"

11 15/16"

3 7/16"

9"

Drawer Construction

11½"

9¼"

D

C

E

U

3 7/16

Drawer 9¼"

9⅛"

Nail & Glue Frame To Ends.

6"

Back 37¾"

Back 3/4"

FIG. 10

Z

Grain

A

Grain

20½"

Table Board ⅞"×18"×40¼" B

W → Fasten Table Bd. To End With Screws Thru This Strip.

Glue stile To End

M

⅞"

18 5/8"

A End ⅞×20½"×42¾"

Floor ⅞"×17⅞"×40¼"

S

strips To Support Floor

Profile No 4

2¼"

FIG. 3

2¼"

W

be made and fastened to the ends with ¾″-x-¾″ strips, screwed to them and to ends (A) to support both. (See Figs. 2 and 3.)

You can now fasten the bottom frame, which holds the doors, to ends (A). Stiles (M) can be glued to ends (A), and so can rail (L) be glued to floor (S). The upper ends of stiles (M) and board (K) are fastened to the bottom of the table board with ¾″-x-¾″ strips, as shown in Fig. 2.

You should now be ready to make and fasten the back (R). This is made of random-width boards, whose edges are joined with lap joints, as shown in Fig. 8. It is nailed to the rabbets cut into the back edges of ends (A), to table board (B), to floor (S), and to shelf (T).

All that now remains to be done is to make and fit both doors, and the three drawers. Little more need be said here regarding these, except to say that cross-

FIG. 1

section details shown at the left in Fig. 2 pretty well show how doors are made; and details of the drawers in Fig. 9 show their construction.

I have shown square, hardwood pegs used to strengthen glued mortise-and-tenon joints, where stiles and rails are joined together. These are not found on the piece shown in the photograph, or on the door on the right in my drawing. Pegs give additional strength to such mortise-and-tenon joints, and add, rather than detract, from the appearance.

The door latches are brass, and the lever holding the door shut rotates as shown in Fig. 7.

BILL OF MATERIAL

Cherry

2 Ends (A) ⅞" x 20½" x 42¾"
1 Table board (B) ⅞" x 18" x 40¼"
1 Top shelf (C) ⅞" x 11½" x 43½"
1 Back above shelf (D) ⅞" x 5" x 42"
2 Brackets (E) at ends of (D) ⅞" x 3¼" x 9¼"
1 Rail above drawers (F) ⅞" x 1¼" x 40"
1 Rail below drawers (G) ⅞" x 2" x 40"
2 Stiles between drawers (H) ⅞" x 1" x 5½"
2 Ends of drawer frame (I) ⅞" x 2" x 6½"
1 Front of dry sink (J) ⅞" x 6" x 42"
1 Board between doors (K) ⅞" x 8½" x 15½"
1 Bottom rail (L) ⅞" x 2¼" x 38¾"
2 Stiles (M) ⅞" x 3" x 20"
4 Door stiles (N) ⅞" x 2" x 14½"
4 Door rails (O) ⅞" x 2" x 12½"
2 Door panels (P) ¾" x 10¾" x 11¼"
3 Drawer fronts (Q) ⅞" x 3⁷⁄₁₆" x 11¹⁵⁄₁₆"

Back, random width boards (R) ¾" x ? x 37¾" (See Fig. 8.)

Poplar

1 Floor (S) ⅞" x 17⅞" x 40¼"
1 Shelf under drawers (T) ¾" x 8⅜" x 40¼"
6 Strips to keep drawers level when pulled out (U) ¾" x 1¼" x 8⅜"
2 Drawer guides (V) ¾" x 1" x 8⅜" and 2 guides ¾" x 1⅛" x 8⅜"
Strips of wood (W) ¾" x ¾" x lengths as needed to support floor, shelves, and table board
6 Drawer sides (X) ⅝" x 3⁷⁄₁₆" x 9"
3 Drawer backs (Y) ⅝" x 3⁷⁄₁₆" x 11¹⁵⁄₁₆"

Birch Plywood

3 Drawer bottoms ¼" x 8⅜" x 11⅛"

ELEVEN

Small Cherry Dry Sink

BEFORE KITCHENS HAD PIPED-IN RUNNING WATER, dirty dishes were washed with water heated on the kitchen stove, and then placed on wooden racks in the trough of a dry sink similar to the one shown here. When dry, the dishes were put back into cupboards, and cooking utensils stored in the bottom of the dry sink.

Though rarely used today for its former purpose, one now finds them used as sideboards and serving tables in the dining room, to hold snacks or toys and games in dens and rumpus rooms, and even as utility tables in bedrooms, as is the case with the one shown in Fig. 1.

To build the dry sink, first make the two ends (A), and rabbet the back edges where the plywood back is to be nailed to them, and also rabbet ends at the top where the frame is attached to it with wood screws. This frame, shown in some detail in Figs. 4 and 5, is put there to hold the upper part of the cupboard section together, and also as a base for the trough bottom. Wood screws through this frame hold the trough in place, as shown in Fig. 3. The front rail of the frame also acts as a door and drawer stop, and because the drawer front goes all the way to the bottom edge of the trough front (J), it is necessary to reduce the width of the drawer sides on both drawers to fit them under the frame.

Because of the somewhat unusual manner of fastening the trough to the lower section, anyone wishing to reproduce this piece of furniture should follow steps in its construction in the following sequence:

1. Make ends (A), and the two front legs (B).

2. Make rail (C), and fasten it to legs (B) with mortise-and-tenon joints, as shown in Fig. 2. Then fasten legs (B) to ends (A) with glue, and a few 6-penny finish nails.

3. Make the frame, consisting of rails (O) and (P), and assemble these with mortise-and-tenon joints, as shown in Figs. 4 and 5.

4. Make boards (Q), and fasten these to the frame with wood screws, as shown in Figs. 4 and 5. (The width of board [Q] in Fig. 5 is dimensioned correctly, but is shown narrower than its actual width in this exploded view.)

5. Fasten the frame with wood screws to the tops of ends (A). Ends of the front rail (O) may be glued to the ends of the cupboard, but put no glue where the cross rails (P) are fastened to them.

6. Make the trough, and fasten it to the frame with wood screws from below, as shown in Fig. 3.

7. Make boards to support the drawers. These should be fastened with wood screws to the bottom edges of (Q), and held in place with strips of wood screwed to the inside of legs and ends, as shown in

Figs. 2 and 3. Guide strips, to keep drawers running straight, should be glued and bradded to (Q) and (R).

8. Make the cupboard floor, and fasten it to ends (A), legs (B), and rail (C). It is fastened to (A), (B), and (C) with supporting strips of wood, and has been left to be fastened last in order that operations 1 to 7 could be accomplished more easily. After fitting drawers, nail on the back.

Doors and drawers should now be made, and fitted into places provided for them. The brass door latch used here is like the one used to latch the doors on the Pine Dutch Cupboard, and is shown in detail in Fig. 12 in Chapter Twenty-two. An elbow catch like the one shown in Fig. 6 may be used to hold the left-hand door when closed. The **H**-hinges are also made of brass.

Door panels are never glued into door frames, but are merely held in place by fitting them loosely into grooves cut into the rails and stiles. Mortise-and-tenon joints are glued, and should be pinned with square hardwood pegs driven into drilled holes whose diameter is the same as the thickness of the pegs. Fig. 7 shows drawer construction details. Beading on drawer fronts, and also that found on one edge of the leg and on top of rail (C), could be glued on, but I prefer molding these with an electric hand router, and/or wood-carving chisels, right on the piece of which they are a part.

FIG. 1

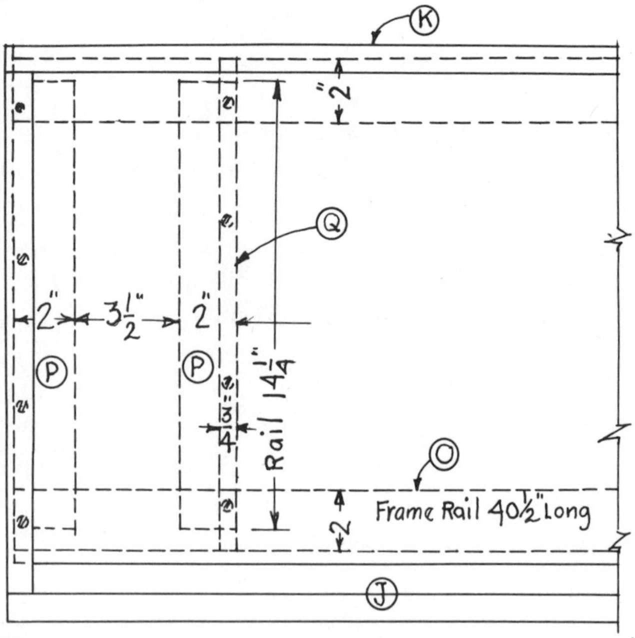
K
2"
Q
2" 3½" 2"
P
P
Rail 14¼"
¾
O
Frame Rail 40½" Long
2"
J

FIG. 4

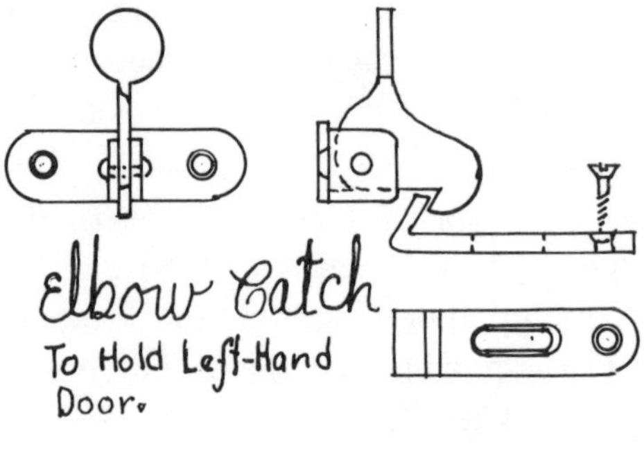
Elbow Catch
To Hold Left-Hand Door.

FIG. 6

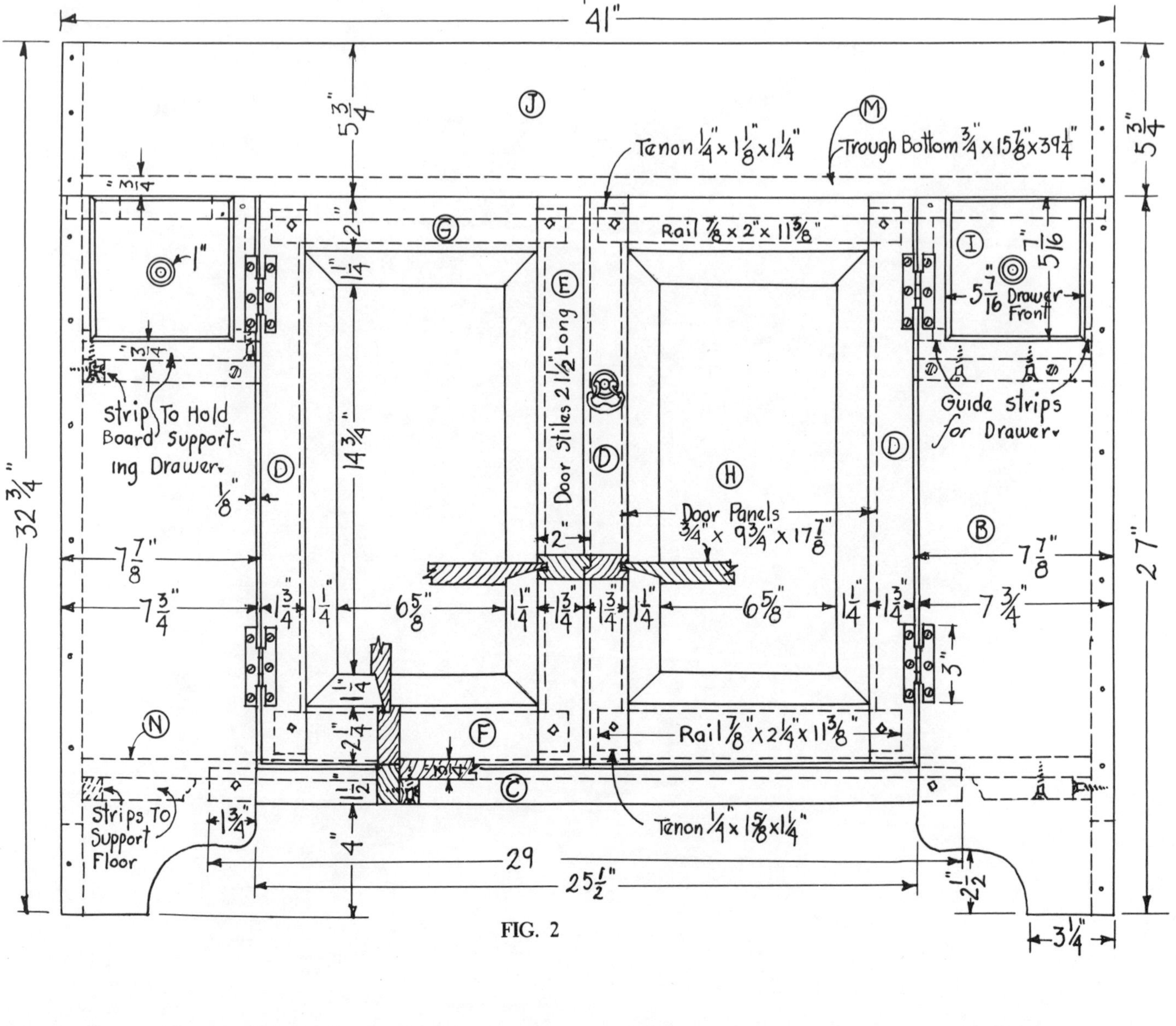
41"
J
5¾"
M
Tenon ¼" x 1⅛" x 1¼"
Trough Bottom ¾" x 15⅞" x 39¼"
5¾"
¾"
2"
G
Rail ⅞" x 2" x 11⅜"
I
1"
1¼"
E
7/16"
5 7/16
Drawer Front
¾"
Door Stiles 21½" Long
Strip To Hold Board Supporting Drawer.
Guide strips for Drawer.
14¾"
D
D
D
H
⅛"
Door Panels ¾" x 9¾" x 17⅞"
B
32¾"
7⅞"
2"
7⅞"
27"
7¾"
1¾"
1¼"
6⅝"
1¼"
1¾"
1¾"
1¼"
6⅝"
1¼"
1¾"
7¾"
3"
1¼"
N
2¼"
F
Rail ⅞" x 2¼" x 11⅜"
1½"
C
Strips To Support Floor
1¾"
4"
Tenon ¼" x 1⅝" x 1¼"
29
25½"
2½"
3¼"

FIG. 2

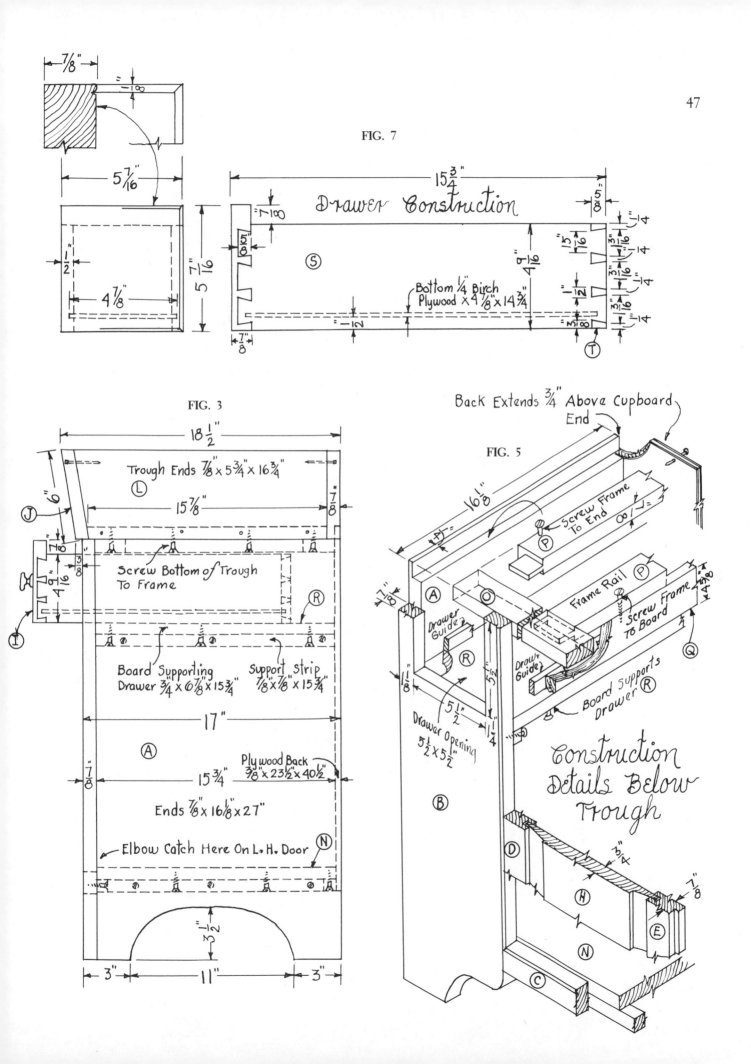

FIG. 7

Drawer Construction

7/8"

5 7/16"

5 7/16"

1/2"

4 7/8"

15 3/4"

5/8"

4 9/16"

S

Bottom 1/4" Birch
Plywood × 4 7/8" × 14 3/4"

7/8"

T

FIG. 3

18 1/2"

Trough Ends 7/8" × 5 3/4" × 16 3/4"
L

15 7/8"

7/8"

J

6"

Screw Bottom of Trough
To Frame

R

Board Supporting
Drawer 3/4 × 6 7/8 × 15 3/4"

Support Strip
7/8" × 7/8" × 15 3/4"

17"

A

Plywood Back
3/8" × 23 1/2" × 40 1/2"

15 3/4"

7/8"

Ends 7/8 × 16 1/8 × 27"

Elbow Catch Here On L.H. Door

N

3 1/2"

3"

11"

3"

Back Extends 3/4" Above Cupboard
End

FIG. 5

16 1/8"

Screw Frame
To End

P

A

O

Frame Rail

P

Screw Frame
To Board

Q

Drawer
Guide

R

Drawer
Guide

Board Supports
Drawer R

1 1/8"

5 1/2"

5 1/2"

1 1/4"

Drawer Opening
5 1/2" × 5 1/2"

B

D

H

3/4"

E

7/8"

N

C

Construction
Details Below
Trough

BILL OF MATERIAL

Cherry

2 Ends (A) ⅞″ x 16⅛″ x 27″
2 Front legs (B) ⅞″ x 7⅞″ x 27″
1 Rail below doors (C) ⅞″ x 1½″ x 29″
3 Door stiles (D) ⅞″ x 1¾″ x 21½″
1 Door stile (E) ⅞″ x 2″ x 21½″
2 Door rails (F) ⅞″ x 2¼″ x 11⅜″
2 Door rails (G) ⅞″ x 2″ x 11⅜″
2 Door panels (H) ¾″ x 9¾″ x 17⅞″
2 Drawer fronts (I) ⅞″ x 5⁷⁄₁₆″ x 5⁷⁄₁₆″
1 Trough front (J) ⅞″ x 6″ x 41″
1 Trough back (K) ⅞″ x 5¾″ x 41″
2 Trough ends (L) ⅞″ x 5¾″ x 16¾″
1 Trough bottom (M) ¾″ x 15⅞″ x 39¼″

Poplar

1 Floor (N) ¾″ x 15¾″ x 39¼″

2 Long frame rails (O) ⅞″ x 2″ x 40½″
4 Short frame rails (P) ⅞″ x 2″ x 14¼″
2 Partition boards between drawers and cupboard (Q)
    ¾″ x 4⅝″ x 15¾″
2 Supporting boards under drawers (R) ¾″ x 7″ x
    15¾″
4 Drawer sides (S) ½″ x 4⁹⁄₁₆″ x 15½″
2 Drawer backs (T) ⅝″ x 4⁹⁄₁₆″ x 5⁷⁄₁₆″
Support strips for floor, and for drawer supports (U)
    ⅞″ x ⅞″ in various lengths

Birch Plywood

1 Back (V) ⅜″ x 23½″ x 40½″
2 Drawer bottoms (W) ¼″ x 4⅞″ x 14¾″

Queen Anne Hunt Table

HUNT BOARDS, OR HUNT TABLES, ARE SO named because they were originally used as sideboards on which to serve refreshments after hunting trips. Some are taller than table height, which is usually about 30 inches, and food served from them is eaten with the guests standing rather than sitting. This one is table height so it may be used either way, and it functions equally well as a dining table. Some hunt tables have a drop leaf on only one side of the table; this one has drop leaves on both sides.

FIG. 1

50

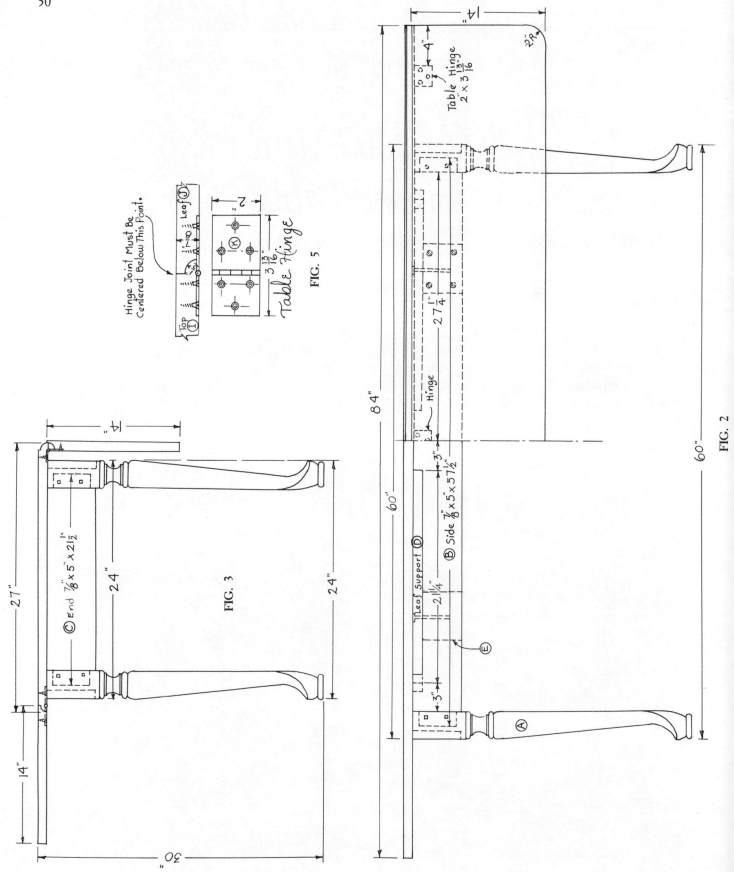

FIG. 5

Hinge Joint Must Be
Centered Below This Point.

Top Ⓘ

Hinge Leaf Ⓙ

Ⓚ

2"

3 13/16"

Table Hinge

FIG. 3

4"

27"

24"

Ⓒ End 7/8" x 5 x 21 1/2"

14"

24"

30"

FIG. 2

14"

4"

2 R"

Table Hinge
2" x 3 13/16"

84"

60"

27 1/4"

Hinge

3"

Leaf Support Ⓓ

Ⓑ Side 7/8" x 5 x 57 1/2"

2 11/4"

Ⓔ

3"

Ⓐ

60"

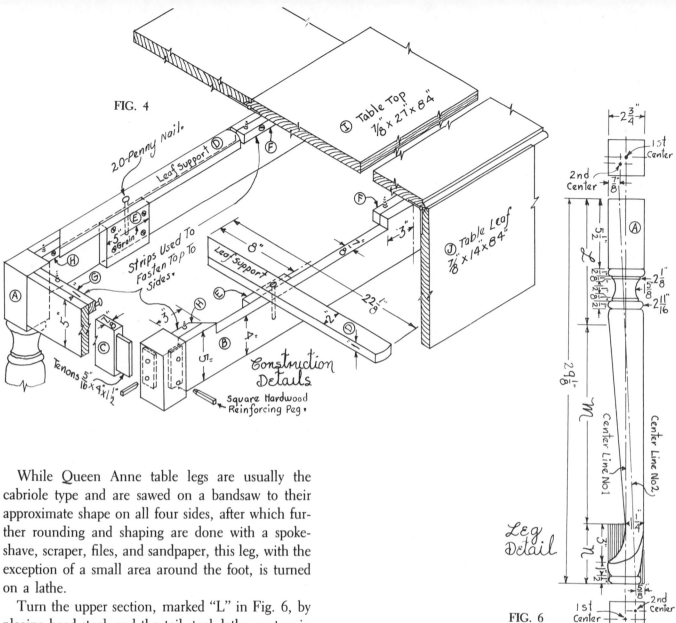

FIG. 4

20-Penny Nail.

Leaf Support D

Table Top I
7/8" x 27" x 84"

Table Leaf J
7/8" x 14" x 84"

Strips Used To
Fasten Top To
Sides.

Leaf Support

8"

3"

22 1/8"

2"

Tenons 5/16" x 4" x 1 1/2"

Construction
Details

Square Hardwood
Reinforcing Peg.

Leg
Detail

FIG. 6

2 3/4"

1st Center

2nd Center

7/8"

5 1/2"

2 1/8"

2 1/8"

1 5/8"

2 1/8"

2 11/16"

Center Line No.1

Center Line No.2

29 1/8"

3"

1 1/2"

5/8"

1st Center

2nd Center

2 3/4"

While Queen Anne table legs are usually the cabriole type and are sawed on a bandsaw to their approximate shape on all four sides, after which further rounding and shaping are done with a spokeshave, scraper, files, and sandpaper, this leg, with the exception of a small area around the foot, is turned on a lathe.

Turn the upper section, marked "L" in Fig. 6, by placing head-stock and the tail-stock lathe centers in the middle of both ends, marked "1st center" in Fig. 6. After turning section "L," relocate the head- and tail-stock centers as indicated by "2nd center" locations in Fig. 6. When this has been done you can turn section "M." Draw a full-sized cardboard pattern of the foot from Fig. 6. Trace its outline on one side of the stock and bandsaw it to shape by removing the shaded portions of section "N." Then trace the outline on an adjacent side of the stock. After you have sawed off the shaded areas from these sides, you are ready to round and finish shaping the foot.

Glued mortise-and-tenon joints are used to hold legs and table aprons together. Squared, hardwood wooden pegs, driven into drilled 3/16-inch holes reinforce these joints, as shown in Figs. 2, 3, and 4. Table leaves are supported when raised by leaf supports (D), which swing out from the table frame, as shown in Fig. 4. An axis for these is provided by using a 20-penny nail, which is about the right length, as a fulcrum. Backing blocks (E) are fastened with glue and wood screws to the inside of the long rails so the holes for the nails can be drilled.

The tabletop should be glued up from narrower boards, which reduces the danger of warping. Rule joints are made with matching molding cutters on the spindle shaper to join leaves to the top. Fig. 5 shows how table hinges are fastened to join these to each other properly. It is important to center the hinge joint directly below the place specified in the enlarged detail shown in Fig. 5. The hinge leaves must be mortised into the undersides of the top and leaves as shown. When properly fitted, table leaves may be raised and lowered without having the joint bind or gape open when raised or lowered.

BILL OF MATERIAL

Walnut

4 Legs (A) 2¾″ x 2¾″ x 29⅛″
2 Sides (B) ⅞″ x 5″ x 57½″
2 Ends (C) ⅞″ x 5″ x 21½″
4 Leaf supports (D) 1″ x 2″ x 22⅛″
4 Backing blocks to hinge leaf supports (E)
  1⅛″ x 4″ x 5″

2 Strips to fasten top to table frame (F) 1″ x 1″ x 6″
2 Strips to fasten top to table frame (G) 1″ x 1″ x 18½″
4 Strips to fasten top to table frame (H) 1″ x 1″ x 3″
1 Tabletop (I) ⅞″ x 27″ x 84″
2 Table leaves (J) ⅞″ x 14″ x 84″
6 Drop-leaf table hinges (K)

THIRTEEN

Pembroke Table

LADY PEMBROKE, AN ENGLISHWOMAN, IS SAID to have ordered Thomas Sheraton to build a small, light drop-leaf table with a drawer in one end, and since the late 1700s, tables falling roughly into this category have been called Pembroke tables. Later on, small, light, delicately proportioned tables of this kind were made in other styles, but the name came into common usage over a period of time, the designation applying to all small, light tables of this kind.

To build the table, first make the four legs (A). Strips of maple $\frac{1}{16}$ inch wide are inlaid on two outside surfaces of each leg, as on the table shown in Fig. 1. However, if strips of celluloid inlay are substituted for the maple strips on this table, the legs can be stained without discoloring the celluloid, which merits consideration of the substitution. Wider strips of inlay, like those at the bottom of the legs, and the banding below the drawer, must be masked with tape to prevent discoloration before applying stain. Shallow grooves, just a shade less deep than the thickness of the $\frac{1}{16}$-inch inlay, can be made with a scratch stock. Thus the inlay, after being glued in place, protrudes above the surface of the leg just enough to enable one to sand it level with the wood. Fig. 6 shows where to put the inlay.

Lay out places to be mortised on each leg and cut these mortises just a little more than $\frac{7}{8}$ inch deep.

Then make rails (B) for both sides, rail (C) for the back, and rail (E) to go under the drawer. Cut tenons on these and fit them to their respective mortises. Saw and trim places on top of side rails (B), where the support strips for table leaves are to go. Rabbet the lower edge of rail (E) for the inlay banding, and glue this to the rabbeted edge. Inlay strips, exactly the same, or closely resembling those shown in Fig. 1,

FIG. 1

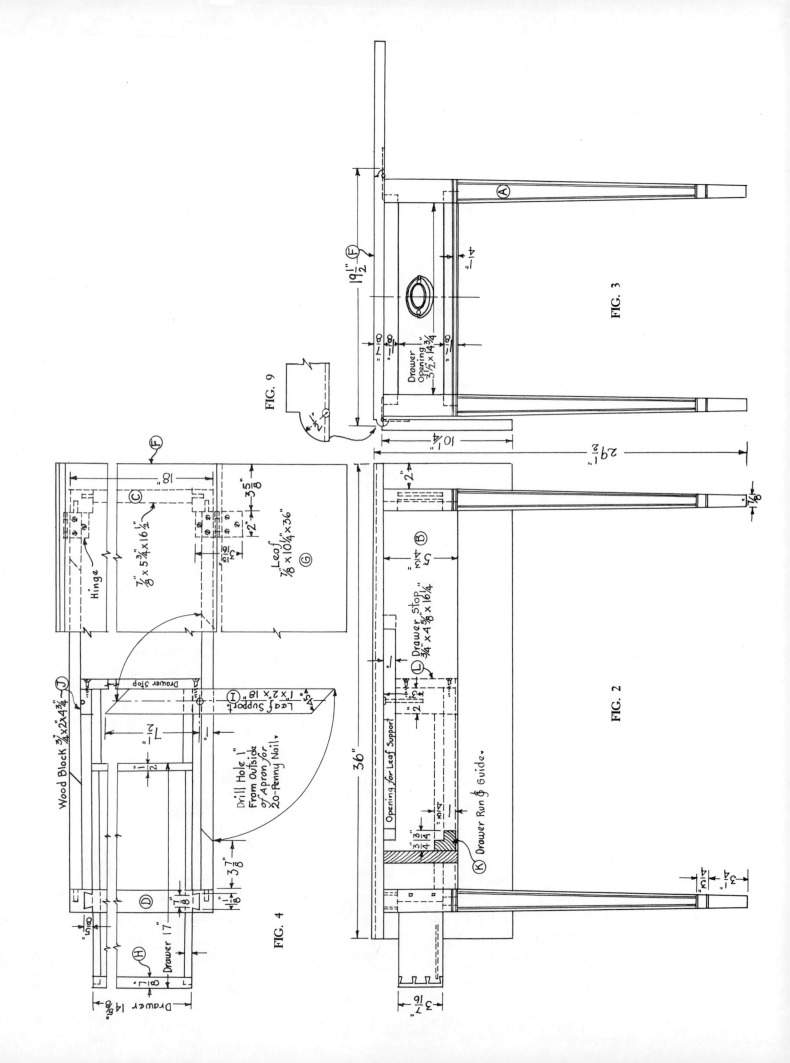

FIG. 3

FIG. 9

FIG. 2

FIG. 4

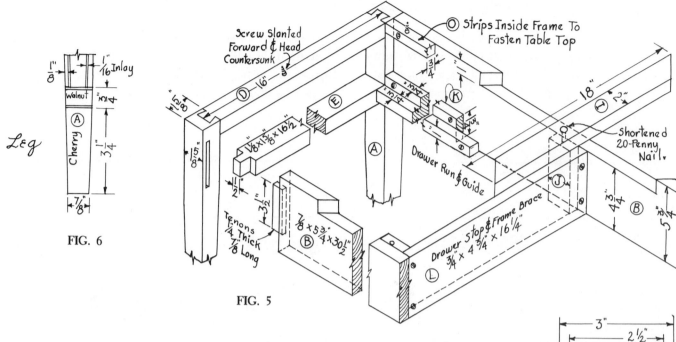

Leg

FIG. 6

FIG. 5

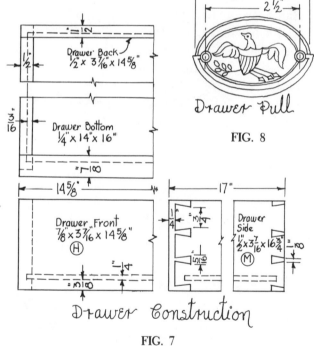

Drawer Pull

FIG. 8

Drawer Construction

FIG. 7

may be purchased at low cost in a variety of designs from full-color mail order catalogs.*

Make rail (D). After shaping the dovetails on both ends, place each on top of the legs to mark the places to be cut out to hold them.

Make a trial assembly of the legs and rails, but before you glue up the frame make blocks (J) and fasten them with wood screws to the insides of rails (B). Then drill holes to hold the shortened 20-penny nails, used as axes for supporting strips (I). The nail heads must be sunk level with the upper sides of these supporting strips, so top (F) can be drawn down tight against the table rails with wood screws.

Supporting strips (I) are positioned to come flush with the outside of rails (B) when the table leaves are down, as the arcs drawn in Fig. 4 will show you.

Glue up the table frame. Make the drawer runs. Drawer run and guide are one piece, as shown in Figs. 2 and 5. Fasten these to rails (B) with wood screws, as in Fig. 5. Then make and fasten drawer stop (L), which also helps strengthen the frame at its center.

Make the drawer and fit it to the opening. Drawer construction is shown in Fig. 7.

Make the tabletop (F) and leaves (G). The rule

*Catalogs may be obtained from Albert Constantine, 2050 Eastchester Road, New York, N.Y. 10461.

joint, where leaves and top come together, should be made with matching shaper cutters. One part of this joint, made on both edges of top (F), is shown in Fig. 9. The center of the table leaf hinge barrel must line up with the vertical line of the fillet directly above it for this joint to function properly when raising or lowering the leaves.

Table-leaf hinges are recessed into both top and

leaf to bring them flush with the undersides of both. When leaves and top have been properly fitted with hinges, lay the assembled top upside down on a flat surface such as a worktable or floor, and with the frame properly located on the underside of (F), screw the frame to it with wood screws. Strips (O) are fastened to the inside of the frame with wood screws so this can be done.

BILL OF MATERIAL

Cherry

4 Legs (A) 1⅝″ x 1⅝″ x 28⅝″
2 Side rails (B) ⅞″ x 5¾″ x 30½″
1 Back rail (C) ⅞″ x 5¾″ x 16½″
1 Rail above drawer (D) 1⅛″ x 1⅝″ x 16″
1 Rail below drawer (E) 1⅛″ x 1⅝″ x 16½″
1 Tabletop (F) ⅞″ x 19½″ x 36″
2 Leaves (G) ⅞″ x 10¼″ x 36″
1 Drawer front (H) ⅞″ x 3⁷⁄₁₆″ x 14⅝″
2 Leaf support strips (I) 1″ x 2″ x 18″
2 Wood blocks to hold fulcrum nails (J) ¾″ x 2″ x 4¾″

Poplar

2 Drawer runs and guides (K) 1½″ x 1¾″ x 15⅜″
1 Drawer stop and frame brace (L) ¾″ x 4¾″ x 16¼″
2 Drawer sides (M) ½″ x 3⁷⁄₁₆″ x 16¾″
1 Drawer back (N) ½″ x 3⁷⁄₁₆″ x 14⅝″
Strips to fasten top to frame (O) ¾″ x ¾″ x lengths as needed

Birch Plywood

1 Drawer bottom ¼″ x 14″ x 16″

FOURTEEN

Dough Trough

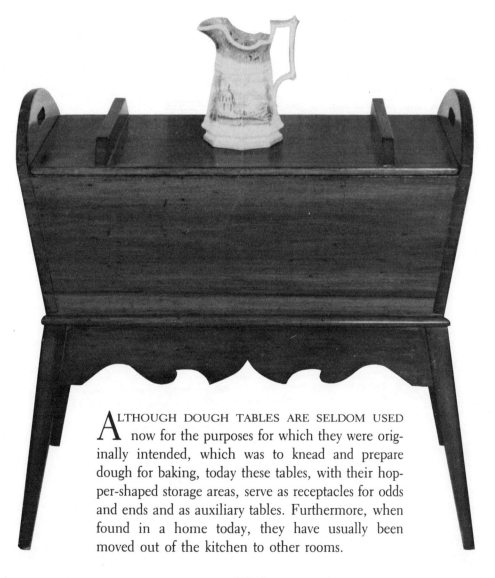

Although dough tables are seldom used now for the purposes for which they were originally intended, which was to knead and prepare dough for baking, today these tables, with their hopper-shaped storage areas, serve as receptacles for odds and ends and as auxiliary tables. Furthermore, when found in a home today, they have usually been moved out of the kitchen to other rooms.

FIG. 1

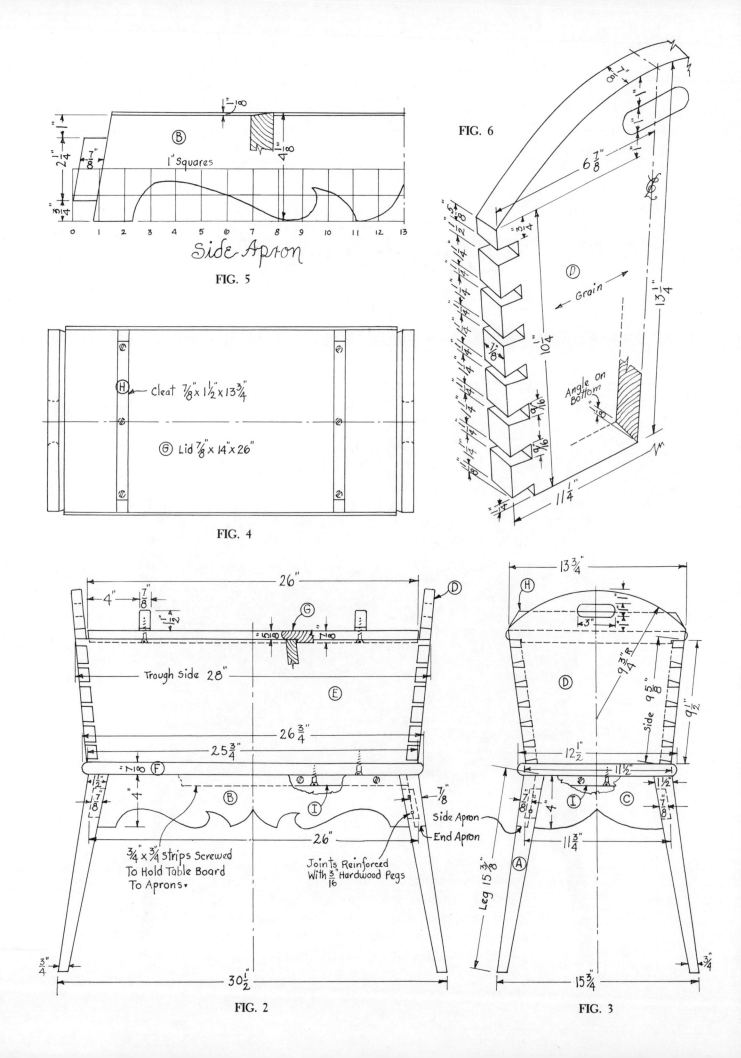

FIG. 6

FIG. 5

Side Apron

B
1" Squares

FIG. 4

H → Cleat ⅞" x 1½" x 13¾"

G → Lid ⅞" x 14" x 26"

D
Grain
Angle on Bottom

FIG. 2

26"
4"
Trough side 28"
E
26¾"
25¾"
F
B
I
3/4" x 3/4" Strips Screwed To Hold Table Board To Aprons.
Joints Reinforced With 3/16" Hardwood Pegs
26"
30½"
¾"

FIG. 3

13¾"
H
3"
9¾" R
D
Side 9⅝"
9½"
12½"
11½"
I
C
Side Apron
End Apron
11¾"
A
Leg 15⅜"
15¾"
¾"

Poplar was the wood most frequently used in their construction because it did not transfer objectionable odors to dough or other food, and the fact that wide boards in this material were, and still are, available was another consideration for choosing it for this purpose. Provided the table is not to be used for preparing food, other woods such as walnut, cherry, and pine may be substituted to build the dough trough.

To make the dough trough, first make the legs (A). Lay out and cut mortises to which aprons (B) and (C) are to be joined.

Saw aprons (B) and (C) to sizes given in the Bill of Material. Do not saw the bottom edges to shape until tenons on the ends of the aprons have been cut to size and fitted to their respective mortises. When this has been accomplished, plane the top edges to the angle required to make them even with the tops of the legs. Then saw bottom edges to shape on the bandsaw, and file and sandpaper these edges. Glue mortise-and-tenon joints, and drill $\frac{3}{16}$-inch holes for the squared hardwood reinforcing pegs shown in Fig. 2.

Make the trough next, starting with ends (D). Details for the layout of these are shown in Fig. 6. Saw the dovetail angles, going with the grain in Fig. 6, with a dovetail saw. Notice that the ends of the dovetails are angled slightly across the ends of (D), and these lines should be drawn using the sliding T-bevel instead of a try square. When the dovetail saw cuts have been made, most of the waste may be removed with parallel saw cuts on the bandsaw where pins cut on the ends of trough sides (E) are to be joined to the tails on (D). If the bandsaw table can be tilted to conform to the angles of the lines on the ends of (D), this will be easier.

True up dovetails with chisel and file, if necessary. Then make trough sides. Place the dovetails you made on ends (D) upon the ends of (E), to which they are to be joined and, with a sharp point of an awl, lay out the angles of the pins on the ends of (E). Saw the angles of these with a dovetail saw, and again remove the waste between the pins on the bandsaw. When all joints have been properly fitted, glue the dovetail joints.

Make the table board, and use wood screws to fasten it to the bottom edges of the trough. Then screw $\frac{3}{4}$"-x-$\frac{3}{4}$" strips to tops of aprons inside the frame, and with more wood screws fasten the frame to the bottom of the trough.

Make the lid. Both long edges of the lid are rabbeted on the lower side to hold the lid in place on top of the trough. (See cross-sectioned detail in Fig. 2.) Make two cleats and fasten them with wood screws to the top of the lid to keep it from warping. (See Fig. 4.)

BILL OF MATERIAL

Poplar

4 Legs (A) $1\frac{1}{2}$" x $1\frac{1}{2}$" x $15\frac{3}{8}$"
2 Side aprons (B) $\frac{7}{8}$" x $4\frac{1}{8}$" x 26"
2 End aprons (C) $\frac{7}{8}$" x $4\frac{1}{8}$" x $11\frac{3}{4}$"
2 Trough ends (D) $\frac{7}{8}$" x $13\frac{1}{4}$" x $13\frac{3}{4}$"

2 Trough sides (E) $\frac{7}{8}$" x $9\frac{5}{8}$" x 28"
1 Table board (trough bottom) (F) $\frac{7}{8}$" x $12\frac{1}{2}$" x $26\frac{3}{4}$"
1 Lid (G) $\frac{7}{8}$" x 14" x 26"
2 Cleats for lid (H) $\frac{7}{8}$" x $1\frac{1}{2}$" x $13\frac{3}{4}$"
Strips to fasten table board to aprons (I) $\frac{3}{4}$" x $\frac{3}{4}$" x lengths as needed

FIFTEEN

Curly Maple Side Table

THIS SMALL CURLY MAPLE SIDE TABLE MAY BE used as a lamp stand alongside an easy chair, or as a bedside table. The beautiful ripple effect of the figured grain is such an attractive attribute that the table will be sure to impress any viewer favorably.

As always, when this kind of wood is selected, planing must be carefully done on the jointer or surface planer. Boards should be passed across the blades of the machine at the slowest possible speed, and blades should be sharp and adjusted to make very shallow cuts. Hand-planing should be avoided. After planing it by machinery to approximately the thickness needed, further smoothing must be done by scraping and sanding the surface.

Turn the legs first (A). Lay out and cut mortises. Then make tenons on sides, back, and rails and fit them to the leg mortises. Make places to hold leaf supports (K) on upper edges of both sides (D). An 8-penny common nail may be used as an axis to rotate this support, as shown in Figs. 2 and 4. A hole large enough to rotate the support easily should be drilled into each of the two supports needed. When the top has been fastened to the frame, these nails will stay in place.

Make and fit the drawers before making and fastening the tabletop. Drawer runs (M) and drawer guides (N) are fastened to the legs, and to sides (D), with wood screws, as shown in Fig. 5. Drawer con-

FIG. 1

FIG. 7

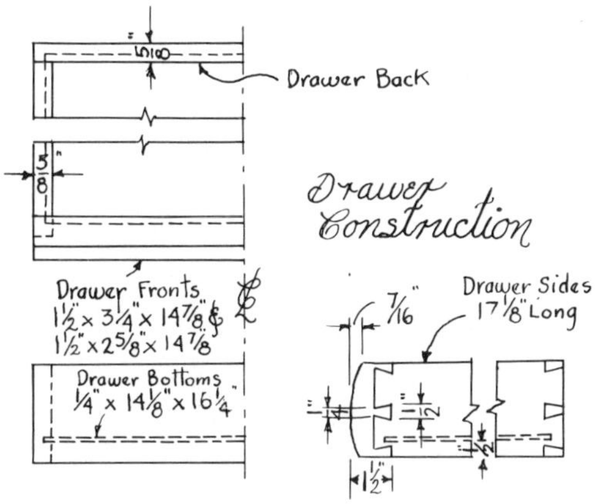
Drawer Back
Drawer Construction
Drawer Fronts 1 1/2" x 3 1/4" x 14 7/8" & 1 1/2" x 2 5/8" x 14 7/8"
Drawer Bottoms 1/4" x 14 1/8" x 16 1/4"
Drawer Sides 17 1/8" Long
7/16"
1 1/2"

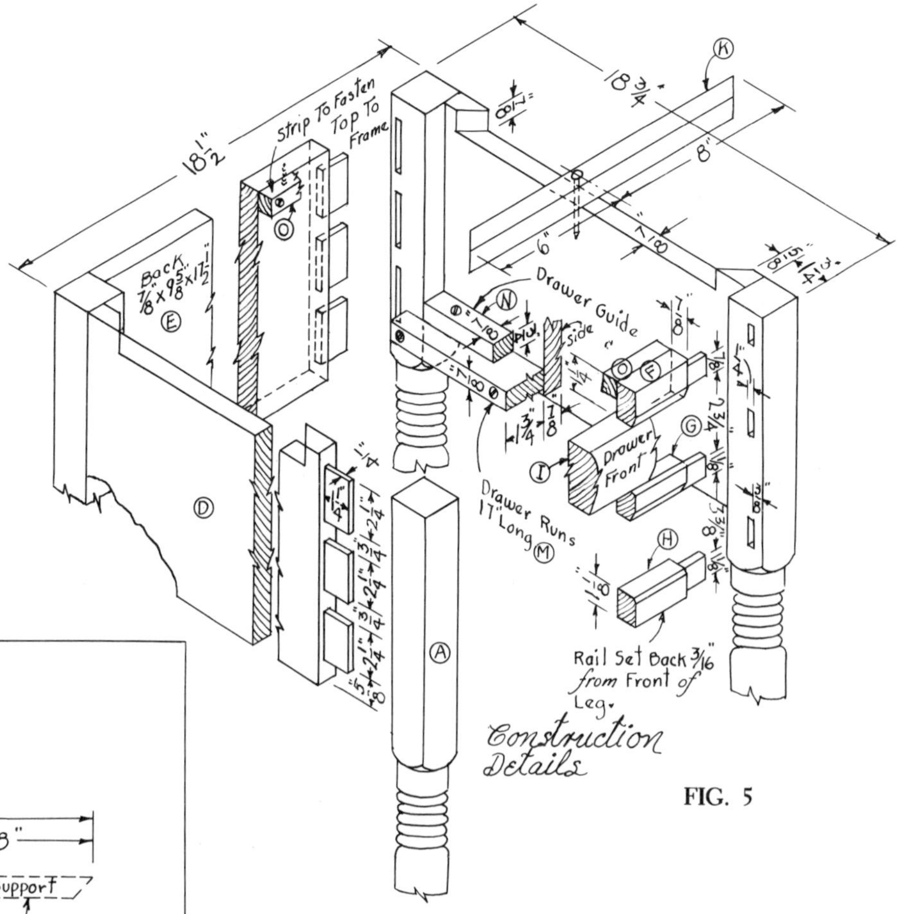
18 1/2"
Strip To Fasten Top To Frame
18 3/4"
8"
6"
Back 7/8" x 9 5/8" x 17 1/2"
Drawer Guide
Side
Drawer Front
Drawer Runs 17" Long
Rail Set Back 3/16" from Front of Leg.
Construction Details
A B C D E F G H I K M N O

FIG. 5

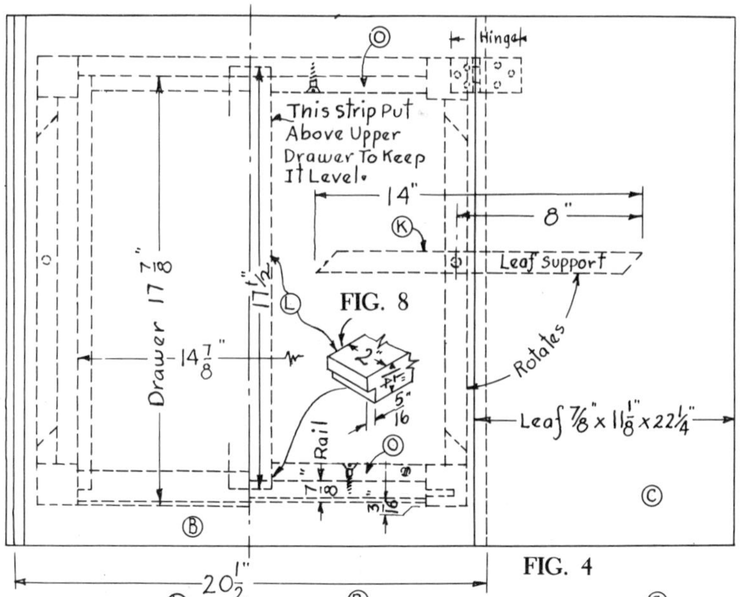
Hinge
This strip Put Above Upper Drawer To Keep It Level.
14"
8"
Leaf Support
Rotates
Drawer 17 7/8"
17 1/2"
14 7/8"
2"
5/16"
Rail
Leaf 7/8" x 11 1/8" x 22 1/4"
20 1/2"
O K L B C

FIG. 8

FIG. 4

FIG. 9

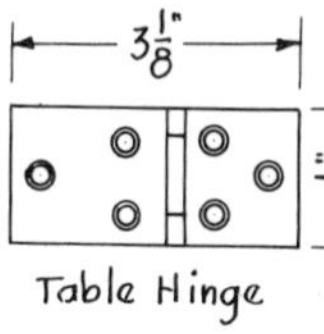
3 1/8"
1 1/2"
Table Hinge

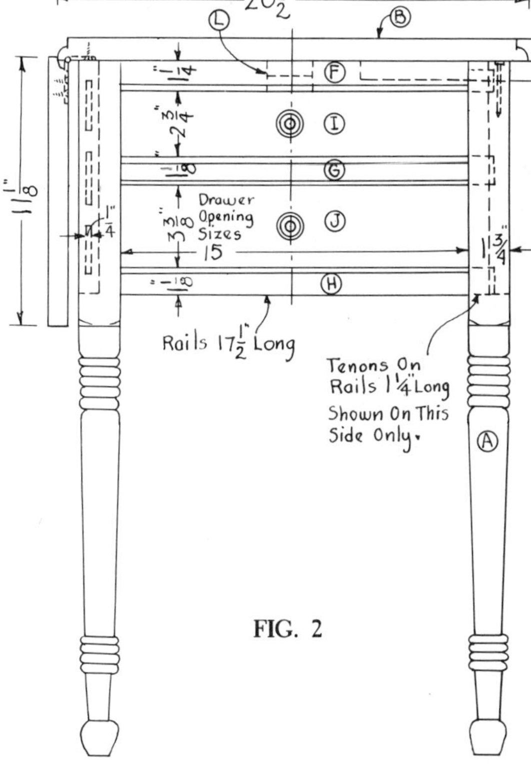
11 1/8"
Drawer Opening Sizes
15
1 3/4"
Rails 17 1/2" Long
Tenons On Rails 1 1/4" Long Shown On This Side Only.
B C L F I G J H A

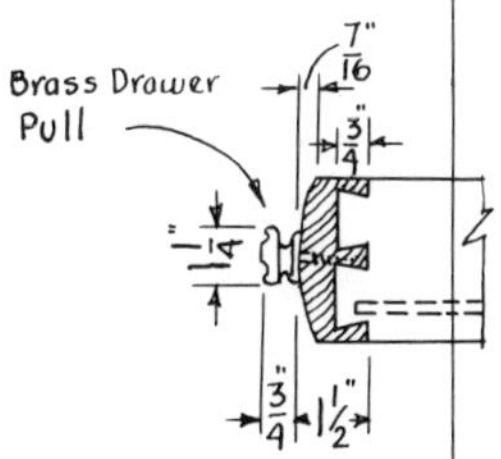
Brass Drawer Pull
7/16"

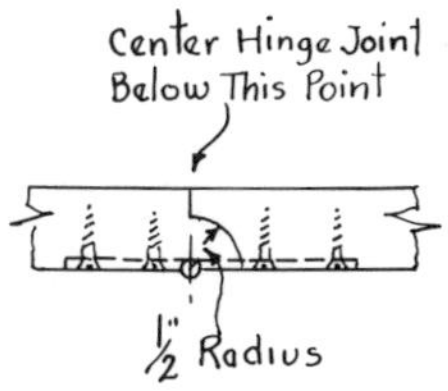
Center Hinge Joint Below This Point
1/2 Radius

FIG. 10

FIG. 2

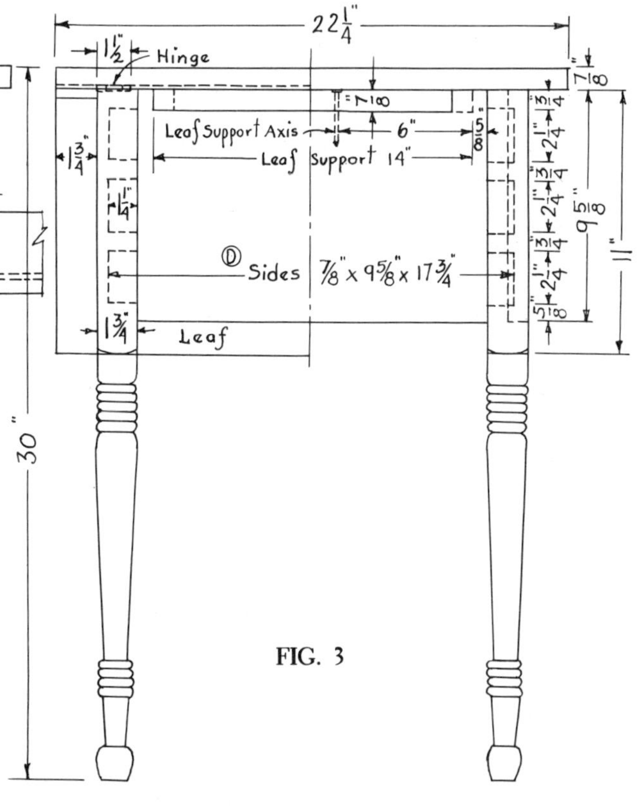
22 1/4"
1 1/2"
Hinge
Leaf Support Axis
6"
Leaf Support 14"
Sides 7/8" x 9 5/8" x 17 3/4"
Leaf
30"
11"
D

FIG. 3

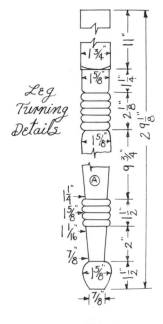

Leg Turning Details

FIG. 6

struction is shown in Fig. 7. Rails above and below the drawers are set back ³⁄₁₆ inch, as shown in Fig. 4, which permits the bulge at the middle of the drawer front to come flush with the outside faces of both front legs when the drawers are pushed all the way back. Drawer joints are dovetailed together.

Leaves (C) are joined to the top (B) with rule joints, as shown in Fig. 2. The table hinge used here is shown in Fig. 9. It is important to center the hinge leaf joint in line with the upper edges of the tabletop joint, as shown in Fig. 10, so that it will work properly when leaves are raised and lowered.

To fasten the top to the table frame, four ³⁄₄″-x-³⁄₄″ strips are fastened with wood screws to the inside of rail (F), and to the inside of back (E), as shown in Fig. 5. Wood screws through these strips, and two more through strip (L) will securely hold top (B) in place. For details see Figs. 4 and 5.

BILL OF MATERIAL

Curly Maple

4 Legs (A) 1⅞″ x 1⅞″ x 29⅛″
1 Tabletop (B) ⅞″ x 20½″ x 22¼″
2 Table leaves (C) ⅞″ x 11⅛″ x 22¼″
2 Table sides (D) ⅞″ x 9⅝″ x 17¾″
1 Table back (E) ⅞″ x 9⅝″ x 17½″
1 Rail above drawers (F) ⅞″ x 1¼″ x 17½″
1 Rail between drawers (G) ⅞″ x 1⅛″ x 17½″
1 Rail below drawers (H) ⅞″ x 1⅛″ x 17½″
Upper drawer front (I) 1½″ x 2⅝″ x 14⅞″
Lower drawer front (J) 1½″ x 3¼″ x 14⅞″

Plain Maple

2 Leaf supports (K) ⅞″ x ⅞″ x 14″

1 Strip above drawer to hold it level (L) 1¼″ x 2″ x 17½″

Poplar

4 Drawer runs (M) ⅞″ x 1¾″ x 17″
4 Drawer guides (N) ¾″ x ⅞″ x 15¼″
2 Drawer sides ⅝″ x 3¼″ x 17⅛″
2 Drawer sides ⅝″ x 2⅝″ x 17⅛″
1 Drawer back ⅝″ x 3¼″ x 14⅞″
1 Drawer back ⅝″ x 2⅝″ x 14⅞″
4 Strips to fasten top to frame (O) ¾″ x ¾″ x 6⅜″

Birch Plywood

2 Drawer bottoms ¼″ x 14⅛″ x 16¼″

SIXTEEN

Slant-Top Curly Maple Desk

THE SHEER BEAUTY OF CURLY MAPLE, USED TO build this handsome desk, must be seen to be believed. When curly maple is inculcated into a design as beautiful as this desk, the results are little short of fantastic. Because wood as beautifully marked as the kind found here is not in plentiful supply, and because of the difficulties involved in preparing it for purposes of the kind shown here, pieces of furniture of such obvious quality are rare and become highly prized heirlooms.

First of all, the wood must be carefully selected. Then it must be prepared for use by careful machine operations. The fact that early pieces of furniture similar to this were produced with primitive tools and no power-driven saws, planers, and sanders is something to be marveled at, for those of us having access to power-driven machinery. Planing wood like this with hand tools is almost out of the question. It may be hand-sawn, scraped with properly sharpened edge tools, sanded and filed, but trying to hand-plane it is extremely hazardous. Cutting tools on power-driven machinery used on wood of this kind must be sharp, and even then must be operated with great skill.

To build the desk, plane and saw the wood to sizes slightly thicker, wider, and longer than the sizes given in the Bill of Material. If you have a surface planer, set it for a series of very light cuts to plane it. If a surface planer is not part of your equipment, a good idea is to have surfacing done in a planing mill. Leave about 1/16 inch more thickness than you will require on finished pieces to allow you to glue boards edge-to-edge where wide boards are needed, such as ends, lid, and table board. The additional thickness will also be needed to dress down other pieces when

FIG. 1

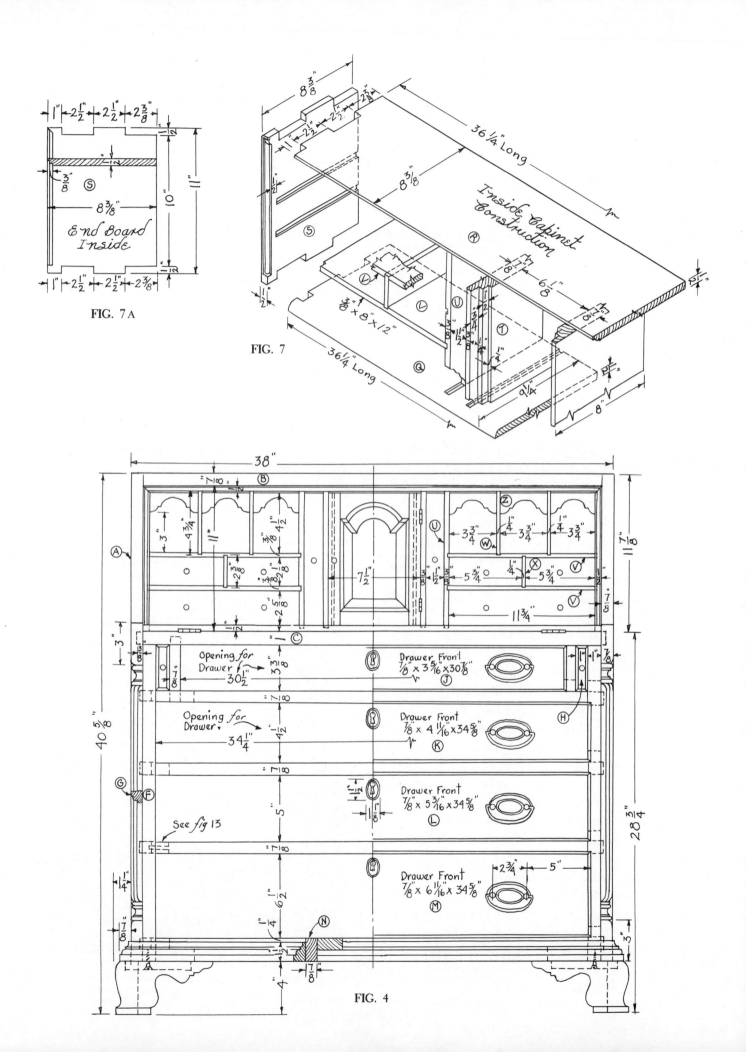

FIG. 7A

End Board Inside

Inside Cabinet Construction

FIG. 7

Opening for Drawer

Drawer Front
7/8" x 3 5/16 x 30 7/8"

Opening for Drawer

Drawer Front
7/8" x 4 11/16 x 34 5/8"

See fig 13

Drawer Front
7/8" x 5 3/16" x 34 5/8"

Drawer Front
7/8" x 6 11/16" x 34 5/8"

FIG. 4

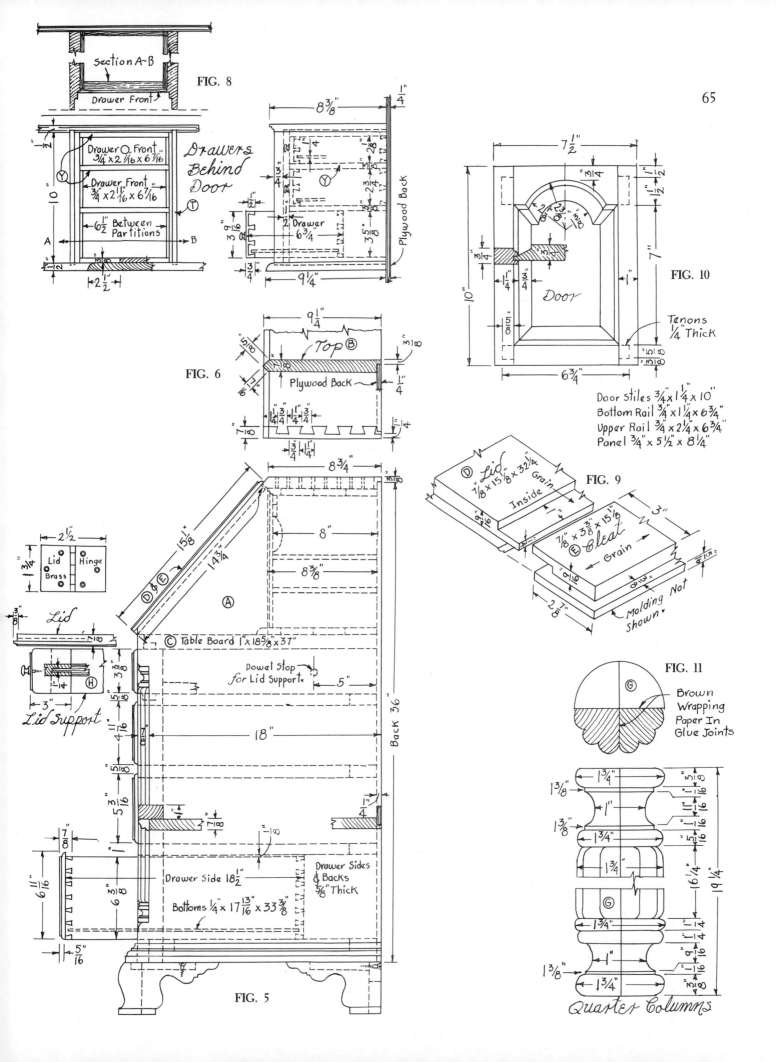

Section A-B

FIG. 8

Drawer Front

Drawer O. Front
3/4 x 2 1/16 x 6 7/16

Drawers
Behind
Door

Drawer Front
3/4 x 2 1/16 x 6 7/16

6 1/2" Between
Partitions

10"

A   B

2 1/2"

Plywood Back

2 Drawer
6 3/4

8 3/8"

FIG. 10

7 1/2"

3/4

Door

10"

6 3/4"

Tenons
1/4" Thick

Door Stiles 3/4" x 1 1/4" x 10"
Bottom Rail 3/4" x 1 1/4" x 6 3/4"
Upper Rail 3/4" x 2 1/4" x 6 3/4"
Panel 3/4" x 5 1/2" x 8 1/4"

9 1/4"

Top B

Plywood Back

FIG. 6

Lid
7/8 x 15 5/8 x 32 1/4

Inside

Grain

FIG. 9

7/8 x 3 3/8 x 15 5/8
Cleat

Grain

2 5/8"

Molding Not
Shown.

8 3/4"

8"

8 3/8"

15 3/8"

14 3/4"

D & E

A

2 1/2"

Lid
Brass   Hinge

Lid

Lid Support

3"

H

C Table Board 1" x 18 5/8" x 37"

Dowel Stop
for Lid Support.   5"

18"

Back 36"

FIG. 11

G

Brown
Wrapping
Paper In
Glue Joints

Drawer Side 18 1/2"

Drawer Sides
& Backs
5/8" Thick

Bottoms 1/4" x 17 13/16" x 33 3/8"

6 11/16"

6 3/8"

5/16"

FIG. 5

1 3/4"

1"

1 3/8"

1 3/4"

1 3/4"

1 3/8"

19 1/4"

16 1/4"

G

1 3/4"

1"

1 3/8"   1 3/4"

Quarter Columns

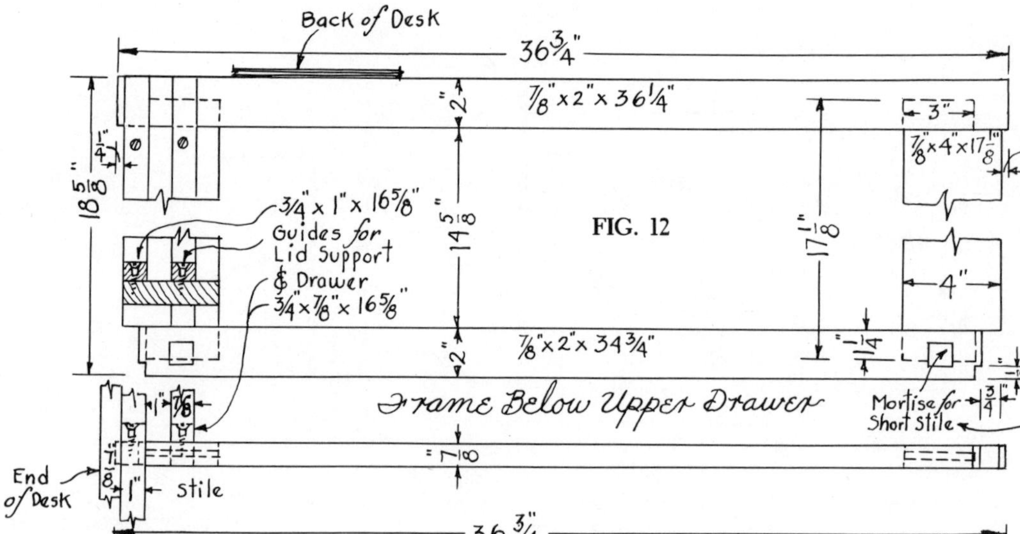
Back of Desk
36 3/4"
7/8" x 2" x 36 1/4"
3"
7/8" x 4" x 17 1/8"
3/4" x 1" x 16 5/8"
Guides for Lid Support & Drawer
3/4" x 7/8" x 16 5/8"
4"
7/8" x 2" x 34 3/4"
Frame Below Upper Drawer
Mortise for Short Stile
End of Desk
Stile

FIG. 12

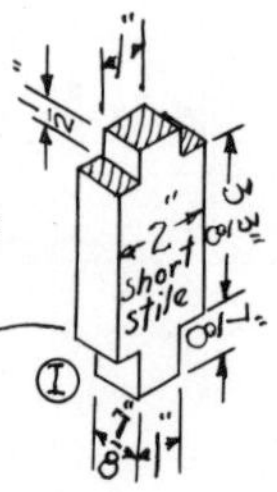
2"
Short Stile
Ⓘ

FIG. 16

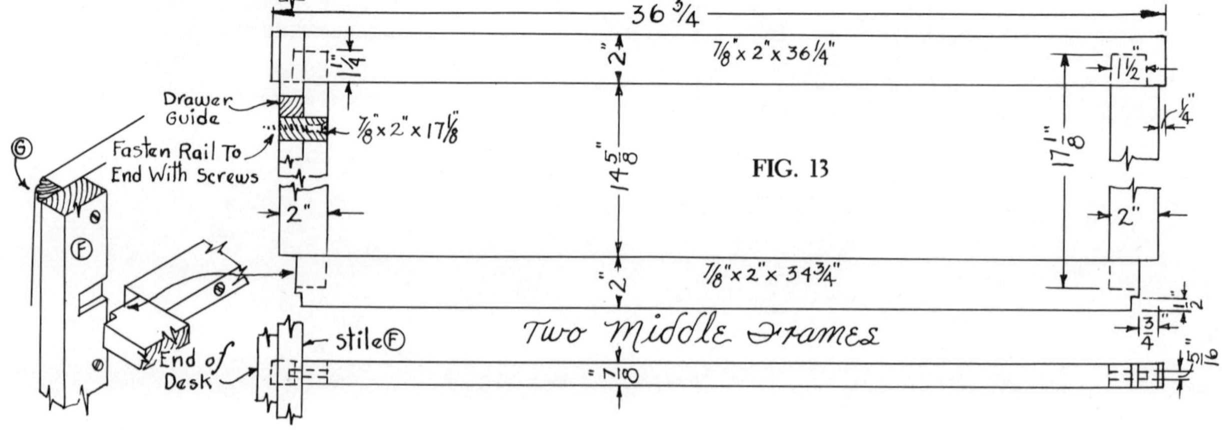
36 3/4"
7/8" x 2" x 36 1/4"
Drawer Guide
7/8" x 2" x 17 1/8"
Fasten Rail To End With Screws
Ⓖ
Ⓕ
2"
7/8" x 2" x 34 3/4"
Two Middle Frames
Stile Ⓕ
End of Desk

FIG. 13

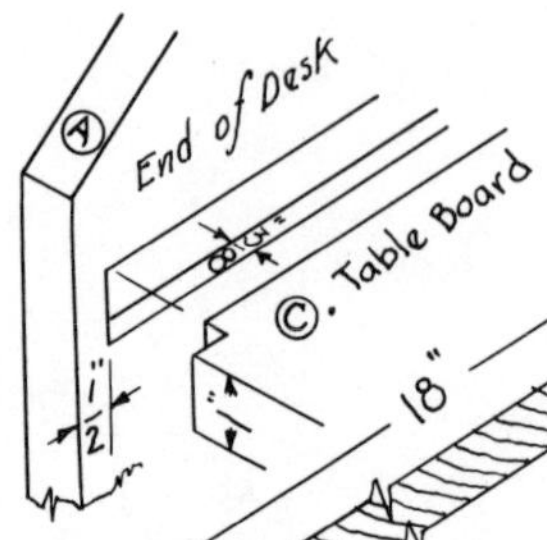
Ⓐ
End of Desk
Ⓒ. Table Board

FIG. 18

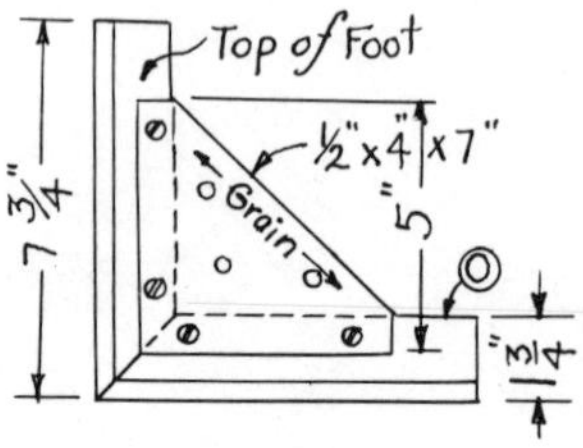
Top of Foot
1/2" x 4" x 7"
Grain
5"
7 3/4"
Ⓞ
1 3/4"

FIG. 14

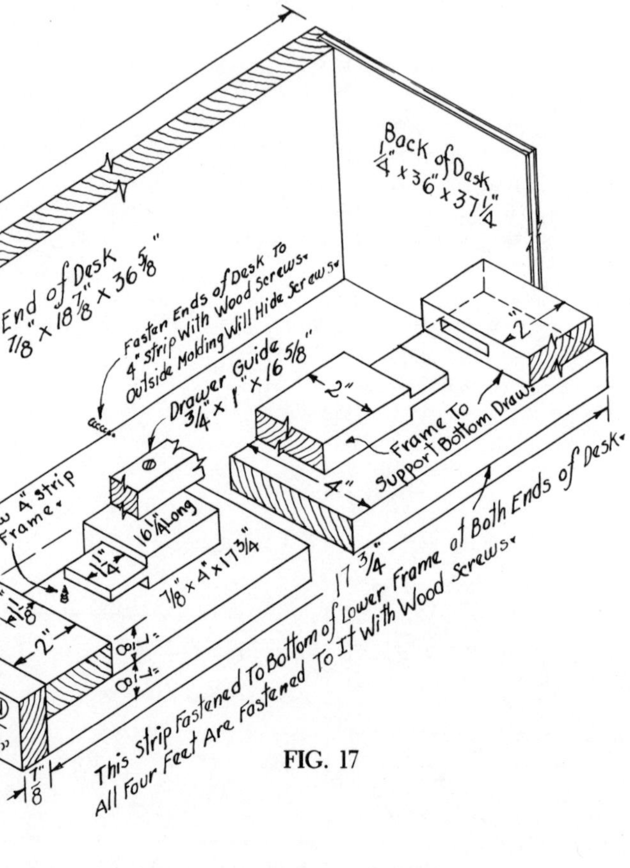
18"
Back of Desk 1/4" x 36" x 37 1/4"
Ⓐ End of Desk 7/8" x 18 7/8" x 36 5/8"
Fasten Ends of Desk To 4" Strip With Wood Screws. Outside Molding Will Hide Screws.
Drawer Guide 3/4" x 1" x 16 5/8"
2"
Frame To Support Bottom Draw.
4"
Gain
Ⓕ
Screw 4" Strip To Frame.
16 1/4 Long
7/8" x 4" x 17 3/4
17 3/4"
This Strip Fastened To Bottom of Lower Frame at Both Ends of Desk.
All Four Feet Are Fastened To It With Wood Screws.
Ⓝ
Ⓞ
4"
2 3/4"

FIG. 17

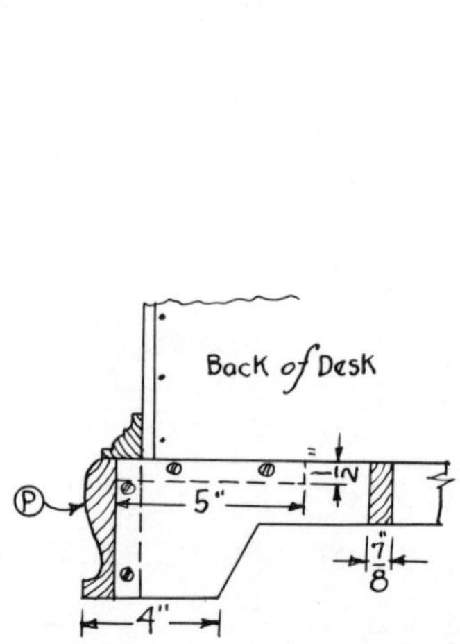
Back of Desk
Ⓟ
5"
4"

FIG. 15

FIG. 2

scraping or sanding them smooth. After the wood has been planed, the grain markings will show sufficiently clear to allow good matching where glue joints have to be made. Final scraping and sanding to thickness should be done only after full-width boards have been made. Unless the equipment is available in your own shop, I suggest having the final dressing to thickness done on a three-drum sander at a planing mill. This should ensure smooth, almost flawless surfaces, and provide uniform thicknesses.

Ends (A) should be made first. I have digressed a bit here from the construction of the desk shown in the photographs by adding the sections above and below the quarter-columns to the width of the ends, instead of making these areas part of the quarter-columns. My way of doing it makes the joints less noticeable and should improve the appearance here.

Frames to support the large drawers should be made before gains are cut into stiles (F) to which they are to be joined. The table board should also be sanded to its proper thickness before grooves are cut into desk ends to hold it. As a rule it is easier to fit boards like this to the groove rather than the other way round, but in this instance we advise the change because the nature of the material and its preparation makes this reversal of procedure more desirable.

When the two ends, frames, and table board joints are ready, make a trial assembly of these parts, clamping them together. The rabbeting on the back edges of ends (A) should have been done, and the stiles (F) should be screwed fast to the ends prior to the trial assembly.

Short stiles (I), shown in Fig. 16, should be ready and put in place at this time also. Guide strips for drawers, and for the slides supporting the lid, may be screwed to the frames later, before the table board and the frames are permanently fastened to the ends

FIG. 3

of the desk. Frame ends are glued to the desk ends only where they are joined to the gains, cut into stiles (F) (Fig. 17) and into gains in back where the back rails of the frames, shown in Figs. 12 and 13, are extended beyond the frame end rails. Gains in back are needed to support the upper three frames only. The bottom frame gets adequate support from the wood screws that secure the 4-inch strips under the frame to the desk ends. The wood screw through rail (N) (Fig. 17), and nails through the back of the desk give further support. The front rail of the bottom frame may also be glued to rail (N). End rails of the two middle frames should also be fastened to the desk ends with two or more wood screws from the inside, as shown in Fig. 13. Do not glue end rails of frames to desk ends. If this is done it will almost surely cause desk ends (A) to split, so use only wood screws here.

Once you are satisfied that drawer frames and table board will join up properly, lay out and make dovetail joints to join desk top (B) to ends (A). These joints should be made and fitted together, but not yet glued. Once again make a trial assembly of both ends of the desk, table board, desk top (B), and one or more drawer frames, to be sure all go together as they should. But before fastening these parts together permanently with glue, first build the inside cabinet, details of which are shown in Figs. 7, 7A, and 8. Details and sizes for doing this will also be found in Figs. 4 and 5.

Fitting this inside cabinet to the upper part of the desk will be much easier if it is done before the main frame is permanently put together, although desk ends, table board, and drawer frames may be permanently joined before the inside cabinet is fastened in place. Top (B), however, should be glued in place after the inside cabinet frame has been made and put in place, to ensure a good fit.

My drawing does not show how the six pigeonhole arches are fastened. They may be glued to cabinet top (R), and also to 1¼-inch-long triangular-shaped sticks, glued to their backs and to the partitions on each side.

Make and fit the lid (D). The method of joining cleats (E) to (D) is shown in Fig. 9. There is always some likelihood of warping or splitting on a lid as wide as this when it is glued to two cleats whose grain goes in opposite directions. However, if the wood used has been well seasoned, this danger is minimized somewhat. Also the fact that a number of finishing coats of varnish are applied to both sides of the lid also helps. Use glue sparingly on the joints, which will provide some assurance this won't happen. A better method of joining cleats to the lid would be to make the tongue-and-groove narrower, and cut three through mortise-and-tenon joints, one near each end and one at the middle of the cleat, and put glue on the mortise-and-tenon joints only.

Fit hinges—and lock if there is to be one—to the lid and table board, and make certain the lid will fit

down snugly on the slanted edges and on the edge of the desk top. Actually, it is a good idea to try fitting this lid during a final trial assembly of the frame, because once these parts are glued you may have trouble making a good fit.

After all the above preparations have been completed, you may glue the frame together. Do not nail on the plywood back of the desk until all drawers have been made and fitted to their openings. Lid support slides may be made after the frame has been glued together. However, bore a ½-inch hole 5 inches from the back, and glue the dowel stop into each slide, so it will protrude from the side next to the short stile (I). This prevents the slide support from being pulled clear out. (See Fig. 5.)

Make and fit the small paneled door, shown in Fig. 10, to the inside cabinet. It is easier to fasten the hinges to partition (T) on the right before the partition is glued to boards (R) and (Q). Inside edges of door stiles and rails have quarter-round molding, which should be done on a shaper. The bevel angle on the three straight sides of the panel may be made by tilting the saw blade, or table on your table saw, to an angle of about 25 degrees, with the panel held upright against the ripping fence. First outline the middle of your panel with saw cuts about ⅛ inch deep before tilting the saw for the bevel-angle cuts. The arching at the top of the panel will have to be formed with chisels, preferably wood-carving chisels. Saw marks should then be scraped and sanded smooth. A small ball-bearing friction catch will keep the door latched.

The shaft from which the two quarter-columns are made is glued up using four 1″-x-1″ sticks, and with heavy brown wrapping paper in the glue joints, as shown in Fig. 11. Turn the column on the lathe, and then shape the beading either with wood-carving chisels, or by mounting the column in a jig so the beading can be formed on a shaper. If V-shaped grooves are first carefully cut along vertical guidelines with a carver's V-tool, the rounding of the bead is easily accomplished with a carver's skew chisel afterward; the columns may be sanded smooth with fine sandpaper folded over a thin stick of wood, one edge of which has been trimmed to knife-blade thickness.

After forming the beading, split the four sections apart by carefully driving a wide chisel into the joints at one end of the column. Glue both quarter-columns into place on the desk.

All drawers are put together with carefully made dovetail joints. Enough details for making these are given in Fig. 5 for the big drawers, and in Fig. 8 for the small drawers. Always lay out dovetail joints so the pins are noticeably narrower than the tails. An exception to this rule will be found on the dovetail joints on top of the desk, though even this may be changed to conform to this rule. Observe carefully the sizes of drawer parts and drawers to get enough clearance so the drawers will slide in and out easily without binding, and make doubly sure of this before gluing drawer joints. On drawers made like the large ones, almost no trimming to get a proper fit is possible once they are glued together. Some trimming is possible on the small drawers, because there are no protruding moldings. However, the thin drawer sides offer little leeway for trimming. Drawer bottoms are not glued to the drawer sides but are held in place without glue.

Moldings are easily formed on the shaper if the shaping is done on one or both edges of fairly wide boards. Once formed, the molding is then ripped off on the table saw to its proper size. Base moldings may be glued to the desk.

Figs. 14 and 15 show how the feet are put together. The front feet are mitered and the miter joints are then glued together. Triangular plates of wood help hold the two sides of the feet together, and serve to fasten the feet to the desk with wood screws. Molding 4 inches wide to shape the feet, as shown at (P) in Fig. 15, may be roughly formed to a shape approximating the one shown at (P), on the table saw. Use a plank 1¾ inches thick and long enough to make the six sides needed for both front and back feet when forming this molding. Make a series of saw cuts, raising or lowering the saw blade to achieve a shape roughly conforming to the shape shown at (P). This shape may be drawn on one, or both, ends of the plank with a marker, to be easily observed as the shaping takes form. After shaping, sand the outside, then saw each of the six sides to the shapes shown in Figs. 4 and 5, and assemble them as shown in Figs. 14 and 15. Fasten them to the bottom of the desk with glue and wood screws.

Now fit all hardware to drawers.

BILL OF MATERIAL

Curly Maple *

2 Ends (A) ⅞" x 18⅞" x 36⅝"
1 Desk top (B) ⅞" x 9¼" x 37½"
1 Table board (C) 1" x 18⅝" x 37"
1 Desk lid (D) ⅞" x 15⅛" x 32¼"
2 Lid cleats (E) ⅞" x 3⅜" x 15⅛"
2 Stiles (F) 1" x 2" x 23⅝"
4 Sticks to turn quarter-column shaft (G) 1" x 1" x 20" †
2 Lid support slides (H) 1" x 3⅜" x 16¹⁵⁄₁₆" and 2 pieces 1" x 3" x 3⅜"
2 Short stiles between upper drawer and lid support slides (I) ⅞" x 2" x 4¾"

1 Upper drawer front (J) ⅞" x 3⁵⁄₁₆" x 30⅞"
1 Drawer front (K) ⅞" x 4¹¹⁄₁₆" x 34⅝"
1 Drawer front (L) ⅞" x 5³⁄₁₆" x 34⅝"
1 Drawer front (M) ⅞" x 6¹¹⁄₁₆" x 34⅝"
1 Rail below bottom drawer (N) ⅞" x 1¾" x 36¼"
2 Front feet 4 pieces (O) 1¾" x 4" x 7¾"
2 Back feet (P) 1¾" x 4" x 7⅜"

* Other fine cabinet hardwoods, like cherry, walnut, or mahogany, could be substituted here to build a piece of good quality.

† The four are glued together with brown wrapping paper in the glue joints. After turning the shaft to size, and shaping the beading, the four may be separated with chisels.

Plain Maple

1 Base for inside cabinet (Q) ½″ x 9¼″ x 36¼″
1 Top for inside cabinet (R) ½″ x 8⅜″ x 36¼″
2 Ends for inside cabinet (S) ½″ x 8⅜″ x 11″
2 Partitions at both sides of door (T) ⅞″ x 8″ x 10¼″
2 Partitions between vertical drawers and pigeonholes (U) ⅜″ x 8″ x 10¼″
4 Shelves to hold small drawers (V) ⅜″ x 8″ x 12″
4 Partitions between pigeonholes (W) ⅜″ x 8″ x 4¾″
2 Paritions between small drawers (X) ⅜″ x 8″ x 2⅜″
4 Shelves behind door (Y) ⅜″ x 6¾″ x 7″
6 Pigeonhole arches (Z) ⅜″ x 1½″ x 3¾″

Cherry—Small Door in Cabinet (See Fig. 10)

2 Stiles ¾″ x 1¼″ x 10″
1 Top rail ¾″ x 2¼″ x 6¾″
1 Bottom rail ¾″ x 1¼″ x 6¾″
1 Panel ¾″ x 5½″ x 8¼″

Poplar—Large Drawers

2 Drawer sides, upper drawer ⅝″ x 3¼″ x 18½″
2 Drawer sides, second drawer ⅝″ x 4⅜″ x 18½″
2 Drawer sides, third drawer ⅝″ x 4⅞″ x 18½″
2 Drawer sides, lower drawer ⅝″ x 6⅜″ x 18½″
1 Drawer back, upper drawer ⅝″ x 3¼″ x 30⅜″
1 Drawer back, second drawer ⅝″ x 4⅜″ x 34⅛″
1 Drawer back, third drawer ⅝″ x 4⅞″ x 34⅛″
1 Drawer back, lower drawer ⅝″ x 6⅜″ x 34⅛″

Poplar—Small Drawers

4 Drawer sides ¼″ x 2⁹⁄₁₆″ x 8″
8 Drawer sides ¼″ x 2¹⁄₁₆″ x 8″
2 Drawer sides ¼″ x 3½″ x 6½″
2 Drawer sides ¼″ x 2¹¹⁄₁₆″ x 6½″
2 Drawer sides ¼″ x 2¹⁄₁₆″ x 6½″
2 Drawer backs ⅜″ x 2⁹⁄₁₆″ x 11¹¹⁄₁₆″

4 Drawer backs ⅜″ x 2¹⁄₁₆″ x 5¹¹⁄₁₆″
1 Drawer back ⅜″ x 3½″ x 6⁷⁄₁₆″
1 Drawer back ⅜″ x 2¹¹⁄₁₆″ x 6⁷⁄₁₆″
1 Drawer back ⅜″ x 2¹⁄₁₆″ x 6⁷⁄₁₆″

Poplar

1 Stretcher between back feet ⅞″ x 4″ x 39½″
4 Triangular plates for tops of feet ½″ x 4″ x 7″

Poplar—Frame Below Upper Drawer

1 Rail ⅞″ x 2″ x 36¾″
1 Rail ⅞″ x 2″ x 34¾″
2 Rails ⅞″ x 4″ x 17⅛″
2 Guide strips ¾″ x 1″ x 16⅝″
2 Guide strips ¾″ x ⅞″ x 16⅝″

Poplar—Two Middle Frames

2 Rails ⅞″ x 2″ x 36¾″
2 Rails ⅞″ x 2″ x 34¾″
4 Rails ⅞″ x 2″ x 17⅛″
4 Guide strips ¾″ x 1″ x 16⅝″

Poplar—Bottom Frame

2 Rails ⅞″ x 2″ x 36¼″
2 Rails ⅞″ x 2″ x 16¼″
2 Rails under bottom frame ⅞″ x 4″ x 17¾″
2 Drawer guides ¾″ x 1″ x 16⅝″

Birch Plywood

1 Desk back ¼″ x 36″ x 37¼″
1 Upper drawer bottom ¼″ x 17¹³⁄₁₆″ x 29¾″
3 Drawer bottoms ¼″ x 17¹³⁄₁₆″ x 33⅜″
2 Small drawer bottoms ¼″ x 7¼″ x 11⁷⁄₁₆″
4 Small drawer bottoms ¼″ x 7¼″ x 5⁷⁄₁₆″
3 Small drawer bottoms ¼″ x 6³⁄₁₆″ x 5⅞″

SEVENTEEN

Hepplewhite Chest of Drawers

THE CHEST OF DRAWERS SHOWN IN FIG. 1 is a handsome eighteenth-century design with French feet. Though probably produced by a cabinetmaker in a rural area workshop, its obvious refinements make it well worth reproducing.

The striped veneer drawer fronts, bell-shaped flower inlays, and crescent-shaped marquetry on the skirt lend an air of distinction here.

A reproduction, using this design as a model, could be done in a number of ways. If beautifully figured, solid mahogany is used for drawer fronts, the cross-grained borders can be added by gluing them to shallow rabbets, cut deep enough to make the surface of the drawer front level and smooth with very little sanding once the border veneer has been glued on. Although the bell-shaped flower inlays, and the marquetry lunette on the skirt, accentuate the areas on which they appear, the chest would still be quite handsome without them.

Crescent-shaped marquetry, already made up into a variety of designs, is available and may be purchased from mail-order firms selling to home craftsmen in small lots.* (Books, instructions, and supplies needed to make veneering and marquetry as easy as possible to those not already familiar with the craft

FIG. 1

*Marquetry may be purchased from Albert Constantine, 2050 Eastchester Road, New York, N.Y. 10461, among others.

are also sold by these suppliers.) The sizes shown in the drawing of this chest may be altered somewhat to adapt the apron to what is available. It may be more

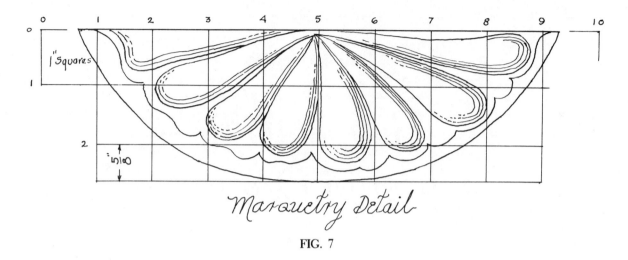

Marquetry Detail

FIG. 7

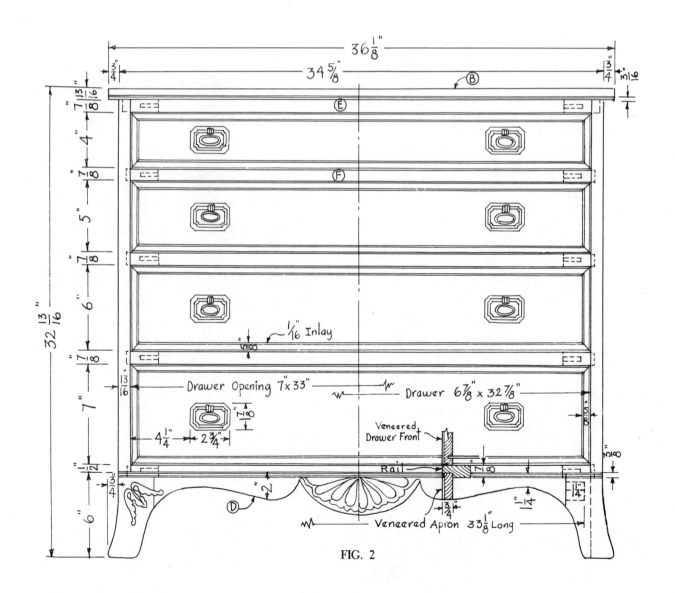

FIG. 2

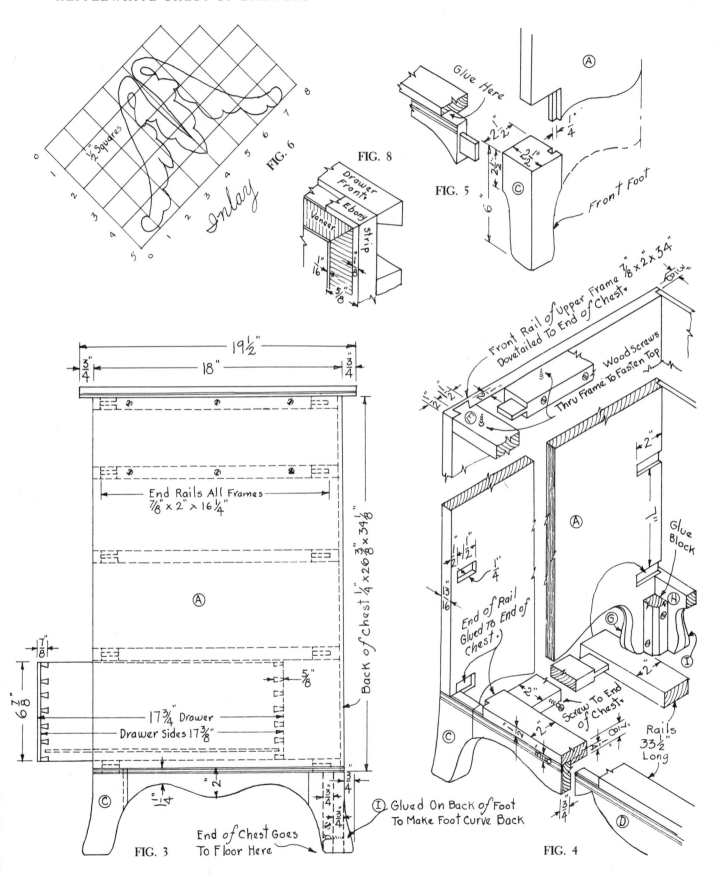

½" Squares

Inlay FIG. 6

FIG. 8

Drawer Front

Veneer

Ebony Strip

1/16"

5/8"

Glue Here

Ⓐ

2½"

¼"

2½"

2½"

6"

Ⓒ

FIG. 5

Front Foot

Front Rail of Upper Frame 7/8" x 2" x 34"
Dovetailed To End of Chest.

Glue

Wood Screws
Thru Frame To Fasten Top

Ⓔ

1½"

2"

2"

Ⓐ

Glue Block

End of Rail
Glued To End of
Chest.

1½"
2"

¼"

3/16"

Ⓖ

Ⓗ

Ⓘ

2"

2"

Screw To End
of Chest.

Rails
33½"
Long

Ⓒ

3/4"

Ⓓ

Ⓘ Glued On Back of Foot
To Make Foot Curve Back

FIG. 4

19½"

18"

3/4"

3/4"

End Rails All Frames
7/8" x 2" x 16¼"

Back of Chest ¼" x 26 3/8 x 34 3/8

Ⓐ

1/8"

5/8"

6 7/8"

17 3/4" Drawer
Drawer Sides 17 3/8"

Ⓒ

2"

1¼"

3/4"

End of Chest Goes
To Floor Here

FIG. 3

difficult to find suitable substitutes for the bell-shaped inlay on the feet, so here it may be necessary to duplicate the design shown if the inlay is used. The inlay used on this chest is maple.

I am of the opinion that the additional interest, or beauty, achieved by veneering skirts or aprons below drawers is more than offset by the damage it will sustain from contact with mop handles and exposure to other hazards which may loosen it. If I were building one like it, I would use solid wood here, with the possible exception of the marquetry decorating the central portion. Even here I would keep a narrow border of solid wood around the curved area to protect it.

To build the chest of drawers, first make two ends (A). Because front feet are made of one-piece solid stock, only the feet at the back are extended to the floor as part of the two ends. (A) is notched at the bottom and fastened to the foot with a short tongue-and-groove joint. This is shown in Fig. 5. Since the foot in the rear is flared out both at the side and at the back, wood ¾ inch thick and 3¼ inches wide is glued to the side of (A) for this purpose, and another piece ¾ inch thick and 2½ inches wide is glued to the stretcher at the back, as shown at the bottom of Fig. 3.

The whole base of this chest could be built as a separate unit consisting of four feet and stretchers fastened to them with mortise-and-tenon joints like the one shown on the foot at the right in Fig. 2. End (A) could then be made 6 inches shorter in length. The full ⅞-inch thickness of the front rail in the frame supporting the bottom drawer could then be exposed, and the base could be fastened to its lower side with wood screws, and sticks of wood fastened with glue and wood screws inside the apron. If this method is used, it will be best to make the front rail of the bottom frame like the front rail of the upper frame, and dovetail it to the ends of the chest.

When both ends of the chest have been made, make the five frames to support the drawers. The upper frame is also the one to which the top (B) is fastened with wood screws, as shown in Fig. 4. The front rail of this frame is ½ inch longer than front rails of the lower frames, for reasons already noted.

This helps hold the tops of ends (A) more securely. The shorter extensions on front and back rails on the other frames, and wood screws through end rails, will keep the other frames in place.

A trial assembly of frames and ends should be made and drawer opening sizes checked. Drawers should now be made. If solid wood is to be used for drawer fronts, dovetail joints like those shown in Figs. 3 and 8 can be laid out and the joints made. If drawer fronts are to be veneered, white pine can be substituted for mahogany for these. Veneer may be bought by the square foot. Some come in widths from 6 inches to 12 inches, and 3 feet long—large enough for these drawer fronts.

Cross-grain veneer trim for borders may be bought in rolls 1 inch wide. Line inlays such as those shown in Fig. 1, in 1/16-inch widths, are available in celluloid. The advantages of using celluloid instead of wood for this purpose is that celluloid will not take stain, and so will not change color when stain is applied to the wood around it—an obvious advantage in this instance.

To veneer drawer fronts like these, first cut drawer fronts to size. Then make the dovetail joints and be sure the drawer slides into the opening freely when the drawer is assembled. Cut rabbets around all four edges of the drawer front for the ⅛"-x-⅜" strips of ebony, or other wood you may want to substitute, which is to be glued to the drawer front after veneering it to protect edges of the veneer. Cut veneer for the center of the panel to exact size. Use a good straightedge and a veneer saw to trim edges with the grain. A thin-bladed knife may be used to trim ends. In the back of the veneer put masking tape along each edge so that it extends far enough over the side to allow you to add both the 1/16-inch inlay strips and borders of cross-banded veneer. These are flexible enough so you can push them tightly against the edges of the veneer. Now turn the veneer, face side up, and put veneer tape over these joined-together pieces to hold them together on the outside, because the masking tape must be removed from the back of the veneer before it can be glued to the drawer front. Place the drawer front over the back of the veneer to make sure the two are exactly the same size before applying contact cement to both veneer and drawer front.

Contact cement is a superior adhesive for gluing veneer to boards. However, it must be used with care. Cut a piece of brown wrapping paper to a width ⅛ inch narrower than the area of the drawer front you plan to veneer and ¼ inch shorter. This paper is called a slip sheet. When the cement has dried for thirty minutes or more, test it by sliding a piece of brown paper across the surface. If the paper does not slide over the covered surface without sticking, allow more drying time. When the glued surface passes the paper test, apply a second coat of cement on both surfaces, and allow this to dry until it again passes the paper test.

Lay the slip sheet on the face of the drawer front with ⅛ inch of the wood exposed on one edge, and ¼ inch exposed at one end. Now carefully lay the veneer on the drawer front so the ¼ inch of exposed wood at the end and the ⅛ inch of exposed wood along one side come together. This must be carefully done, because once contact is made, no adjustment is possible. Use a veneer roller to press the veneer firmly against the drawer front as you pull the slip sheet away a little at a time until both surfaces adhere to each other firmly.

The ebony strip of wood shown in Fig. 8 may now be glued to the drawer front, or some other kind of hardwood strip may be substituted here. This protects the edges of the veneer once the strips are in place. White glue in a squeeze bottle, which dries more slowly, may be used to glue the strips to the drawer front.

The veneer tape may be removed with a moistened cellulose sponge that has no soap on it. Avoid wetting the wood around the tape as much as possible, and moisten only a small portion of the tape at a time. Loosen one end of the tape with a very blunt knife and peel it off slowly and carefully. Final cleanup may be done with a properly sharpened cabinet scraper blade. If this is done carefully, the scraper should not gouge the veneer. Some very careful sanding with very fine garnet paper may be needed also.

While tops on chests like this may be veneered, solid tops are more serviceable and durable, and since they constantly hold things which could easily damage a veneered surface, it is better to make them of solid wood.

The bell-shaped decoration on the feet was inlaid with maple, probably at least ⅛ inch thick. The ornament to be used for this should be at least ⅛ inch thick, and should be sawed to shape on a jigsaw, and its edges carefully smoothed with files. Shading of edges is done by holding them in preheated sand to singe the wood, a refinement of this decoration worth some extra trouble. Lay the inlay on the wood and carefully trace its outline on the foot. Lower the wood where it is to go to a depth a little less than the thickness of the ornament. This will allow you to chisel and sand it level with the surface to which it is glued after the glue has dried.

The lunette on the center of the apron may be sawed from an oval-shaped marquetry by halving it, and may be applied with contact cement or with white glue.

BILL OF MATERIAL

Mahogany

2 Ends (A) ¹³⁄₁₆″ x 18″ x 32″
1 Top (B) ¹³⁄₁₆″ x 19½″ x 36⅛″
2 Feet (C) 3¼″ x 3¼″ x 6″

1 Front apron (D) ¾″ x 3″ x 33⅛″
1 Front rail, upper frame (E) ⅞″ x 2″ x 34″
4 Front rails for four lower frames (F) ⅞″ x 2″ x 33½″
1 Drawer front ⅞″ x 3⅞″ x 32⅞″
1 Drawer front ⅞″ x 4⅞″ x 32⅞″

1 Drawer front ⅞″ x 5⅞″ x 32⅞″
1 Drawer front ⅞″ x 6⅞″ x 32⅞″
2 Blocks glued to back feet (G) ¾″ x 3¼″ x 6″

Poplar

2 Drawer sides ⅝″ x 3⅞″ x 17⅜″
2 Drawer sides ⅝″ x 4⅞″ x 17⅜″
2 Drawer sides ⅝″ x 5⅞″ x 17⅜″
2 Drawer sides ⅝″ x 6⅞″ x 17⅜″
1 Drawer back ⅝″ x 3⅞″ x 32⅞″
1 Drawer back ⅝″ x 4⅞″ x 32⅞″

1 Drawer back ⅝″ x 5⅞″ x 32⅞″
1 Drawer back ⅝″ x 6⅞″ x 32⅞″
5 Back frame rails ⅞″ x 2″ x 33½″
10 End rails for frames ⅞″ x 2″ x 16⅛″
1 Rail for base at back (H) ¾″ x 5⅝″ x 34⅜″
2 Blocks glued to rear of back feet (I) ¾″ x 2½″ x 5⅝″

Birch Plywood

4 Drawer bottoms ¼″ x 16⅜″ x 32⅛″
1 Back ¼″ x 26⅜″ x 34⅛″

EIGHTEEN

Three-Drawer Pennsylvania Walnut Chest

THIS THREE-DRAWER CHEST OF WALNUT, AN early type, typical of those found among the Pennsylvania Dutch in eastern Pennsylvania, belonged to my grandmother, Margaretta Borneman. The bracket feet and the brasses, with the exception of the lost escutcheon plate, are original. The hand-forged iron hinges and lock are also still in place and in good condition. In Fig. 9 I show a hinge, and in Fig. 10 a lock, quite similar to those on this chest. These closely resemble hinges and lock on an older walnut chest inherited from his father by my nephew. In an earlier book,* I showed detailed working drawings from which this lock may be made, so because the one on this chest is fashioned in much the same way, I'm substituting a facsimile in Fig. 10 for the lock on this chest. The similarity of hand-made locks on many of these old chests leads me to believe they were made from patterns which closely resembled each other.

Exact duplicates of the Chippendale-style drawer pulls and escutcheon plates, shown in Fig. 11, may be impossible to find after all these years, but others quite similar to these are obtainable, and may be substituted.†

Other substitutions I've taken the liberty of making in my drawings for those found on the chest in Fig. 1 are a frame in place of a wide board to support the drawers, and plywood bottoms for the drawers instead of solid lumber found on all old pieces of this kind. Such construction is an improvement. The frame under the drawers will not swell to a greater width, or shrink to a width which is narrower, and the same is true of the plywood drawer bottoms. My drawings provide for such changes in the width of the floor of the chest, as shown in Fig. 3.

To build the chest, glue up pieces for front (A), ends (B), and back (C). Front and ends of this chest were made from single wide boards, and if boards of such width are available, so much the better. However, since lumber as wide as this is hard to come by, your only choice may be to glue several narrower boards together. This is not so important when making the back of a chest, but was considered a feature imparting quality to old pieces of this kind. Lumber used for a chest of this kind should be thoroughly dried and seasoned to prevent checking, warping, and other defects.

The small ends of the pins on the dovetail joints are somewhat narrower in Fig. 1 than I show them to be in Fig. 2, making the pitch of the angle a bit greater; but making them as I show them is easier. In

* *Masterpiece Furniture Making*, Stackpole Books, 1979, Harrisburg, Pennsylvania 17105.

† These may be purchased from Ball and Ball Brasses, Exton, Pennsylvania 19341.

Fig. 1 this narrow end of the pin is closer to being ⅛ inch.

Before cutting and fitting the dovetails, cut grooves in ends and back of the chest to hold the floor (L) and the frame which supports the drawers. When you make the floor, reduce its thickness enough so it will fit loosely enough into these grooves to allow it to expand and contract ¼ inch or more provided for this purpose in the grooves in the back of the chest. Front edges of floor and frame should be glued to (A) and to rail (E), to fasten them securely there, but floor (L) and rails (N) and (M) should not be glued to ends (B) or to back (C).

When floor (L) and the frame have been properly fitted to the grooves, lay out and saw the dovetails on front (A), and on back (C). This may be done on the bandsaw, provided you have one with a table wide enough. If you don't have a bandsaw big enough to do this on boards of this width, use a dovetail saw to make the cuts going in the same direction as the grain, and then a coping saw across the grain to remove the waste. Some trimming with a thin-bladed chisel may then be required before laying out lines for the dovetail pins on ends (B).

Take note that the bottom of back (C) is dovetailed to the backs of rear feet (I), as shown more clearly in

FIG. 1

Fig. 13. So, feet (I) should be made, and the dovetailing can then be done to join them to the back.

Front (A), ends (B), rail (E), and stiles (F) should be made, and glued to each other before the back of the chest is glued to the ends. Grooves to hold the till must also be cut into the back and front, as shown in Fig. 5. Make till sides (S) and (T), floor (U), and lid (V), and make trial assemblies of all the following: (A), (B), (C), (E), (F), and (L). Also make, fit, and glue together the frame that supports the drawers. Details needed to make this frame are found in Fig. 13.

When all the above are ready, place the frame which supports the drawers, and the floor, into the grooves cut into ends (B). Then glue stiles (F) to rail (E). Front (A) may then be glued to ends (B). Rail (E) and stiles (F) may then be glued to the front and ends of the chest. Then glue till sides (S) and (T) to till floor (U). Place these and lid (V) into places provided in front (A), and then glue back (C) to ends (B).

Next, make the front feet (H), as shown in Fig. 12. The miter joint, where the two sides of the foot come together, is glued. A hardwood spline, ⅛ inch or more thick, fitted to grooves up the middle of this mitered joint, would help strengthen the joint, and making the grooves on the table saw would not be difficult.

The large molding from which both sides of front feet and one side of back feet are made can be roughly formed with parallel saw cuts on the table saw, until a shape approximating that on the left-hand side of the foot pattern shown in Fig. 6 is formed. If carefully done, this ogee curve can then be smoothed down with scraping blades and sandpaper. The stopped rabbet which holds the triangular-shaped plate (R) can be partly made on the table saw with a dado head, and then finished with a chisel. It is best to do this before bandsawing the foot to shape. Use a miter box to saw the miter joint. Then saw the curves on the right-hand side of Fig. 6 to shape on the bandsaw.

When the front feet have been made, glued up,

and the triangular-shaped plates screwed and glued to the tops, and when holes for the dovetails at the bottom of back (C) have been chiseled out, then the front and back feet may be joined together with strips of wood (Q), screwed to the tops of triangular plates (R). Then (Q) may be fastened to the bottom of the frame which is under the drawers, with wood screws, as shown in Fig. 12. Later, when molding is glued to the tops of the feet, to rail (E), and to ends (B), these feet will be held securely in place.

Make the three drawers. Form the molding on all four edges of the drawer fronts with shaping cutters, and the lips on three edges of each drawer front on the table saw. Then make all drawer sides and backs, and saw the dovetails for these on the bandsaw. Chisel out the holes on both ends of the drawer fronts to hold the drawer sides. Cut grooves in drawer fronts, sides, and backs to hold the drawer bottoms, and glue the dovetail joints. Do not glue drawer bottoms to drawer sides, but leave these joints unglued. Be sure every drawer fits into its opening so it will slide in and out freely before gluing the dovetail joints.

Make the lid last. Here again, several boards must be glued together to make a lid as wide as this, unless you have the good fortune to have lumber this wide. A glued-top is less apt to warp or split, but as Fig. 1 shows, glue joints sometimes open because the cleats to which both ends of the top are joined do not shrink or swell like the lid, because the grain runs in the opposite direction. Cleats are grooved and mortised to hold the tongues and tenons made on the lid ends. The molding on three edges of the lid is cut to shape only after the cleats have been glued to the lid.

Wrought-iron hinges like those shown in Fig. 9 are recommended if they can be found or made. Otherwise heavy offset brass chest hinges may have to be substituted, inferior though the substitution may be. The same is true of the lock. The wrought-iron one is the proper kind, but a more modern type may have to be substituted.

FIG. 5

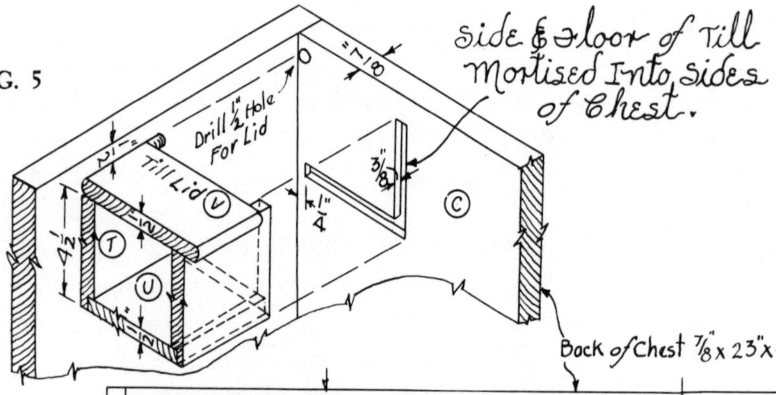
Side & Floor of Till Mortised Into Sides of Chest.
Drill 1/2" Hole For Lid
Till Lid
V
T
U
C
3/8"
4 1/2"
7/8"

FIG. 9

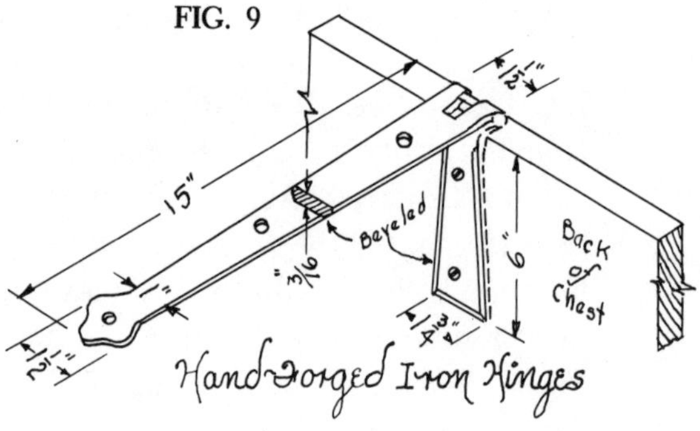
15"
1 1/2"
1"
Beveled
3/16"
6"
4 3/4"
2 1/2"
Back of Chest
Hand-Forged Iron Hinges

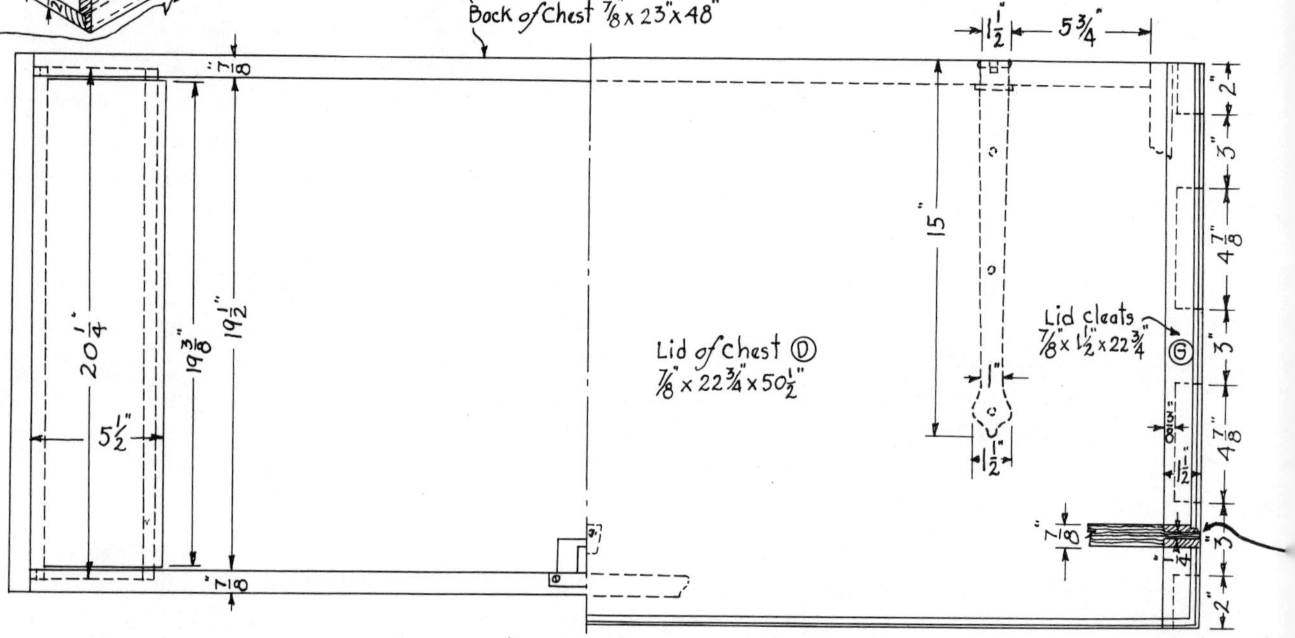
Back of Chest 7/8 x 23" x 48"
1 1/2"
5 3/4"
7/8"
20 1/4"
19 3/8"
19 1/2"
5 1/2"
15"
Lid of Chest D
7/8" x 22 3/4" x 50 1/2"
1"
1 1/2"
Lid cleats
7/8" x 1 1/2" x 22 3/4"
G
2"
3"
4 7/8"
3"
4 7/8"
3"
2"

FIG. 4

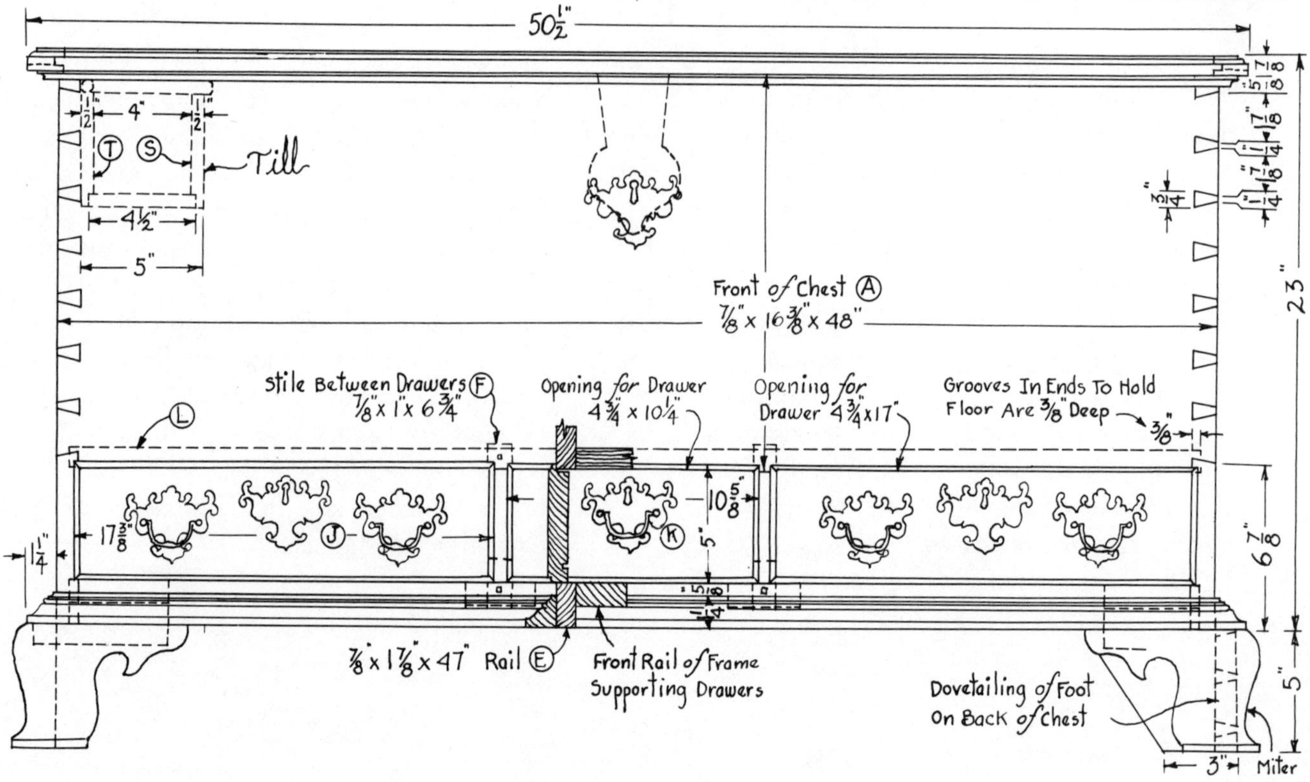
50 1/2"
4"
1/2"
T S
Till
4 1/2"
5"
Front of Chest A
7/8" x 16 3/8" x 48"
23"
3/4"
Stile Between Drawers F
7/8" x 1" x 6 3/4"
Opening for Drawer
4 3/4 x 10 1/4
Opening for Drawer 4 3/4 x 17"
Grooves In Ends To Hold Floor Are 3/8" Deep
3/8"
L
17 3/8
J
10 5/8
K
5"
6 7/8"
1 1/4"
7/8" x 1 7/8" x 47" Rail E
Front Rail of Frame Supporting Drawers
Dovetailing of Foot On Back of Chest
5"
3"
Miter

FIG. 2

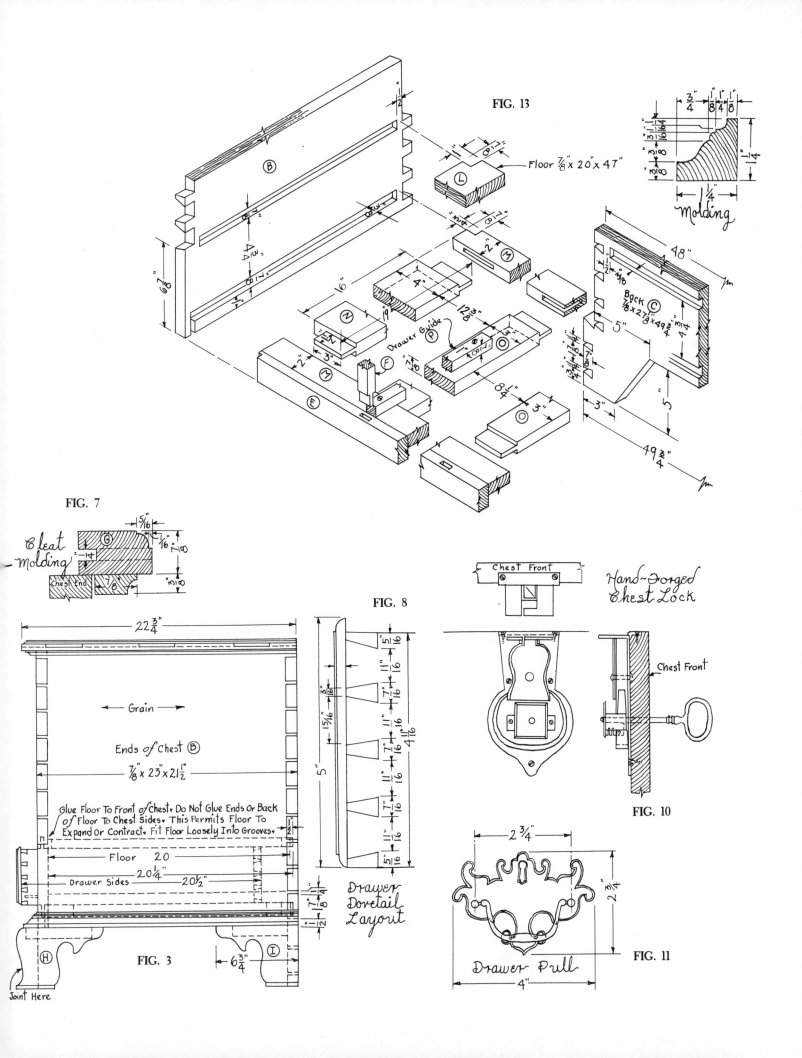

FIG. 13

Floor 7/8" x 20" x 47"

Molding

Back C
7/8" x 27 3/8" x 49 3/4"

48"

FIG. 7

Cleat molding

G
Chest End

FIG. 3

22 3/4"

← Grain →

Ends of Chest B
7/8" x 23" x 21 1/2"

Glue Floor To Front of Chest. Do Not Glue Ends Or Back of Floor To Chest Sides. This Permits Floor To Expand Or Contract. Fit Floor Loosely Into Grooves.

Floor 20

Drawer Sides 20 1/4"   20 1/2"

H   I

Joint Here

6 3/4"

FIG. 8

Drawer Dovetail Layout

Chest Front

Hand~Forged Chest Lock

Chest Front

FIG. 10

Drawer Pull

2 3/4"

2 3/4"

4"

FIG. 11

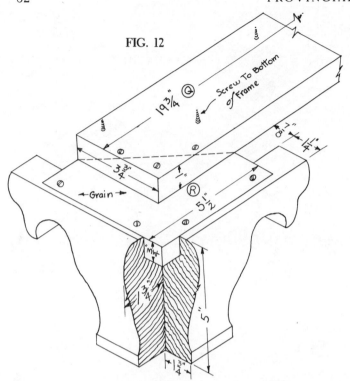

FIG. 12

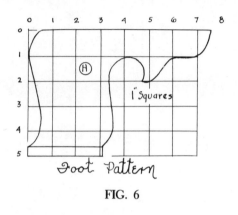

Construction of Front Feet

Sides of Front Feet Are Joined With A Miter And Held Together On Top With A Triangular Plate Fastened To The Feet With Glue & Wood Screws. The 3¾ x 19¾ Strip Going from Front To Back Foot Is Used To Fasten The Feet To The Frame Under The Drawers.

Foot Pattern

FIG. 6

BILL OF MATERIAL

Walnut

1 Front of chest (A) ⅞″ x 16⅜″ x 48″
2 Ends (B) ⅞″ x 23″ x 21½″
1 Back (C) ⅞″ x 27⅛″ x 49¾″
1 Lid (D) ⅞″ x 22¾″ x 50½″
1 Rail below drawers (E) ⅞″ x 1⅞″ x 47″
2 Stiles between drawers (F) ⅞″ x 1″ x 6¾″
2 Lid cleats (G) ⅞″ x 1½″ x 22¾″
2 Front feet 4 pieces (H) 1¾″ x 5″ x 7½″
2 Back feet 2 pieces (I) 1¾″ x 5″ x 6¾″
2 Drawer fronts (J) ⅞″ x 5″ x 17⅜″
1 Drawer front (K) ⅞″ x 5″ x 10⅝″
Molding under lid ⅜″ x ⅞″ x 100″ (approx.)
Molding above feet 1¼″ x 1¼″ x 100″ (approx.)

Poplar

1 Chest floor (L) ⅞″ x 20″ x 47″
2 Rails in frame under drawers (M) ⅞″ x 2″ x 47″

2 Rails in frame under drawers (N) ⅞″ x 4″ x 19″
2 Rails in frame under drawers (O) ⅞″ x 3″ x 19″
2 Drawer guides (P) ⅞″ x 1″ x 19¾″
2 Strips above feet (Q) 1″ x 3¾″ x 19¾″
2 Triangular plates in feet (R) ¾″ x 5¼″ x 8″
1 Till side (S) ½″ x 4½″ x 20¼″
1 Till side (T) ½″ x 4½″ x 19½″
1 Till bottom (U) ½″ x 4½″ x 20¼″
1 Till lid (V) ½″ x 5½″ x 20¼″

Poplar

6 Drawer sides ⅝″ x 4¹¹⁄₁₆″ x 20½″
2 Drawer backs ⅝″ x 4¹¹⁄₁₆″ x 16⅞″
1 Drawer back ⅝″ x 4¹¹⁄₁₆″ x 10⅛″

Birch Plywood

2 Drawer bottoms ¼″ x 16⅛″ x 19¾″
1 Drawer bottom ¼″ x 9⅜″ x 19¾″

NINETEEN

North European Carved Chest

THIS CHEST, WITH ITS LAVISHLY CARVED front is of North European origin, possibly Danish or Norwegian, as the type of carving found on its front seems to indicate. Walnut wood used to build one like it would be ideal material, though white oak or some other hardwood could be substituted.

The original, shown in Fig. 1, has a lid slightly rounded to a convex shape on top, an element I have dispensed with in my working drawings, because the

FIG. 1

FIG. 4 Carving Pattern

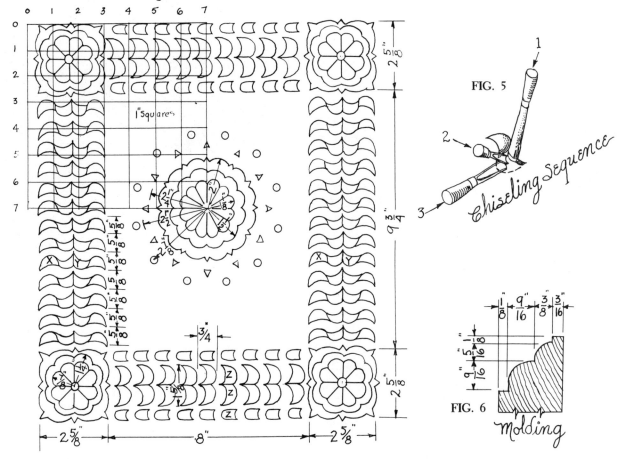

1"squares

FIG. 5

Chiseling Sequence

FIG. 6 Molding

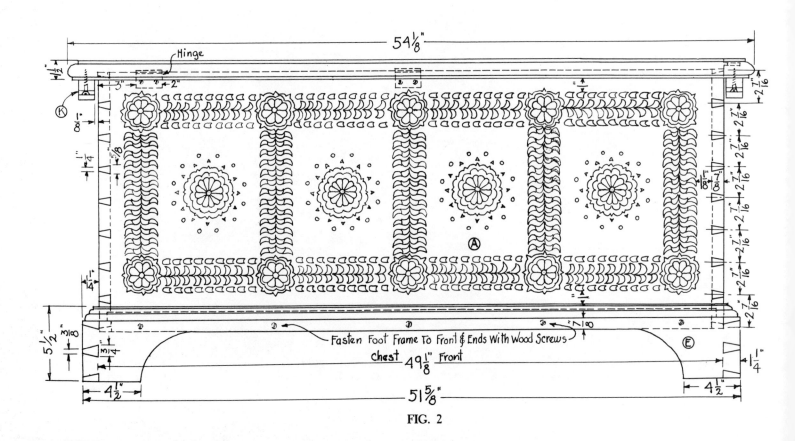

Hinge

Fasten Foot Frame To Front & Ends With Wood Screws

Chest 49⅛" Front

FIG. 2

difficulties involved in reproducing this somewhat unusual feature do not seem to be worth the trouble such construction would involve. The substitution of a flat lid seems better and of greater practical value to me. I have also substituted brass chest hinges for the hardwood dowels used as fulcrums on the rear ends of the hinge strips on this chest. Iron handles, like those shown in the photograph, are not shown on the drawings, and if some are to be used on a reproduction they will have to be fashioned from mild steel on a forge.

To build the chest, glue up boards to make front (A), ends (B), and back (C). When sanded smooth, lay out the dovetail joints, and cut and fit these to each other.

Draw a full-sized pattern like the one shown in Fig. 4, the design of which may be transferred to the wood with carbon paper if light-hued wood like maple or oak is used. Lines transferred on wood as dark as walnut with carbon paper may not show as clearly. In this case, cut openings where the pattern is marked "X" and "Y," on both sides of the pattern, with carving gouges. Heavier pencil lines may then be drawn around these. By turning the pattern over on its opposite side after the first openings have been traced, the whole pattern may be drawn. Openings marked "Z" may be cut out in their entirety instead of removing only half sections like "X" and "Y."

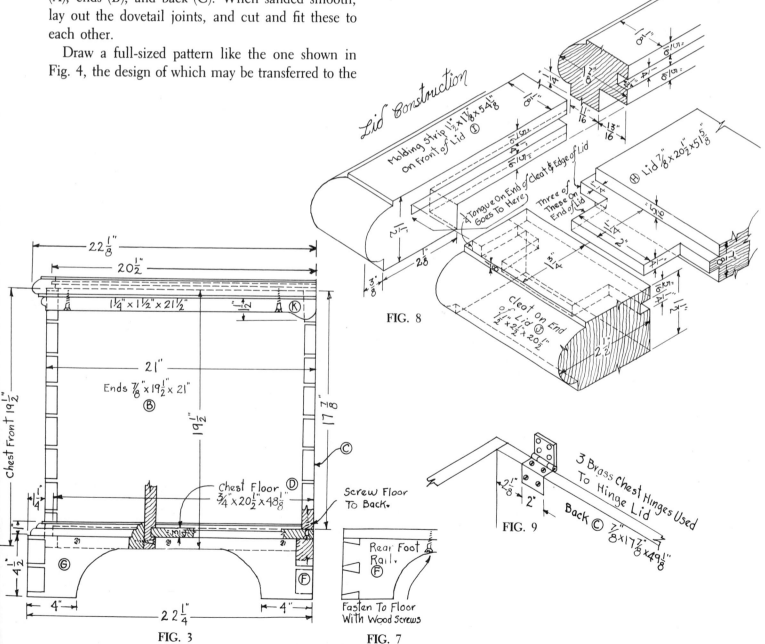

FIG. 8

FIG. 3

FIG. 7

FIG. 9

Rosettes, like those on all four corners of the pattern and those in the center, may be laid out by first drawing compass circles, and then outlining individual segments. Some tedious work is involved in doing all this, but this is unavoidable.

Fig. 5 shows the chiseling sequence to follow when carving the areas marked "X" and "Y" in Fig. 4. I suggest experimenting on a practice block before undertaking to carve the chest front itself.

When the carving has been done, cut grooves to hold the floor into the front and ends of the chest on the inside. These grooves are ⅜ inch deep. The floor extends to the outside of the chest at the back, and is fastened to the lower edge of the back with wood screws, as shown in Fig. 3. When the floor has been made, fit it into these grooves. It should not be necessary to glue the floor to the chest sides, because the grooves are deep enough to hold it in place without doing this. Drill holes along lower edges of front (A), and ends (B), and countersink these on the inside for screw heads, so the base can be fastened to sides and ends with wood screws as shown in Figs. 2 and 3. When the floor has been fitted to these grooves, put the floor into the grooves, glue the dovetail joints, and with wood screws fasten the rear edge of the floor to the back.

Make stretchers (E), (F), and (G) for the base, and shape the molding on upper edges of (E) and (G) as shown in Fig. 6. Then lay out dovetail joints, and cut and fit these. When this has been done, form the feet by bandsawing them to shape, as shown in Figs. 2, 3, and 7. Glue the dovetail joints, being sure the frame fits snugly around both ends and the front of the chest. You have more leeway when fastening rail (F) at the back, and it is possible to plane and sand the joined members there to even up the surface.

Make the lid. Glue up (H), and plane and sand it. Cut molding strip (I) and both cleats (J) to thickness, width, and lengths, shown in Fig. 8, and cut mortises, grooves, and rabbet on inside edges where they are joined to (H). Cut tongues and tenons on both ends and front of (H) and fit all joints before shaping the molding on cleats (J) and molding strip (I). If the molding is cut on (I) and (J) before gluing the joints, strips of wood should protect the molding when applying pressure with clamps.

When the lid has been glued up and fitted to the chest, chest hinges may be used to fasten it to the back, as shown in Fig. 9. Unless the length of the lid is shortened, which it could be if hinge strips (K) are not used, these should be made and fastened to both ends of the lid.

BILL OF MATERIAL

Walnut

Chest front (A) ⅞" x 19½" x 49⅛"
2 Chest ends (B) ⅞" x 19½" x 21"
1 Chest back (C) ⅞" x 17⅞" x 49⅛"
1 Chest floor (D) ¾" x 20½" x 48⅛"
1 Front stretcher for feet (E) 1¼" x 5½" x 51⅝"

1 Rear foot rail (F) 1¼" x 4½" x 51⅝"
2 Foot stretchers for ends (G) 1¼" x 5½" x 22¼"
1 Lid (H) ⅞" x 20½" x 51⅝"
1 Molding strip for front of lid (I) 1½" x 1⅞" x 54⅛"
2 Cleats on ends of lid (J) 1½" x 2½" x 20½"
2 Hinge strips under lid ends (K) 1¼" x 1½" x 21½"

TWENTY

Small
Tulip and Aster Chest

TULIP AND ASTER CHESTS, SIMILAR TO THE one shown in Fig. 1, apparently originated in Connecticut. They were also sometimes called sunflower chests.

Distinguishing features were the use of oak for framework and panels. Wide pine boards, however, were used to make the lids, backs, and floors of these chests. The chests were made with three carved

FIG. 1

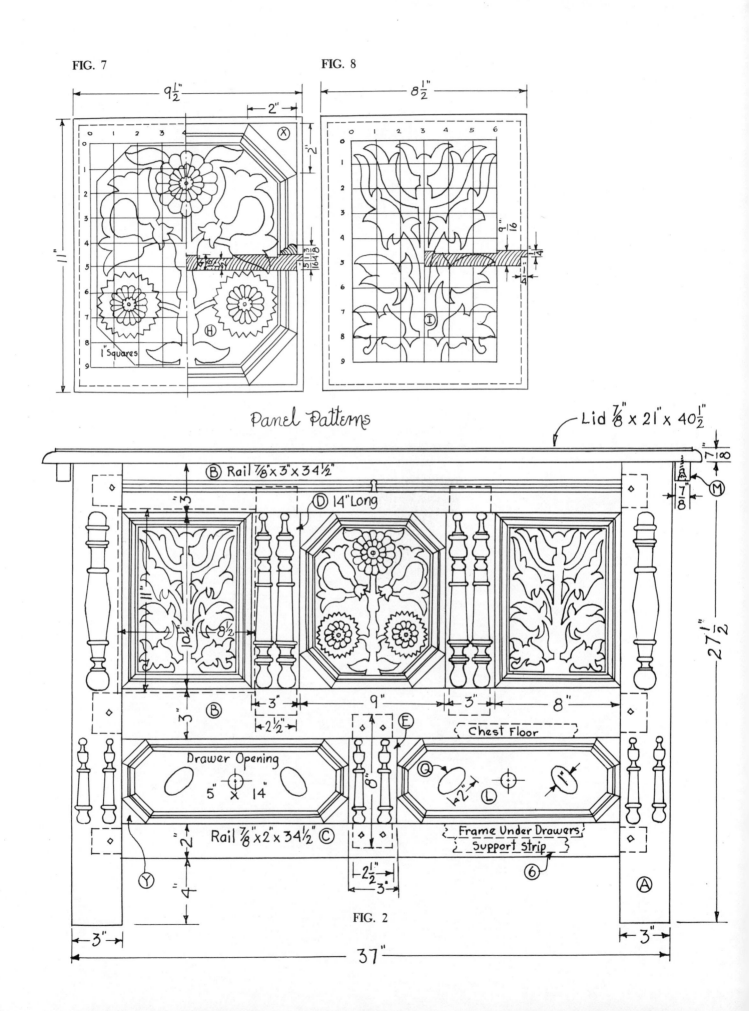

FIG. 7

FIG. 8

1" Squares

Panel Patterns

Lid ⅞" x 21" x 40½"

B Rail ⅞" x 3" x 34½"

D 14" Long

Chest Floor

Drawer Opening
5" x 14"

Frame Under Drawers
Support Strip

Rail ⅞" x 2" x 34½" C

FIG. 2

37"

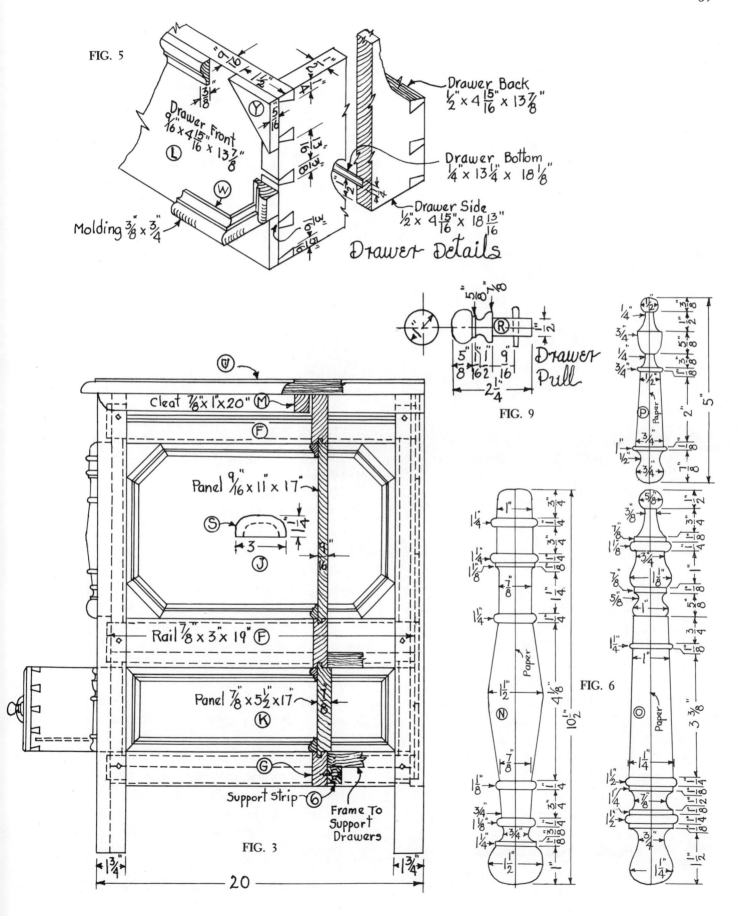

FIG. 5

Drawer Front
$\frac{9}{16}" \times 4\frac{15}{16}" \times 13\frac{7}{8}"$
Ⓛ

Ⓨ

Ⓦ

Molding $\frac{3}{8}" \times \frac{3}{4}"$

Drawer Back
$\frac{1}{2}" \times 4\frac{15}{16}" \times 13\frac{7}{8}"$

Drawer Bottom
$\frac{1}{4}" \times 13\frac{1}{4}" \times 18\frac{1}{8}"$

Drawer Side
$\frac{1}{2}" \times 4\frac{15}{16}" \times 18\frac{13}{16}"$

Drawer Details

Ⓡ

Drawer Pull

FIG. 9

Ⓟ Paper

FIG. 6

Ⓝ Paper

Ⓞ Paper

Ⓤ

Cleat $\frac{7}{8}" \times 1" \times 20"$ Ⓜ

Ⓕ

Panel $\frac{9}{16}" \times 11" \times 17"$

Ⓢ

Ⓙ

Rail $\frac{7}{8}" \times 3" \times 19"$ Ⓕ

Panel $\frac{7}{8}" \times 5\frac{1}{2}" \times 17"$
Ⓚ

Ⓖ

Support strip Ⓖ

Frame To
Support
Drawers

FIG. 3

$1\frac{3}{4}"$ $1\frac{3}{4}"$

20

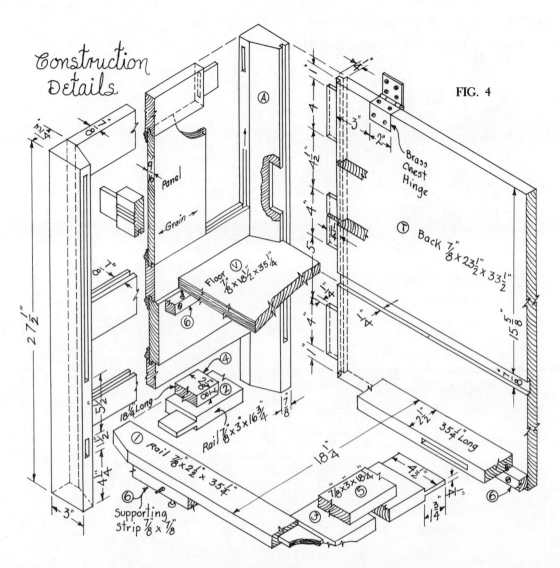

Construction Details

FIG. 4

panels on front, in the upper part, and usually two drawers below these extending the distance occupied by the three panels above them. On this chest two smaller drawers are substituted for the two-tiered longer drawers usually found on such chests.

Typical decorations were the three circular carved flowers on the center panel, and the carving with surfaces raised by lowering the background around the designs, left flat (as shown in the photograph), and in Figs. 2, 7, and 8 on the working drawings. Other typical features used to decorate these chests are the molding bordering panels and drawer fronts, and the split turnings and turtle-shaped bosses glued to the frame, panels, and drawer fronts. For this chest I recommend using maple to make these, because maple

is better suited for this type of turning, and its finish and coloring. Split turnings were painted black to simulate ebony wood. Moldings around panels and drawer fronts were colored a dark red hue. All in all these chests were pretty fancy household items for the times when they first appeared.

The chest shown here is smaller than typical models from which the design is adapted. The smaller size adapts it better to small rooms in which space saving is a factor to be taken into consideration.

To build the chest, make and shape the four legs. They are chamfered on the inside, so as not to have the corners protrude inside the chest compartment. Lay out and cut mortises and grooves to hold rails and panels.

Make rails (B), (C), (F), and (G), and stiles (D) and (E). Cut tenons on all rails and stiles, and fit them to their respective mortises. Cut grooves into all four legs where tongues of panels, and back, are to be joined to them. Make back (T). Then make a trial assembly of legs, rails, stiles, and back. When this has been done, cut grooves into rails (B), (C), (F), and (G); and into both edges of stiles (D) to hold panels. Cut ¼-inch tongues on all four edges of each panel, and fit these to their respective grooves. Cut the molding on the front of the top rail, and on the top rails on both ends of the chest. Use a router bit properly shaped to do this with an electric hand router if the equipment is available, or carve it with wood-carving chisels.

Carve the three panels. With the exception of the three flowers in the center panel, all this is accomplished by lowering the background around the design to a depth of ¹⁄₁₆ inch or so, and then carefully smoothing the background. Carver's gouges will shape the flowers, the grooves of the petals being quite shallow in depth. Full-sized patterns can be made from the drawings shown in Figs. 7 and 8.

When panels have been carved, and the floor of the chest made, you should be ready to glue together posts, rails, stiles, and floor. The chest floor fits into a groove in the back, and panels (K) and strips (6) help support both ends of the floor. The front edge of the floor should be glued to rail (B). Panels should not be glued to rails, stiles, or legs, but left loose in the grooves holding them, and with a bit of clearance to permit changes in width with change of seasons.

The frame holding up the two drawers should now be made. It is held together with mortise-and-tenon joints, as shown in Fig. 4, and is supported and held in place by supporting strips (6), fastened with wood screws to its underside and to the rails and back of the chest. Strips (4) and (5) should be fastened to its upper side to act as drawer guides before the frame is fastened to the chest frame.

Make and fit the drawers. While pine was the wood commonly used for drawer sides, I prefer poplar and advocate substituting it for this purpose. Drawer construction is shown in Fig. 5.

Make enough molding to outline panels and drawers, as shown in the drawings. Also make the triangular-shaped corner blocks (X) and (Y). These and the molding are glued to panels and drawer fronts, with a few brads to help hold them in place.

Bosses on drawer fronts and split turnings may be cut to shape on the lathe. Brown wrapping paper is glued between two strips of wood, which permits separating the two halves easily after turning them on the lathe. The brown paper can be removed from the flat side with a scraper blade, and the turning glued to the chest. All finishing coats should be applied to the turnings and moldings before gluing them in place.

Make the chest lid, and fasten the two oak cleats (M) to the bottom of the lid at both ends with wood screws. Do not glue these to the lid. Use two chest hinges to fasten the lid to the back, as shown in Fig. 4. A chest lock may be installed if so desired, though this is optional. Turned wooden drawer pulls for this chest are shown in Fig. 9.

BILL OF MATERIAL

Oak

4 Legs (A) 1¾″ x 3″ x 27½″
2 Rails (B) ⅞″ x 3″ x 34½″
1 Rail (C) ⅞″ x 2″ x 34½″

2 Stiles between panels (D) ⅞″ x 3″ x 14″
1 Stile between drawers (E) ⅞″ x 3″ x 8″
4 Rails (F) ⅞″ x 3″ x 19″
2 Rails (G) ⅞″ x 2″ x 19″
1 Panel (H) ⁹⁄₁₆″ x 9½″ x 11″

2 Panels (I) $\frac{9}{16}$" x 8½" x 11"
2 Panels (J) $\frac{9}{16}$" x 11" x 17"
2 Panels (K) $\frac{7}{8}$" x 5½" x 17"
2 Drawer fronts (L) $\frac{9}{16}$" x 4$\frac{15}{16}$" x 13$\frac{7}{8}$"
2 Cleats (M) $\frac{7}{8}$" x 1" x 20"

Maple

2 Split turnings; make from 2 pieces (N) $\frac{7}{8}$" x 1¾" x 11"
4 Split turnings; make from 4 pieces (O) $\frac{7}{8}$" x 1¾" x 11"
6 Split turnings; make from 6 pieces (P) $\frac{5}{8}$" x 1¼" x 5½"
4 Bosses; make from 4 pieces (Q) ½" x 1" x 2" *
2 Drawer pulls (R) 1" diam. x 2¼"
2 Handles (S) 1" x 1¼" x 3"

White Pine

1 Back (T) $\frac{7}{8}$" x 23½" x 33½"
1 Lid (U) $\frac{7}{8}$" x 21" x 40½"

*These are glued together with brown wrapping paper between, so they can be split apart after turning them, to shapes as shown in Fig. 6.

1 Floor of chest (V) $\frac{7}{8}$" x 18½" x 35¼"
Molding (W) $\frac{3}{8}$" x ¾" x lengths as needed for drawer fronts and panels
4 Corner blocks for panels (X) $\frac{5}{16}$" x 1½" x 3"
8 Corner blocks for drawer fronts (Y) $\frac{5}{16}$" x 1" x 2$\frac{1}{8}$"

Poplar

(1) Front and back rails, frame under drawers $\frac{7}{8}$" x 2½" x 35¼"
(2) 2 End rails, frame under drawers $\frac{7}{8}$" x 3" x 16¾"
(3) 1 Middle rail, frame under drawers $\frac{7}{8}$" x 4½" x 16¾"
(4) 2 Drawer guides, frame under drawers $\frac{7}{8}$" x 2$\frac{1}{8}$" x 18¼"
(5) 1 Drawer guide, frame under drawers $\frac{7}{8}$" x 3" x 18¼"
(6) Support strips under frame which holds drawers $\frac{7}{8}$" x $\frac{7}{8}$" x lengths as needed
4 Drawer sides ½" x 4$\frac{15}{16}$" x 18$\frac{13}{16}$"
2 Drawer backs ½" x 4$\frac{15}{16}$" x 13$\frac{7}{8}$"

Birch Plywood

2 Drawer bottoms ¼" x 13¼" x 18$\frac{1}{8}$"

TWENTY-ONE

Display Cabinet

THE DISPLAY CABINET, SHOWN IN FIG. 1, IS filled with antique china. It would serve equally well as a display cabinet for prized acquisitions of many other kinds, or as a bookcase.

I have substituted brass **H**-hinges in my drawings for those used on the cabinet shown in Fig. 1, because the substitution is a desirable improvement. A good cabinet door lock could be added if one is needed.

Another substitution I've made is the ¼-inch birch plywood back for the tongue-and-groove jointed, solid wood back that is found on this cabinet. Adherence to older practices when solid stock was used because nothing better was available is in my estimation not justifiable in a reproduction, and the substitution reduces weight.

To make the display cabinet, first make the two ends (A). Both of these are extended all the way to the floor where the back feet are fastened to them, and this makes it possible to fasten the back feet with wood screws from the inside. It is also a better means of support for the great weight of the contents stored in such cabinets, and stiles (D) go to the floor for the same reasons. The parts of the front feet, shown in Fig. 2, are fastened with wood screws to stiles (D) from the back, and after the miter joint has been glued and bradded, and braced with the triangular plate (R), this type of construction makes a sturdy

FIG. 1

93

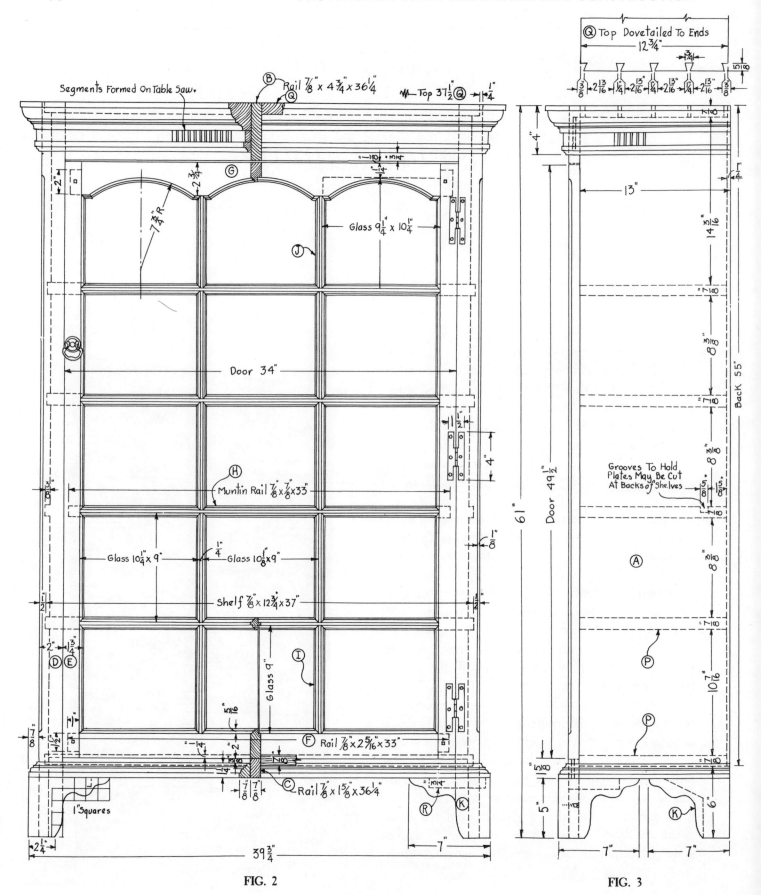

FIG. 2

FIG. 3

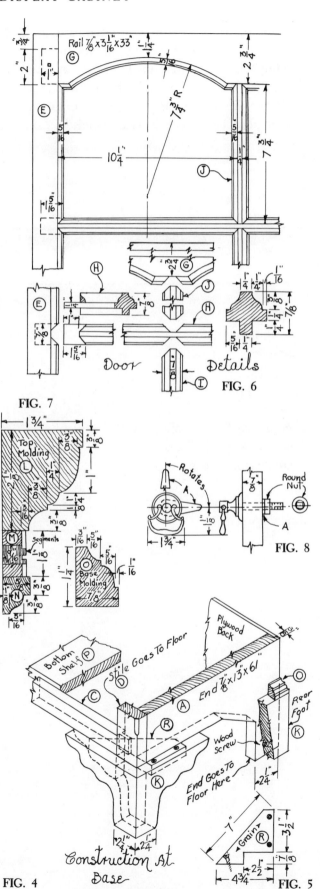

FIG. 7

FIG. 6

FIG. 8

Construction At Base

FIG. 4

FIG. 5

base, as shown in Fig. 4. Feet need not be made until the frame which holds the door has been glued to ends (A).

Rabbet the back edges of ends (A) to hold the plywood back. The back is nailed to the ends and to the shelves, floor, and top. Also cut grooves across the insides of (A) to hold the shelves and floor.

Top (Q) is dovetailed to the ends, as shown at the top of Fig. 3.

Make rails (B), (C), and stiles (D), and the mortise-and-tenon joints to make the front frame which holds the door. Tenons on rail (B) are 5/16 inch thick, 3 inches wide, and 1⅛ inches long. Tenons on rail (C) are 5/16 inch thick, 1⅝ inches wide, and 1⅛ inches long. Chamfer the outside edges of stiles (D), then glue the frame together.

When dovetail joints at the top have been made, make the shelves and floor and glue these to ends (A). When stiles (D) have been glued to ends (A), drive a few finish nails to help hold them in place at the top where the molding will hide them and at the bottom where feet will do the same. Feet and base molding (O) may then be made and fastened in place.

Make the door next. Cut and shape enough molding to make muntin rails (H) and muntin stiles (I) and (J). Make door stiles (E) and mortise them to hold rails (F), (G), and (H), after which the shaping of the molding on the inside edges of stiles (E) can be done. Then make rails (F) and (G). Make and fit tenons on rails (F), (G), and (H) to the mortises in (E) before you saw the arches on rail (G), and also file and sand the bandsawed arches before shaping the molded edge. Now carefully shape the 45-degree angles where moldings are joined to each other, as shown in Fig. 6. Joinery on the door is the most difficult part of building a piece of furniture like this, and it must be done with care. The method of construction shown here is different from the way such work would be done in a planing mill. The way shown on the drawings is a practical way of doing it with the kinds of tools and equipment usually found in home workshops of the kind in which this piece of furniture and others in this book were made. One could, of course, have the door made in a shop where such work is routinely done, but the cost would be a great deal higher.

When the door has been made and fitted to the opening, hinges, latch, and perhaps a lock may be put on. The drawing shows ⅛-inch clearance at the top of the door for easy opening and closing, and enough should be provided on the left for easy opening and closing.

The molding at the top is in three parts. By making it this way, the segments on the frieze of the molding may be formed on the table saw, and the shaped parts may more easily be formed. (See Fig. 7.) When the molding has been put on, cut and fasten the plywood back with nails to ends (A), shelves, and top.

BILL OF MATERIAL

Cherry

2 Ends (A) ⅞″ x 13″ x 61″
1 Top rail (B) ⅞″ x 4¾″ x 36¼″
1 Bottom rail (C) ⅞″ x 1⅝″ x 36¼″
2 Stiles (D) ⅞″ x 2″ x 61″
2 Door stiles (E) ⅞″ x 1¾″ x 49½″
Rail on bottom of door (F) ⅞″ x 2⁵⁄₁₆″ x 33″
Rail with arches at top of door (G) ⅞″ x 3¹⁄₁₆″ x 33″
4 Muntin rails in door (H) ⅞″ x ⅞″ x 33″
8 Muntins (I) ⅞″ x ⅞″ x 9″
2 Muntins (J) ⅞″ x ⅞″ x 7¾″
Feet, 6 pieces (K) ⅞″ x 5″ x 7″
Molding at top (L) 1¾″ x 2⅛″ x 82″ (approx.)
Molding at top (with segments) (M) ⁹⁄₁₆″ x 1⅛″ x 82″ (approx.)

Molding at top (N) ⅝″ x ¾″ x 82″ (approx.)
Base molding (above feet) (O) ⅞″ x 1¼″ x 82″ (approx.)

Poplar or Pine

Shelves and floor, 5 pieces (P) ⅞″ x 12¾″ x 37″
Top (Q) ⅞″ x 12¾″ x 37½″
Triangular-shaped plates for front feet (R) ¾″ x 3″ x 7″

Birch Plywood

Back (S) ¼″ x 37¼″ x 55″

TWENTY-TWO

Dutch Cupboard of Pine

THE DUTCH CUPBOARDS SHOWN IN THIS AND succeeding chapters are without exception somewhat unusual and distinctive examples of types found in rural areas of eastern Pennsylvania. Unlike the open-shelved Welsh dressers and hutches of New England, contents in these are stored behind glass doors, where in addition to displaying them, contents can be kept from collecting dust and dirt. Cupboards as large as these can hold a great deal, a fact easily ascertained by examining our example in Fig. 1; and they are made to serve as sideboards as well as for display and storage purposes. Cooking utensils are often kept on shelves in the lower part.

The most difficult part of building one is making the glass doors. Since all the glazed doors found on these cupboards, and on two corner cupboards found later in the book, were made with home workshop equipment, an innovative method of joinery to make this practicable was used here. This is shown in some detail in Fig. 8. When glued together, with the glass in place, the construction is sound.

For those not equipped with a spindle shaper or with an electrically powered hand shaper and router, with cutters to shape the molding, I recommend having the doors made in a planing mill. Making a lot of moldings in a great variety of shapes can pose problems in a home workshop, where not only the proper equipment but also the skills necessary to do it safely

FIG. 1

97

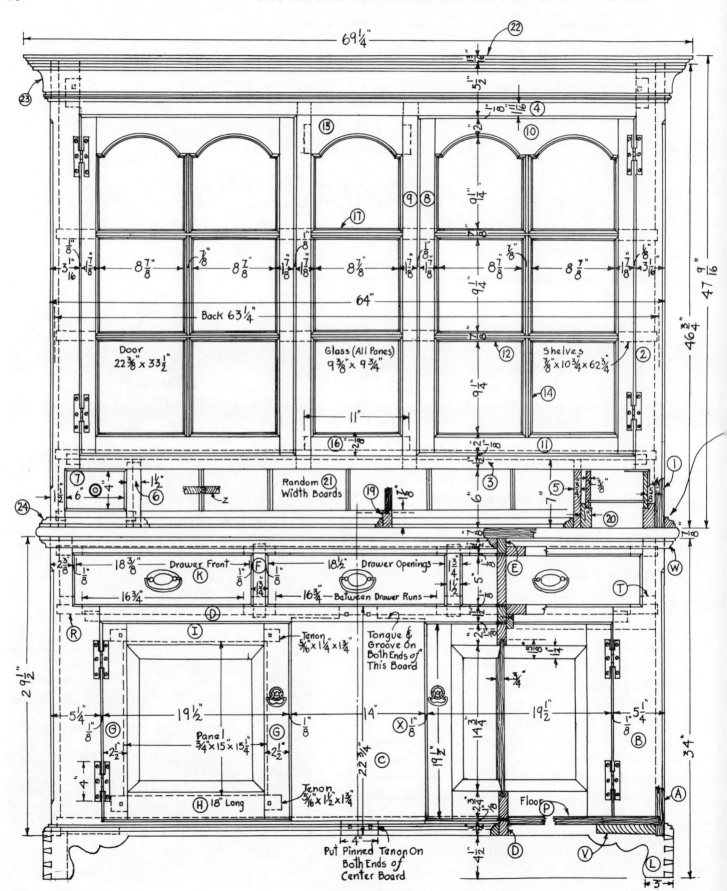

FIG. 2

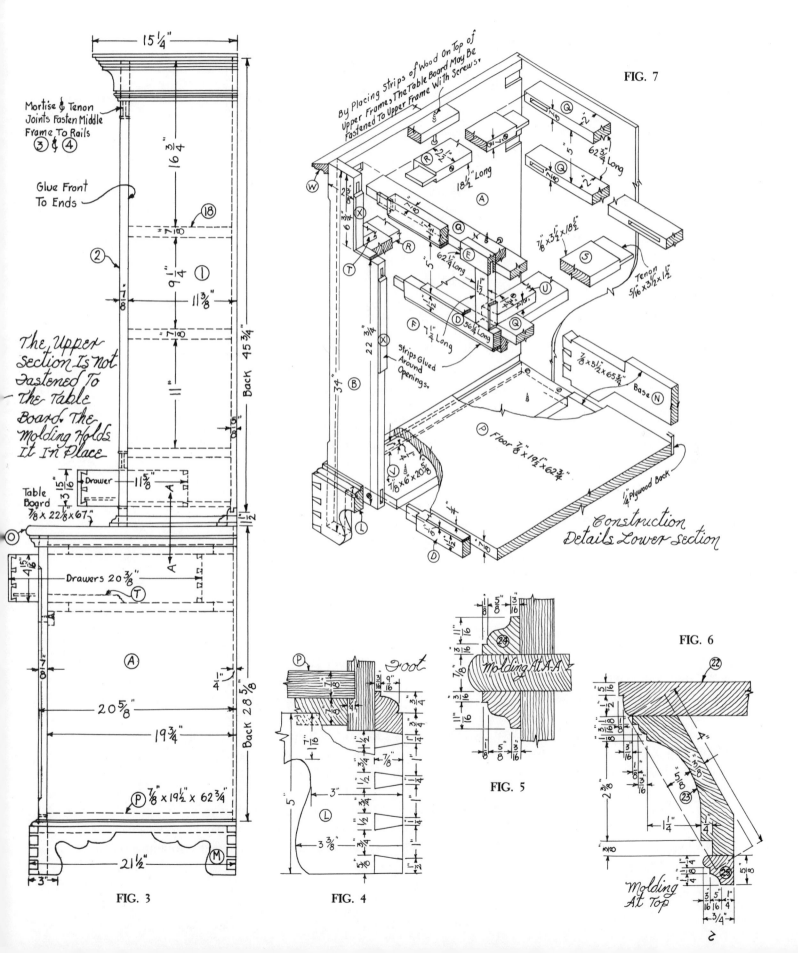

FIG. 7

Mortise & Tenon Joints Fasten Middle Frame To Rails ③ & ④

Glue Front To Ends

The Upper section Is Not Fastened To The Table Board. The Molding Holds It In Place

Table Board 7/8 x 22 3/8 x 67"

FIG. 3

By Placing Strips of Wood On Top of Upper Frames The Table Board May Be Fastened To Upper Frame With Screws.

Strips Glued Around Openings.

Construction Details Lower Section

Foot

Molding At A-A

FIG. 5

FIG. 6

FIG. 4

Molding At Top

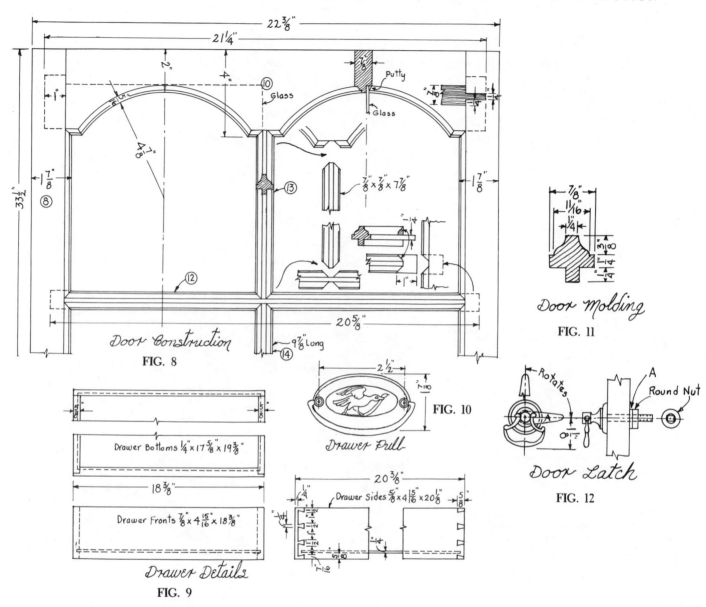

Door Construction

FIG. 8

Door Molding

FIG. 11

Drawer Pull

FIG. 10

Door Latch

FIG. 12

Drawer Details

FIG. 9

and well must be available. Exact reproductions of the molding shapes shown need not be strictly adhered to, but some adaptation of shapes other than those shown may at times be substituted. Indeed, a close examination of Fig. 1 will reveal the fact that I redesigned some of the molding on my drawings to modify and improve those found on the cupboard shown in Fig. 1.

The shape of the muntin molding on these doors is not the shape usually found on such doors (see Fig. 11), but it was made with the cutter on hand, and is

a suitable shape. Strips of wood 7/8″ x 7/8″ are sanded smooth, after which the molding is shaped on both edges for the outside of the door. The rabbets on both edges which hold the glass are then cut on the circular saw. Notches, where moldings are joined at right angles, are carefully sawed out and trimmed with chisels or files.

Ready-made crown moldings in pine are available in places where lumber is sold, and if judiciously chosen such substitutions may be acceptable, though I would prefer reproducing the molding shown in

Fig. 6. The large cove may be cut to its approximate shape on the circular saw, and so may the bottom edge. A hand shaper or spindle shaper is best to shape the top.

LOWER SECTION

Fig. 7 shows the construction of the lower section in greater detail than can be shown in Figs. 2 and 3. A part of stile (B) goes clear to the floor to reinforce the base and thus helps bear the load it must support. Two boards (V), screwed to ends (A) and stile (B) from the outside, help support the floor, and hold the bottom of the cupboard together. The floor and boards (V) are supported on top of base rail (N) in the back.

Floor (P) and shelves (18) in the upper section are glued into grooves cut across ends (A) in the lower part, and ends (1) in the upper part.

Frames to support the drawers are made as shown in Fig. 7. The frame above the drawers is put there to keep the drawers level when pulled out, and the table board is also fastened to it with wood screws. Ends of long rails (Q) are extended ¼ inch beyond rails (R) so they are supported by gains cut into end boards (A). A strip of wood, screwed to the back of rail (D), helps support the front of the frame under the drawers, and strips of wood above the upper frame permit fastening the table board to the upper frame. Wood screws long enough to go through both frame and strips are used for this purpose.

UPPER SECTION

In the upper section, the glazed frame in the middle is fastened to rails (3) and (4) by cutting tenons on the extended ends of stiles (9). Both glazing and finishing should be done on the back of the entire frame holding the doors before it is fastened to ends (1), shelves, and top. The back on the upper section is made of ⅝-inch random-width boards, joined together as shown at (Z) in Fig. 2.

Upper and lower doors are latched as shown in Fig. 12. Molding fastened to the table board on top with glue and brads holds the upper section in place. Large drawers are made as shown in Fig. 9.

BILL OF MATERIAL

LOWER SECTION

Pine

2 Ends (A) ⅞" x 19¾" x 29½"
2 End stiles on front (B) ⅞" x 5¼" x 34"
1 Board between doors (C) ⅞" x 14" x 22¾"
2 Rails above and below doors (D) ⅞" x 1½" x 56¼"
1 Rail above drawers (E) ⅞" x 1½" x 62¼"
2 Stiles between drawers (F) ⅞" x 1½" x 7¼"
4 Door stiles (G) ⅞" x 2½" x 19½"
2 Door rails (H) ⅞" x 2¾" x 18"
2 Door rails (I) ⅞" x 2" x 18"
2 Door panels (J) ¾" x 15" x 15¼"
3 Drawer fronts (K) ⅞" x 4¹⁵⁄₁₆" x 18⅜"

1 Front of base (feet) (L) ⅞" x 5¾" x 65¾"
2 ends of base (feet) (M) ⅞" x 5¾" x 21½"
1 Back of base (feet) (N) ⅞" x 5½" x 65¾"
1 Table board (O) ⅞" x 22⅛" x 67"
1 Floor (P) ⅞" x 19½" x 62¾"
4 Rails, frames above and below drawers (Q) ⅞" x 2" x 62¾"
4 End rails, frames above and below drawers (R) ⅞" x 2½" x 18½"
4 Rails, frames above and below drawers (S) ⅞" x 3½" x 18½"
2 Drawer guides (T) ¾" x 1⅝" x 19½"
2 Drawer guides (U) ¾" x 1¾" x 19½"
2 Boards under floor (V) ⅞" x 6" x 20⅝"

Molding under table board (W) ⅞″ x ¹⁵⁄₁₆″ x 110″ (approx.)

Strips around drawer and door openings (X) ⅛″ x ⅞″ x lengths as needed

6 Drawer sides ⅝″ x 4¹⁵⁄₁₆″ x 20⅛″

3 Drawer backs ⅝″ x 4¹⁵⁄₁₆″ x 18⅜″

Birch Plywood

1 Back for lower section ¼″ x 28⅝″ x 63″

3 Drawer bottoms ¼″ x 17⅝″ x 19⅜″

UPPER SECTION

Pine

(1) 2 Ends ⅞″ x 11⅜″ x 46¾″

(2) 2 Stiles ⅞″ x 3¹⁄₁₆″ x 46¾″

(3) 1 Rail below doors ⅞″ x 1½″ x 62⅞″

(4) 1 Rail above doors ⅞″ x 5½″ x 62⅞″

(5) 2 Boards, small drawer housing ¾″ x 7″ x 10¾″

(6) 2 Stiles, front of small drawer housing ⅞″ x 1½″ x 7″

(7) 2 Drawer fronts ⅞″ x 3¹⁵⁄₁₆″ x 5¹⁵⁄₁₆″

(8) 4 Stiles for doors ⅞″ x 1⅞″ x 33½″

(9) 2 Stiles for glazed panel between doors ⅞″ x 1⅞″ x 36¾″

(10) 2 Top rails, glazed doors ⅞″ x 4″ x 21¼″

(11) 2 Bottom rails, glazed doors ⅞″ x 2″ x 21¼″

(12) 4 Horizontal muntins for doors ⅞″ x ⅞″ x 20⅝″

(13) 2 Vertical muntins for doors ⅞″ x ⅞″ x 7⅞″

(14) 4 Vertical muntins for doors ⅞″ x ⅞″ x 9⅞″

(15) 1 Top rail, glazed panel ⅞″ x 4″ x 11″

(16) 1 Bottom rail, glazed panel ⅞″ x 2⅛″ x 11″

(17) 2 Muntins, glazed panel ⅞″ x ⅞″ x 11″

(18) 3 Shelves ⅞″ x 10¾″ x 62¾″

(19) 1 Rail for base of back ⅞″ x 1⅞″ x 63¼″

(20) 4 Drawer runs and guides 1″ x 2⅛″ x 10¾″

(21) Back ⅝″ x 63¼″ x 45¾″ (random-width boards)

(22) Top ¹³⁄₁₆″ x 15¼″ x 69¼″

(23) Crown molding 1″ x 4″ x 100″ (approx.)

(24) Molding above table board ⅞″ x ¹⁵⁄₁₆″ x 130″ (approx.)

(25) Molding at top ⅝″ x ¾″ x 100″ (approx.)

4 Drawer sides ⅜″ x 3¹⁵⁄₁₆″ x 11⅜″

2 Drawer backs ⅜″ x 3¹⁵⁄₁₆″ x 5¹⁵⁄₁₆″

Birch Plywood

2 Drawer bottoms ¼″ x 5⁷⁄₁₆″ x 10⅝″

TWENTY-THREE

Cherry Dutch Cupboard

THIS DUTCH CUPBOARD IS SMALLER THAN THE pine cupboard shown in Chapter Twenty-two and simpler to build. The cherry wood used to build it gives it a degree of refinement above that found in similar pieces made of the more commonly used woods such as pine or poplar. Walnut or curly maple could be used to build this piece.

While the cupboard is not too large to be built with the upper section permanently fastened to the lower section, it's better if built as shown here, with the upper section merely resting upon the lower section and not fastened to it. This makes it easier to move, should this become necessary.

LOWER SECTION

To build the lower section, make the two ends (A), both of which are extended clear to the floor. This makes it easy to fasten the feet and gives extra strength where it is necessary to have it. Stiles (B) also go to the floor, making it possible to fasten feet (M) and (N) to ends (A) and to stiles (B) with wood screws from the inside. The weight of the contents, which as you can see by looking at Fig. 1, are often quite heavy, makes this extra strengthening of the supporting elements a desirable feature.

Make rails (C), (D), and (E), board (G), and stiles (F), and cut and fit mortise-and-tenon joints to make

FIG. 1

103

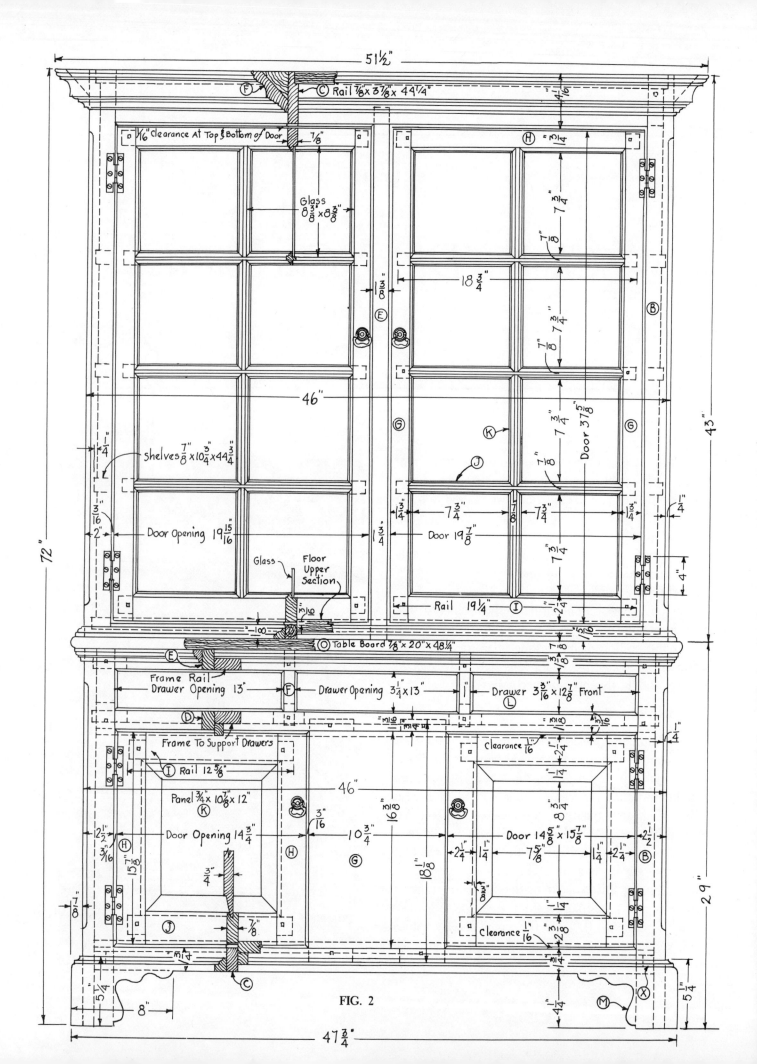

FIG. 2

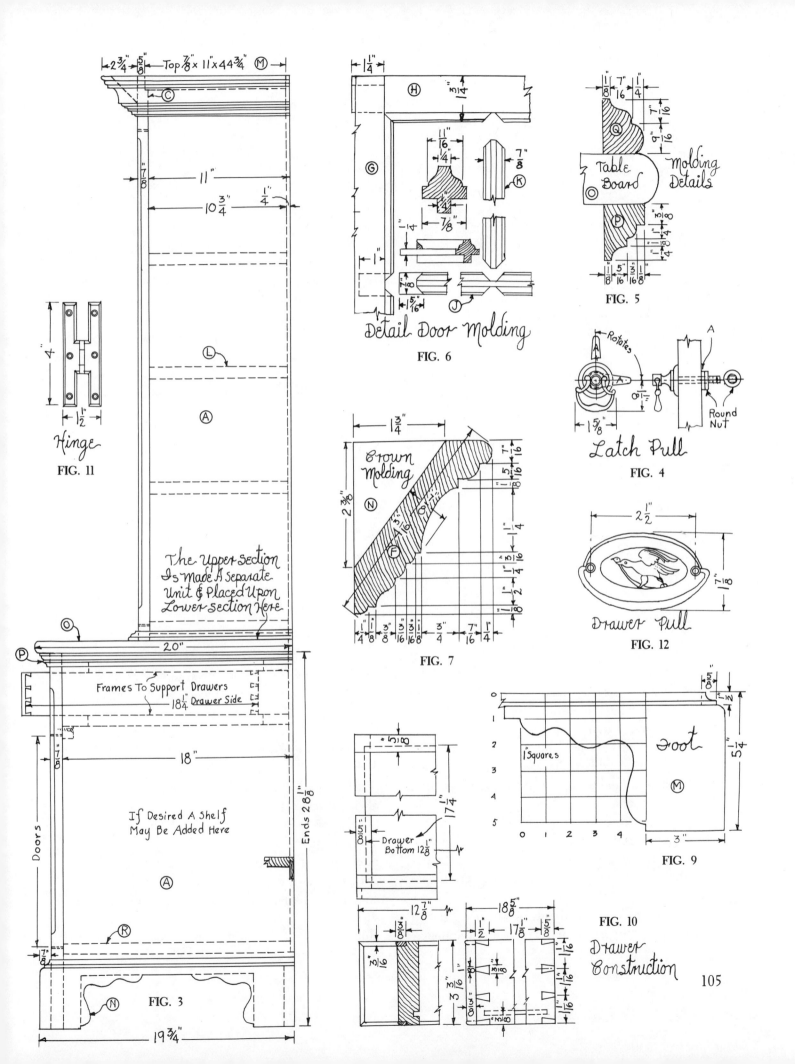

Top 7/8" x 11" x 44 3/4" Ⓜ

2 3/4" 5/8"

Ⓒ

7/8"

11"

10 3/4" 1/4"

Ⓛ

Ⓐ

Ⓗ

1 1/4"

3/14"

Ⓖ

1 1/4"   1/16"   7/8" Ⓚ

7/8"

1 1/4"

1"

7/8"

1 5/16" Ⓙ

Detail Door Molding

FIG. 6

1/8" 7/16" 1/4"

7/16"

Table Board Ⓠ Molding Details

Ⓞ Ⓟ

9/16"

5/16" 5/16"

1/8" 5/16" 1 3/16 1/8"

FIG. 5

Ⓞ

4"

1 1/2"

Hinge

FIG. 11

Rotates A

A A

Round Nut

1 5/8" Latch Pull

FIG. 4

2 1/2"

1 7/8"

Drawer Pull

FIG. 12

The Upper Section
Is Made A Separate
Unit & Placed Upon
Lower Section Here

1 3/4"

Crown Molding

2 3/8"

Ⓝ

Ⓕ

7/16" 5/18" 1/8"

1 1/4"
1 3/16"
1 1/4"
1 1/2"
1 1/8"

1/4" 1/8" 3/8" 3/16" 3/16" 3/4" 7/16" 1/4"

FIG. 7

Ⓞ 20"

Ⓟ

Frames To Support Drawers
18 1/4" Drawer Side

18"

7/8"

If Desired A Shelf
May Be Added Here

Doors

Ⓐ

Ends 28 1/8"

Ⓡ

7/8"

FIG. 3

Ⓝ

19 3/4"

5/18"

17 1/4"

5/18"

Drawer Bottom 12 7/8"

12 7/8"

18 5/8"

3/16"

3 1/6"

1/2" 17 1/8" 5/16"

Drawer Construction

0 1 2 3 4 5

1" Squares

Foot Ⓜ

5/8" 1/2"

5 1/4"

0 1 2 3 4

3"

FIG. 9

FIG. 10

105

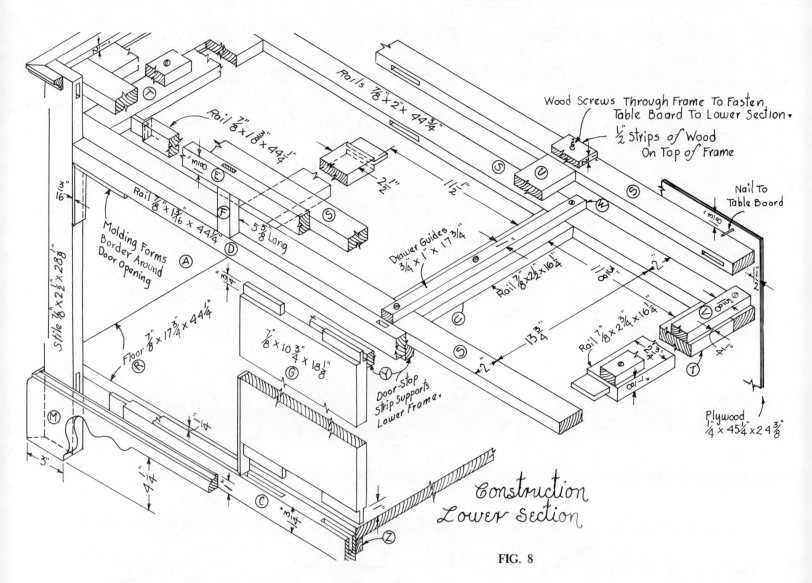

the front frame. Assemble and glue the joints of the frame. Make strips of wood for the 3/16-inch bead molding with which to outline door openings, and fit and glue these around door openings. A few brads may be used to help hold these in place, but they should also be glued fast. Place heavier strips of wood over them and hold these in place with clamps until the glue has set.

Rabbet the back edges of ends (A) to hold the plywood enclosing the back, and cut 1/4-inch-deep grooves across the tops of (A) on the inside, to support the ends of the frames that go over and under the drawers.

Make the two frames, details of which are shown in Fig. 8. The upper frame is fastened to the under-

side of the table board with wood screws, as shown in Fig. 8, but 1/2-inch strips of wood must be placed to fill the spaces between the frame rails and the table board when you do this. Frame and table board should be fastened together before fastening them to ends (A). Rails (S) may be glued to rail (D) and rail (E), to fasten them securely to the frame on the front of the lower section.

Make and fasten drawer guides (V) and (W) to the lower frame with wood screws. Both frames are then fitted into the grooves on the insides of ends (A). It is not a good idea to put glue along the entire length of end rails (T) when fitting them into these grooves, since this could cause cracks to form on ends (A). If glue is used, put only a little on a small area at about the middle of rail (T). The support strip (Y), glued to (D), and fastened with wood screws to (G) and to the bottom of the frame, gives adequate support at the front; and the plywood back, when it is nailed to the backs of the frames, and ends (A), will hold everything together. Nails and wood screws may also be used where molding (Q) will cover them, to help fasten the upper frame.

Make the floor board and fit it into place. Use wood screws to fasten support strips (X) and (Z) to the floor and to ends (A) and rail (C). Make boards (M) and (N) for the feet and shape the molding on their upper edges. Then cut and fit the miter joints where they are joined together, before cutting the feet to shape on the bandsaw. The feet should then be fastened with wood screws to the bottoms of ends (A), with glue to rail (C), and with wood screws to the bottoms of stiles (B). Glue, and several small finish nails, should be used to hold the miter joints together.

Make the drawers. Details showing their construction are shown in Fig. 10. Notice that the narrower bead molding than that which outlines the door openings is, in this instance, glued around the edges of the drawer fronts, into rabbets cut around drawer-front edges, as shown in the cross section in Fig. 10.

When drawers have been made and fitted to their respective openings, make the two paneled doors. Make and fit the mortise-and-tenon joints; cut grooves in rails and stiles to hold panels, and raise the panels on the table saw. Do not glue panels into the grooves, but glue and pin mortise-and-tenon joints. Use ³⁄₁₆-inch hardwood pegs to pin these joints. These square pins are driven into ³⁄₁₆-inch drilled round holes.

UPPER SECTION

Build the upper section. The most difficult parts to build in the upper section are the doors, so it is best to make these first. Cut strips of wood for stiles (G) and for rails (H) and (I), and for muntins (J) and (K). Shape the molding on rails, stiles, and muntins; then make joints to fasten the pieces together. See Figs. 2 and 6 for details showing how these pieces are fitted

and joined to each other. When you have made sure that all joints fit properly, glue rails (H), (I), and (J) to one stile (G) first. This will allow you to glue the short muntins to the muntin rails without having to force them into place, and once you have joined vertical and horizontal muntins together, you can glue rails (H), (I), and (J) to the stile on the opposite side of the door.

Get out stock for both ends (A). Cut ¼-inch-deep grooves across the insides to hold the shelves and top, and rabbet the back edges to fasten the plywood back. Make stiles (B) and (E), and rails (C) and (D). Cut and fit mortise-and-tenon joints to make the front frame. Bevel the outside edges of stiles (B); then glue up the frame. Fit the shelf ends into the grooves and make sure the front frames width equals the width of assembled shelves and ends. Then glue stiles (B) to ends (A). Once the plywood back has been nailed fast to shelves and ends (A), the shelves will stay in place.

Cut, fit, and glue the ³⁄₁₆-inch molding strips around the door openings, and be sure doors fit properly so they can be opened and closed without binding.

Place the upper section on top of the table board, and fit molding (Q) around it.

Make the crown molding. With care, the rough-shaping of this can be started on the table saw and then finished with wood-carving chisels. The molding shape could be somewhat simplified to make this still easier, and result in an even more beautiful molding if you know how. A suggestion is to make the large cove in the middle of the molding wider, and join it to a fillet extended from the top of the reverse curve on the lower part, and at the top of the molding have only one bead instead of two. Details for shaping the crown molding are given in Fig. 7. The triangular-shaped backing (N) is first nailed to the top to form a base to which the crown molding can be nailed, and the molding itself can be made from a board only ⅞ inch thick.

Brass hardware, of the kinds shown in Figs. 4 and 11, may then be put on the doors. This should be taken off again before finishing coats are applied to the wood. Drawer pulls are shown in Fig. 12.

BILL OF MATERIAL

LOWER SECTION

Cherry

2 Ends (A) ⅞″ x 18″ x 28⅛″
2 Stiles (B) ⅞″ x 2½″ x 28⅛″
1 Bottom rail (C) ⅞″ x 1¾″ x 44¼″
1 Rail under drawers (D) ⅞″ x 1³⁄₁₆″ x 44¼″
1 Rail above drawers (E) ⅞″ x 1⅜″ x 44¼″
2 Stiles between drawers (F) ⅞″ x 1″ x 5⅝″
1 Board between drawers (G) ⅞″ x 10¾″ x 18⅛″
4 Door stiles (H) ⅞″ x 2¼″ x 15⅞″
2 Top rails for doors (I) ⅞″ x 2¼″ x 12⅝″
2 Bottom rails for doors (J) ⅞″ x 2⅜″ x 12⅝″
2 Door panels (K) ¾″ x 10⅞″ x 12″
3 Drawer fronts (L) ⅞″ x 3³⁄₁₆″ x 12⅞″
1 Front foot (M) ⅞″ x 5¼″ x 47¾″
2 End feet (N) ⅞″ x 5¼″ x 19¾″
1 Table board (O) ⅞″ x 20″ x 48¼″
Molding under table board (P) ¾″ x 1″ x 88″ (approx.)
Molding above table board (Q) ¹³⁄₁₆″ x 1″ x 72″
   (approx.)
Border moldings around door openings ³⁄₁₆″ x ⅞″ x
   lengths as needed

Poplar

1 Floor (R) ⅞″ x 17¾″ x 44¼″
4 Rails in frames to hold drawers (S) ⅞″ x 2″ x 44¾″
4 End rails, frames to hold drawers (T) ⅞″ x 2¾″ x
   16¼″
4 Rails, frames to hold drawers (U) ⅞″ x 2½″ x 16¼″
2 Drawer guides, bottom frame (V) ¾″ x 1⅝″ x 17¾″
2 Drawer guides, bottom frame (W) ¾″ x 1″ x 17¾″
2 Strips to support floor (X) ⅞″ x ⅞″ x 17¾″
Doorstop and support strip for frame under drawers
   (Y) ⅞″ x 1″ x 44¼″

Support strip for floor (Z) ⅞″ x ⅞″ x 42½″
6 Drawer sides ⅝″ x 3³⁄₁₆″ x 18¼″
3 Drawer backs ⅝″ x 3³⁄₁₆″ x 12⅞″

Birch Plywood

1 Back ¼″ x 45¼″ x 24⅜″
3 Drawer bottoms ¼″ x 12⅛″ x 17¼″

UPPER SECTION

Cherry

2 Ends (A) ⅞″ x 11″ x 43″
2 Stiles (B) ⅞″ x 2″ x 43″
1 Rail above doors (C) ⅞″ x 3⅞″ x 44¼″
1 Rail below doors (D) ⅞″ x 1⅛″ x 44¼″
1 Stile between doors (E) ⅞″ x 1⅜″ x 40⅜″
Crown molding (F) ⅞″ x 4³⁄₁₆″ x 85″ (approx.)
4 Door stiles (G) ⅞″ x 1¾″ x 37⅝″
2 Door rails (H) ⅞″ x 1¾″ x 19¼″
2 Door rails (I) ⅞″ x 2¼″ x 19¼″
6 Horizontal door muntins (J) ⅞″ x ⅞″ x 18¾″
8 Vertical door muntins (K) ⅞″ x ⅞″ x 8⅜″
Border molding around door openings ³⁄₁₆″ x ⅞″ x
   234″ (approx.)

Poplar

4 Shelves (L) ⅞″ x 10¾″ x 44¾″
1 Top (M) ⅞″ x 11″ x 44¾″
Triangular backing for crown molding (N) 1¾″ x
   2⅜″ x lengths as needed

Birch Plywood

1 Back ¼″ x 45¼″ x 42½″

TWENTY-FOUR

Large Cherry Dutch Cupboard

I**T'S SOMEWHAT UNUSUAL TO FIND A DUTCH** cupboard of such a generous size and handsome design as the one shown here. Country-made, by a cabinetmaker well versed in woodworking skills but with little other help in the way of guidelines (such as the ones provided here), this example, and others in the book built by the same person, are of considerable merit. He used nothing more than the picture of a somewhat similar antique cupboard found in Wallace Nutting's *Furniture Treasury* as his model, with roughly drawn details of his own making of parts as occasion and need for them arose in the course of constructing the piece, and one must certainly admire the good results achieved.*

Changes were made, such as reducing the height and number of shelves and panes of glass found in the upper section of the example shown in Nutting's book. Two small drawers and an open area at the bottom of the upper section are additional departures from the model that inspired this piece of furniture. Other changes in size, proportion, and detail are evident as one would expect in a piece with so little to chart the course.

*See Pennsylvania Cupboard #559, Nutting's *Furniture Treasury*, Vol. 1.

FIG. 1

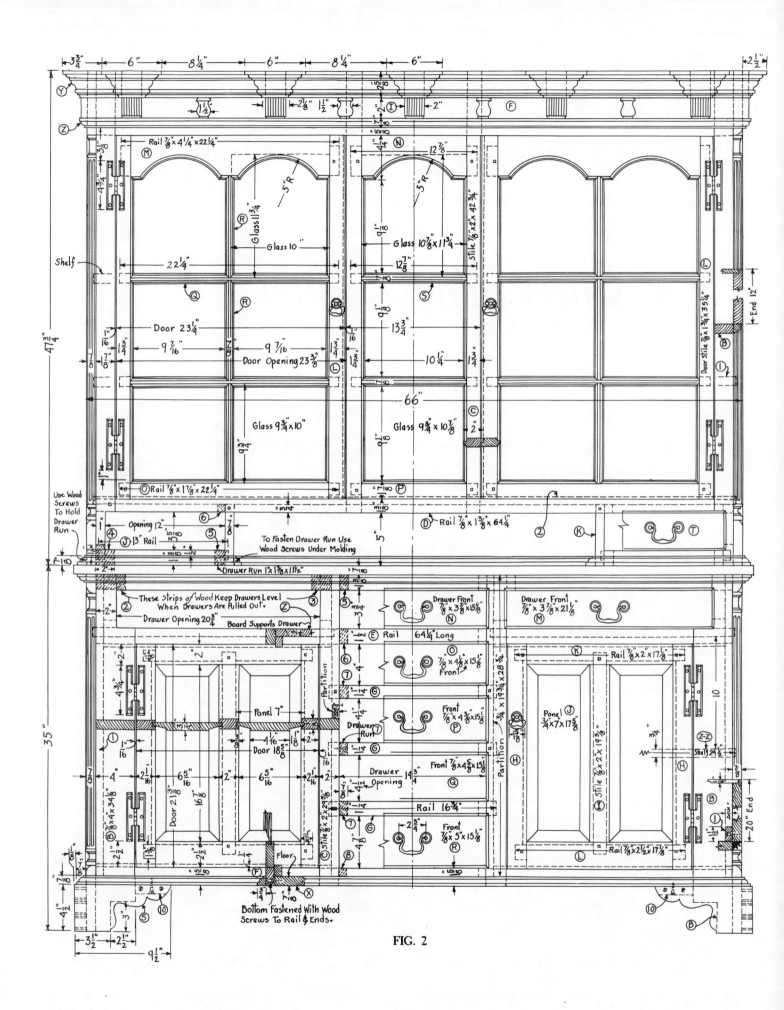

FIG. 2

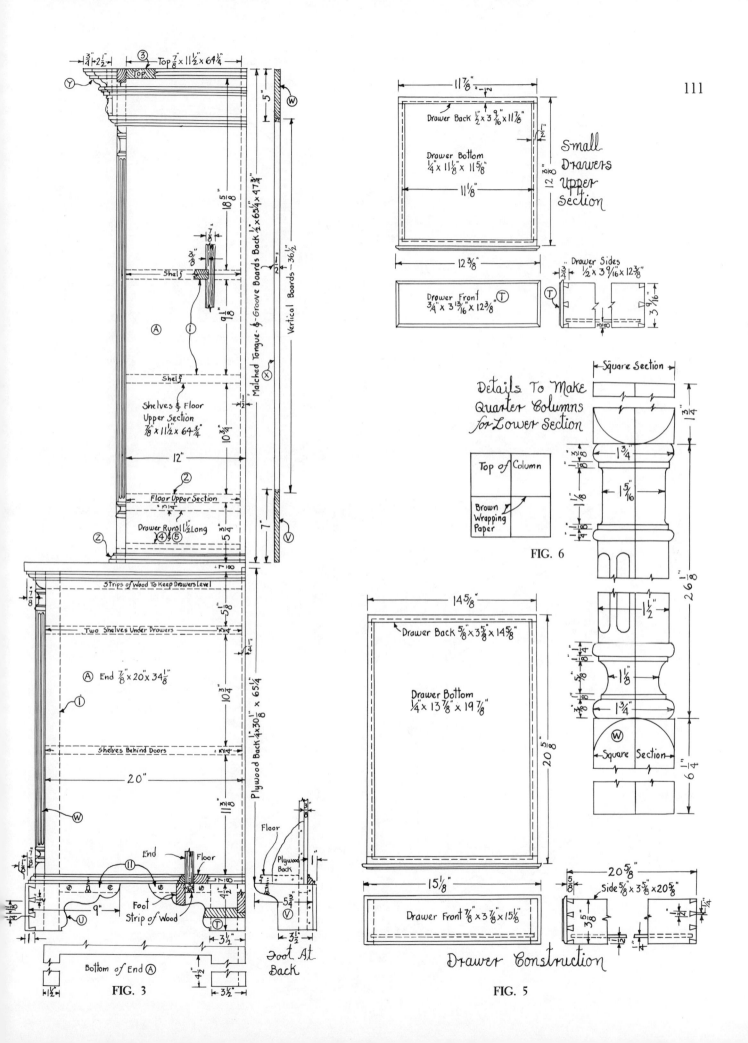

FIG. 3

Small Drawers Upper Section

Details To Make Quarter Columns for Lower Section

FIG. 6

Drawer Construction

FIG. 5

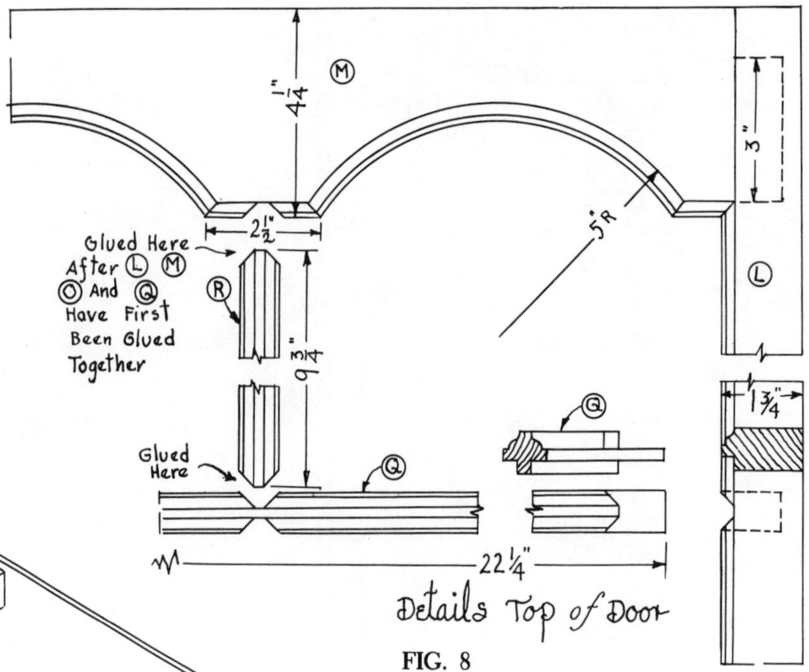

Details Top of Door

FIG. 8

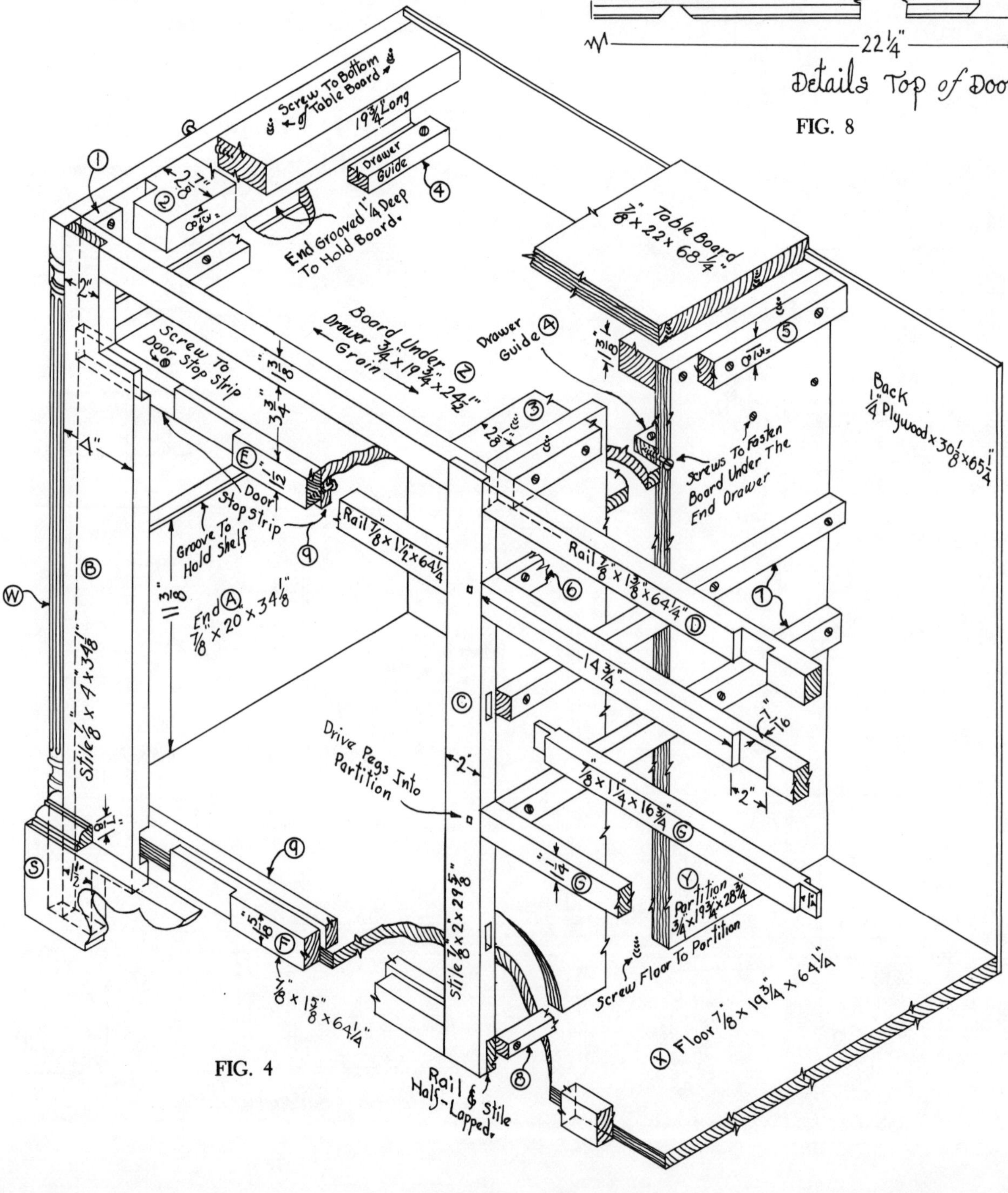

Glued Here
After ⓁⓂ
Ⓞ And Ⓠ
Have First
Been Glued
Together

Glued
Here

$2\frac{1}{2}"$

$9\frac{3}{4}"$

$\frac{1}{4}"$

3"

5° R

$1\frac{3}{4}"$

$22\frac{1}{4}"$

FIG. 4

Screw To Bottom
of Table Board

$19\frac{3}{4}$ Long

Drawer
Guide

$2\frac{7}{8}"$

End Grooved $\frac{1}{4}$ Deep
To Hold Board.

$\frac{7}{8}"$ Table Board
$\frac{7}{8} \times 22 \times 68\frac{1}{4}"$

Board Under Ⓩ
Drawer $\frac{3}{4} \times 19\frac{3}{4} \times 24\frac{1}{2}"$
Grain

Drawer
Guide ④

Screw To
Door Stop Strip

$2"$

$4"$

Groove To
Hold Shelf

Door
Stop Strip

Rail $\frac{7}{8} \times 1\frac{1}{2} \times 64\frac{1}{4}"$

End Ⓐ
$\frac{7}{8} \times 20 \times 34\frac{1}{8}"$

Rail $\frac{7}{8} \times 1\frac{1}{8} \times 64\frac{1}{4}"$

Screws To Fasten
Board Under The
End Drawer

Back
$\frac{1}{4}$ Plywood $\times 30\frac{1}{8} \times 65\frac{1}{4}"$

Stile $\frac{7}{8} \times 4 \times 34\frac{1}{8}"$

$14\frac{3}{4}"$

$2\frac{1}{8}"$

Drive Pegs Into
Partition

$2"$

$\frac{7}{8} \times 1\frac{1}{4} \times 16\frac{3}{4}"$

$4"$

Partition
$\frac{3}{4} \times 19\frac{3}{4} \times 28\frac{3}{4}"$

Stile $\frac{7}{8} \times 2 \times 29\frac{5}{8}"$

$\frac{7}{8} \times 15\frac{5}{8} \times 64\frac{1}{4}"$

Screw Floor To Partition

Rail & Stile
Half-Lapped.

Floor $\frac{7}{8} \times 19\frac{3}{4} \times 64\frac{1}{4}"$

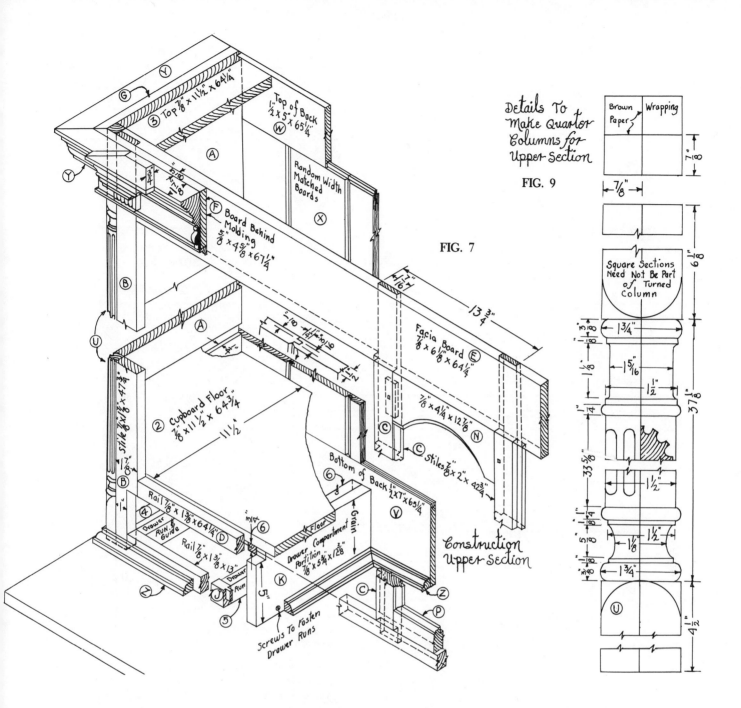

FIG. 7

Details To Make Quarter Columns for Upper Section

FIG. 9

Construction Upper Section

LOWER SECTION

In making the detailed drawings of the piece, shown here, I have made a few changes of my own, such as simplifying the design of the molding at the top. The simpler outline of the molding I have substituted will be easier to make than the one found on this cupboard, an improvement which in no way detracts from the effectiveness of the design but rather enhances its beauty.

The upper section is not fastened to the table board of the lower section but merely rests on its surface, which is the way such large two-section pieces were often made, so moving them from place to place was easily done when this became necessary.

To build the cupboard, make the lower section first.

Cut and glue up stock for ends (A), partitions (Y), floor (X), boards (Z), and shelves (Z-Z). Plane and sand surfaces smooth, then cut grooves on the inside of ends (A), and on the cupboard sides of partitions (Y), to hold shelves (Z) and shelves (Z-Z). Rabbet the back edges of ends (A) to fasten the plywood back later.

Backing strips (1), shown in Figs. 2 and 4, are fastened with wood screws to the inside front edges of

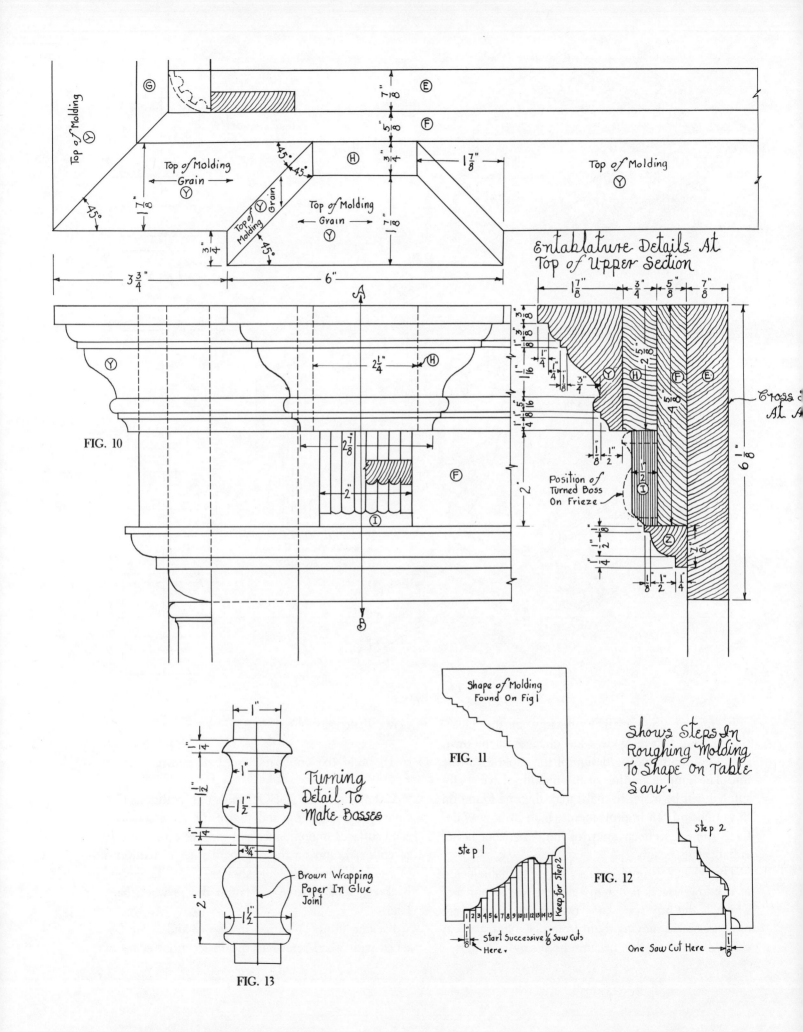

Top of Molding Y

Top of Molding
← Grain →
Y

45° 45°

Top of Molding
Y Grain

Top of Molding
Y Grain

Top of Molding
← Grain →
Y

45°

45°

G

E
$\frac{7}{18}$"

F
$\frac{5}{8}$"

H
$\frac{3}{4}$"

$1\frac{7}{8}$"

Top of Molding Y

$1\frac{7}{8}$"

$\frac{3}{4}$"

1"$\frac{7}{18}$"

Entablature Details At
Top of Upper Section

$3\frac{3}{4}$" 6"

$1\frac{7}{8}$" $\frac{3}{4}$" $\frac{5}{8}$" $\frac{7}{8}$"

A

Y

$2\frac{1}{4}$" H

$2\frac{7}{8}$"

2"

I

2

F

Position of
Turned Boss
On Frieze

Y H F E

Cross
At A

$6\frac{1}{8}$"

Z

FIG. 10

B

Turning
Detail To
Make Bosses

1"

$\frac{1}{4}$"

1"

$1\frac{1}{2}$"

$1\frac{1}{2}$"

$\frac{1}{4}$"

$\frac{3}{4}$"

2

$1\frac{1}{2}$"

Brown Wrapping
Paper In Glue
Joint

FIG. 13

Shape of Molding
Found On Fig 1

FIG. 11

Shows Steps In
Roughing Molding
To Shape On Table
Saw.

Step 1

1 2 3 4 5 6 7 8 9 10 11 12 13 14 15

Keep for Step 2

$\frac{1}{8}$" Start Successive $\frac{1}{8}$" Saw Cuts
Here.

Step 2

FIG. 12

One Saw Cut Here $\frac{1}{8}$"

(A). Stiles (B) are glued to these when the front frame has been made and assembled, and once the quarter-columns are glued into place this makes a strong corner. Stiles (C) are glued and fastened with ³/₁₆-inch-square hardwood pegs to partition (Y) after the front frame has been assembled.

Cut stock for stiles (B) and (C), and for rails (D), (E), (F), and (G). Lay out and cut lap joints and mortise-and-tenon joints to make the front frame, and glue these members together. Make drawer runs and guides (2), (3), (4), (5), (6), (7), and (8). Fasten drawer runs (4), (6), (7), and (8) with wood screws, as shown in Fig. 4, but do not yet screw strips (2), (3), and (5) to (A) and (Y), but save these to screw them fast under the table board before fastening it to the top of the lower section. Otherwise the short height of the opening for the drawers at both ends would make it almost impossible to drive wood screws through (2), (3), and (5) into the table board.

Glue boards (Z) and shelves (Z-Z) to ends (A) and partitions (Y). Then fit floor (X) in place, fastening it to ends (A) and partitions (Y) with wood screws.

Make the drawers. The type of dovetailing, and other details needed to make the upper middle drawer, is shown in Fig. 5, and except for the greater drawer width, both drawers on either side will be made the same way. Dovetail layouts for the four bottom drawers are not shown on the drawings, but should be easy to lay out if pins are kept the same size as those shown in Fig. 5, and tails are varied in width just a little, or one more tail is added in the deeper drawers. It is always a good idea to fit drawers into their respective openings before fastening the back to the cabinet.

Make the two doors. Get out stock for rails (K) and (L), and stiles (H) and (I). Lay out and cut grooves, mortises, and tenons, and fit these together properly. Then make the panels in the manner shown in Fig. 16 in Chapter Twenty-seven. Once these are in place, the mortise-and-tenon joints may be glued up and reinforced with ³/₁₆-inch-square cherry pegs. Do not glue the panels to the frame.

Before putting on hinges, latches, and drawer pulls, make the table board and fasten strips (2), (3),

and (5) to the underside of the table board, as shown in Fig. 4.

If you have not already turned the column shown in Fig. 6, do so now. Flute the column, then split it into four parts by carefully driving a chisel into one end to pry the four sections apart, and glue the quarter-column to edges of (A) and (B).

Make the feet. Cut out stock for these to the lengths, widths, and thicknesses shown in Figs. 2 and 3, but wait to bandsaw them to shape only after the dovetail joints on the front feet, and the butt and dado joints on the back feet have been made. Then fasten these to the stiles, quarter-columns, and ends, with wood screws, as shown in Figs. 2 and 3.

UPPER SECTION

To make the upper section, cut out and sand stock for ends (A), shelves (1), floor (2), and top (3). Cut ¼-inch-deep grooves across the inside of ends (A) to support the floor and shelves, as shown in Fig. 7. Rabbet rear edges of ends (A) to fasten the back after everything else has been put together.

Cut out and sand stock for stiles (B) and (C), and for rail (D) and fascia board (E). Make the lap joints fitting these together. Then lay out and cut mortises into stiles (C) to fasten arched rail (N), lower rail (P), and muntin rails (S). Bandsaw and smooth the arch in (N).

Make both doors, cutting stock for stiles (L), rails (M), (O), and (Q), and muntin styles (R). Bandsaw the arches in (M), and smooth the edges. Set up the shaper to cut molding on all edges which need shaping. Make and fit all joints, as shown in Fig. 2, and in the larger detail, Fig. 8. Glue the frames together.

Turn the column, shown in Fig. 9. In case your lathe bed is too short to make the square top and bottom sections of the column, and the turned shaft all in one piece, you can make the ⅞″ x ⅞″ square sections separately, and glue them in place above and below the turned shaft. Ends (A) and the assembled frame are held together by the glue joints holding shelves, floor, and ends together, and the glue joints used to fasten the quarter-columns in place. Backup strips like those used in the lower section to reinforce the front corners are not put into the upper section, since they would be an encumbrance here.

As previously indicated, I have redesigned and simplified the molding used at the top of the entablature, in order to make reproducing the design easier to accomplish. (See Fig. 10.) The actual shape of the molding found at the top of Fig. 1 is shown in Fig. 11, from which it is evident that the design I have substituted is a decided improvement. The molding shown in Fig. 10 can be cut to its approximate shape on the table saw, as shown in Fig. 12, and it can then be formed to the finished shape with wood-carving chisels and gouges. Careful sanding, after shaping it on strips long enough to make all of it, should result in a satisfactory product. Offset areas on long borders, like the one at the top of the cupboard, are made by sawing the adjoining ends at 45-degree angles on a miter box, as indicated in Fig. 10. This sawing is the more easily done with the top of the upside-down molding resting on the miter box floor. Even the short ¾-inch-long sections of molding, shown in the top view of Fig. 10, can be easily sawed to shape from the ends of a long piece of molding in this way.

Molding, where individual pieces are joined, should be glued, and a few #18 brads may also be used to help hold them in place.

The beaded blocks (I) can be glued to the border under each offset area, and after turning the bosses shown in Fig. 13, these should also be glued to this border.

Hinges, latches, and drawer pulls may now be put in place, though these should all be removed when finishing coats of paints, stain, and varnish are put on.

Before you fasten the molding, make and fasten the top (3) with wood screws to the end and fascia board. The boards (F) and (G) under the molding should also be nailed or screwed fast to the fascia board and to ends (A) at this time.

Panes of glass should be put into the three areas of the center frame, and held in place with putty or glazing compound. This should be done before nailing the back to the cabinet. Doors need not be glazed until all finishing coats have been applied. Rails (M) and (N) must be routed out in back to depths of ¼ inch where tops of glass panes are fitted into the doors and center frame.

Make and nail on the back, consisting of members (V), (W), and (X), shown in Figs. 3 and 7.

The same narrow ⅞"-x-⅞" molding (Z) is put on around the base of the upper section as was used on the lower section. It may be glued and bradded to the base of the upper section, but the upper section is not fastened to the table board of the lower section, but merely rests upon it.

BILL OF MATERIAL

LOWER SECTION

Cherry

2 ends (A) ⅞" x 20" x 34⅛"
2 End stiles on frame (B) ⅞" x 4" x 34⅛"
2 Stiles at middle of frame (C) ⅞" x 2" x 29⅝"
1 Top rail in frame (D) ⅞" x 1⅜" x 64¼"
1 Rail under three upper drawers (E) ⅞" x 1½" x 64¼"

1 Bottom rail in frame (F) ⅞" x 1⅝" x 64¼"
3 Short rails between four bottom drawers (G) ⅞" x 1¼" x 16¾"
4 Door stiles (H) ⅞" x 2" x 21⅜"
2 Door stiles between panels (I) ⅞" x 2" x 19⅜"
4 Door panels (J) ¾" x 7" x 17⅝"
2 Top rails in doors (K) ⅞" x 2" x 17⅛"
2 Bottom rails in doors (L) ⅞" x 2½" x 17⅛"
2 Upper drawer fronts (M) ⅞" x 3⅞" x 21⅛"
1 Upper drawer front (N) ⅞" x 3⅞" x 15⅛"

1 Drawer front (O) ⅞″ x 4⅛″ x 15⅛″
1 Drawer front (P) ⅞″ x 4⅜″ x 15⅛″
1 Drawer front (Q) ⅞″ x 4⅝″ x 15⅛″
1 Drawer front (R) ⅞″ x 5″ x 15⅛″
2 Fronts for feet (S) 1″ x 4½″ x 9½″
2 Sides for feet (T) 1″ x 4½″ x 9″
2 Sides for feet (U) 1″ x 4½″ x 9″
2 Backs for feet (V) 1″ x 4½″ x 5¾″
2 Quarter-columns; make from glued stock (W) ⅞″ x ⅞″ x 34⅛″

Molding around base and under table board ⅞″ x ⅞″ x 220″ (approx.)

Pine

1 Floor (X) ⅞″ x 19¾″ x 64¼″
2 Partitions (Y) ¾″ x 19¾″ x 28¾″
2 Boards under end drawers (Z) ¾″ x 19¾″ x 24½″
2 Shelves (Z-Z) ¾″ x 19¾″ x 24½″

Yellow Poplar

(1) 2 Backup strips to reinforce corners ¾″ x 1½″ x 28¾″
(2) 2 Strips under table board 1⅜″ x 2⅞″ x 19¾″. These are fastened with wood screws to the underside of the table board and to the ends to fasten the two together.
(3) 2 strips under the table board serving the same purpose as (2) 1⅜″ x 2⅛″ x 19¾″
(4) 4 Drawer guides ¾″ x 1¼″ x 19¾″
(5) 2 Strips under table board to keep top middle drawer level when pulling it out. ⅞″ x 1⅜″ x 19¾″
(6) 2 Drawer runs ⅞″ x 1½″ x 19¾″
(7) 6 Drawer runs ⅞″ x 1¼″ x 19¾″
(8) 2 Drawer runs ⅞″ x ¾″ x 19¾″
(9) 4 Doorstop strips at top and bottom of doors ⅞″ x 1″ x 23¼″
(10) 2 Backup strips for feet ¾″ x ¾″ x 3½″
(11) 4 Backup strips for feet ¾″ x ¾″ x 6″
6 Drawer sides, upper three drawers ⅝″ x 3⅝″ x 20⅝″
2 Drawer sides ⅝″ x 3⅞″ x 20⅝″
2 Drawer sides ⅝″ x 4⅛″ x 20⅝″
2 Drawer sides ⅝″ x 4⅜″ x 20⅝″

2 Drawer sides ⅝″ x 4¾″ x 20⅝″
2 Drawer backs ⅝″ x 3⅝″ x 20⅝″
1 Drawer back ⅝″ x 3⅝″ x 14⅝″
1 Drawer back ⅝″ x 3⅞″ x 14⅝″
1 Drawer back ⅝″ x 4⅛″ x 14⅝″
1 Drawer back ⅝″ x 4⅜″ x 14⅝″
1 Drawer back ⅝″ x 4¾″ x 14⅝″

Birch Plywood

2 Drawer bottoms ¼″ x 19⅞″ x 19⅞″
5 Drawer bottoms ¼″ x 13⅞″ x 19⅞″
1 Back for lower section ¼″ x 30⅛″ x 65¼″

UPPER SECTION

Cherry

2 Ends (A) ⅞″ x 12″ x 47¾″
2 Stiles (B) ⅞″ x 1⅞″ x 47¾″
2 Stiles (C) ⅞″ x 2″ x 42¾″
1 Rail (D) ⅞″ x 1⅜″ x 64¼″
1 Fascia board at top (E) ⅞″ x 6⅛″ x 64¼″
1 Board behind molding at top (F) ⅝″ x 4⅝″ x 67¼″
2 Boards behind molding at ends (G) ⅝″ x 4⅝″ x 12⅝″
5 Backup blocks under molding at top (H) ¾″ x 2¼″ x 2⅝″
5 Blocks under molding (I) ½″ x 2″ x 2″
2 Short rails under small drawers (J) ⅞″ x 1⅜″ x 13″
2 Drawer compartment partitions (K) ⅞″ x 12⅜″ x 5¾″
4 Door stiles (L) ⅞″ x 1¾″ x 35¼″
2 Top door rails (M) ⅞″ x 4¼″ x 22¼″
1 Top rail in frame between doors (N) ⅞″ x 4¼″ x 12⅞″
2 Bottom rails in doors (O) ⅞″ x 1⅞″ x 22¼″
1 Bottom rail in frame between doors (P) ⅞″ x 1⅞″ x 12⅞″
4 Muntin rails in doors (Q) ⅞″ x ⅞″ x 22¼″
6 Muntin stiles in doors (R) ⅞″ x ⅞″ x 9¾″
2 Muntin rails in frame between doors (S) ⅞″ x ⅞″ x 12⅞″
2 Small drawer fronts (T) ⅞″ x 3¹³⁄₁₆″ x 12⅜″

2 Quarter-columns; make from 4 glued-together pieces (U) ⅞" x ⅞" x 47¾"

1 Bottom of back (V) ½" x 7" x 65¼"

1 Top of back (W) ½" x 5" x 65¼"

Random-width boards (X) ½" thick x 36½" long for back

Top molding (Y) 1⅞" x 2⅝" x 130" approx. length as needed

Molding at top, around drawer compartments, etc. (Z) ⅞" x ⅞" x 215"

4 Turned bosses, made from 2 split turnings 1½" diam. x 5½" (Fig. 13)

Pine

(1) 2 Shelves ⅞" x 11½" x 64¾"

(2) 1 Floor ⅞" x 11½" x 64¾"

(3) 1 Top ⅞" x 11½" x 64¼"

Poplar

4 Drawer sides ½" x 3⁹⁄₁₆" x 12⅜"

2 Drawer backs ½" x 3⁹⁄₁₆" x 11⅞"

(4) 2 Drawer runs 1⅞" x 2" x 11½"

(5) 2 Drawer runs 1" x 1⅜" x 11½"

(6) 2 Strips to keep drawers level when being pulled out ¾" x ¾" x 11½"

Birch Plywood

2 Drawer bottoms ¼" x 11⅛" x 11⅝"

TWENTY-FIVE

Pine Corner Cupboard

SMALL, COUNTRY-MADE CORNER CUPBOARDS, like the one shown in Fig. 1, are often handsome and, generally speaking, impressive furniture items. Much of this is due to the colorful contents usually found in profusion on shelves behind the glazed doors, but is also due to many well-executed design elements and fine craftsmanship. Despite an occasional lack of sophistication found among these design elements, such as crudely shaped moldings and finials, and some instances in which curves on aprons and pediments leave something to be desired, the results achieved, with but few exceptions, turn out quite well.

In my estimation, this pine corner cupboard, on which I would prefer to see better-shaped moldings, is in other respects a home-workshop item of good quality.

To build the corner cupboard, it may be best to build the door of the upper section first, since this will be the most difficult element to build. It will be easier to make small changes and adjustments on stiles and rails surrounding it, should this become necessary to fit it into place, than it would be on the door itself, once it has been put together.

UPPER SECTION

Make the two door stiles (14) and rail (15). Also get out stock for top rail (16) and muntin rails (17). Then get out ⅞"-x-⅞" stock sufficiently long to make muntins (18) and (19). Before bandsawing arches in rail (16), shape the molding along the entire straight bottom edge of rail (16), and on stiles (14), rails (17), and stile sticks from which (18) and (19) are to be made.

Next, make all mortise-and-tenon joints, and make a trial assembly of stiles (14), rails (15), (16), and (17). Notice that joints come together on a miter where moldings join each other, a detail I call to your attention in the bottom left-hand window of the door in Fig. 2, and in the larger detail shown in Fig. 3. When the mortise-and-tenon joints have been properly fitted, bandsaw the arches and cut the molding around the arches. Then cut the notches and fit the joints where muntins join each other and where they join stiles and rails. Once all these joints are glued, they make a sturdy door.

Make the upper section of the cabinet into which the door fits. First, make the three posts (1) and (2). The angle on one edge of post (1), and one edge of stile (3), where they are joined, is 67½ degrees, as shown in Fig. 5. Edges of the back post (2) are angled to 45 degrees.

Make the floor, the three shelves, and the top (4) for the upper section. The grain on all shelves, floors, and tops runs parallel to the front of the cupboard, and enough boards may be glued edge-to-edge to get the 18-inch widths needed for the upper section, and for the 18⅞-inch widths for the lower section. When the shelves have been planed and sanded to thicknesses of ⅞ inch, cut the ⅜-inch-deep grooves across posts (1) to support shelf ends. Back edges of posts (1) are rabbeted to fasten the plywood backs so their edges are covered. The plywood backs may be nailed to post (2), shelves (4), and posts (1), after the shelves, top, and floor have first been glued into the grooves cut across posts (1).

Then make the front frame, which comprises stiles (3) and pediment board (5). All three of these have a narrow bead molding cut on their edges around the door, and this bead may be formed on the edges with a sharp cutter, or with wood-carving chisels, or it may be formed by rounding the edge of a strip of wood ⅛ inch thick, which is then glued and bradded to the edges of stiles (3) and pediment board (5). Make the mortise-and-tenon joints to fasten pediment board (5) to stiles (3). Be sure to fit the joints so the door has sufficient clearance and it may be opened and closed without binding, being aware that finishing coats may make additional clearance necessary.

Bandsaw the top of pediment board (5) to shape, after first making a full-sized cardboard pattern from the detailed drawing shown in Fig. 6. File and sandpaper the sawed edges.

If joints on outside edges have been carefully made, there should now be no trouble making good tight-fitting glue joints where stiles (3) are joined to posts (1).

Stiles and posts may be nailed fast to top board and floor, if nails are driven in where their heads are hidden later on by moldings.

Make the curved and the straight moldings for the top and the carved rosettes, which are first turned to their circular shape on the lathe. After carving block (8), shown in Fig. 2, fasten it to the pediment board with wood screws from the back. Then screw block (9) to the back to form a base thick enough to hold the finial base. Curved moldings may be fastened with wood screws from the back to the pediment board. Only their lower ends should be glued to the stile; and the mitered joint where the straight and

FIG. 1

curved moldings meet should be glued and further secured with a small brad or two. Glue the rosettes to the top of the pediment board, and then turn the finials shown in detail in Fig. 7.

LOWER SECTION

To make the lower section, follow the procedures you used to make and assemble the upper section, though you should find that building it will be simpler than building the upper section. Take note from the plan view, shown cross-sectioned in the upper part of Fig. 2, that the cabinet of the lower section is only as much wider from front to back as the thickness of the stock used on its front, which is 7/8 inch. Shelf moldings (F) and (G) form a border and stop around the front where the upper and lower sections come together, and act as a fence to hold the upper section properly in place.

You will find the paneled door of the lower section is much easier to make and assemble than the door of the upper section. Panels are raised by first cutting shallow saw kerfs, about 1/8 inch deep on the panel faces to form border lines, leaving the flat middle section a rectangle 6 7/16" x 14 1/2". Then by tilting the table saw, or the saw table, and raising the saw blade high enough to bevel the edges and holding the panel in an upright position when making these cuts, the panel edges will be cut to their proper shape. (See Chapter Twenty-seven, Fig. 16.) After smoothing down the bevels with a cabinet scraper blade, and with sandpaper, the edges should fit into the grooves snugly, but not too tight. Panels should never be glued into the grooves made to hold them, but should be fitted loosely enough to permit the wood to expand or contract with a change in seasons.

Put hinges and door latches on both doors and be sure that doors open and close without binding. All hardware should be removed to apply the finishing coats. Replacing them, once the finish is on, will be easy.

BILL OF MATERIAL

LOWER SECTION

Pine

2 Posts (A) 7/8" x 4 3/4" x 28 1/2"
1 Post (B) 7/8" x 4" x 28 1/2"
2 Stiles (C) 7/8" x 3" x 28 1/2"
1 Rail above door (D) 7/8" x 1 3/4" x 28"
1 Rail below door (E) 7/8" x 2 5/8" x 28"
1 Shelf molding (F) 7/8" x 2 7/8" x 31 1/2"
2 Short shelf moldings (G) 7/8" x 2" x 5 1/2"
Top, floor, shelf 3 pieces (H) 7/8" x 18 7/8" x 36 1/2"
2 Door stiles (I) 7/8" x 1 7/8" x 21 1/2"
1 Door stile (J) 7/8" x 2 1/8" x 20 1/8"
2 Door panels (K) 3/4" x 10 1/16" x 18 1/16"
1 Bottom door rail (L) 7/8" x 2 1/4" x 24"
1 Top door rail (M) 7/8" x 1 7/8" x 24"

Molding under shelves (F) and (G) (N) 7/8" x 7/8" x lengths as needed
Strips to support shelves and top (O) 7/8" x 7/8" x lengths as needed

Birch Plywood

2 Plywood backs (P) 1/4" x 24 1/2" x 23 3/4"

UPPER SECTION

Pine

(1) 2 Posts 7/8" x 4 3/8" x 48"
(2) 1 Post 7/8" x 4" x 48"
(3) 2 Stiles 7/8" x 2 3/4" x 48"
(4) Top, shelves, floor, 5 pieces 7/8" x 18" x 35"

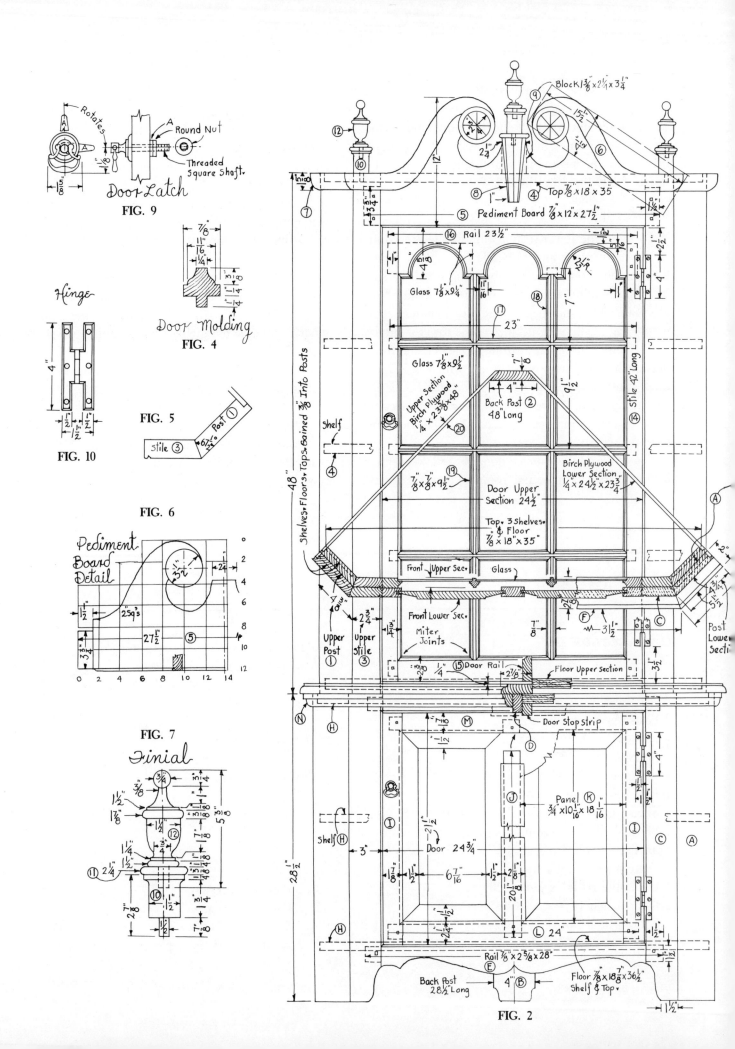

Rotates

A — Round Nut

A

Threaded Square Shaft.

Door Latch

FIG. 9

Hinge

FIG. 5

FIG. 10

Door Molding

FIG. 4

Post ①

Stile ③

FIG. 6

Pediment Board Detail

2 sq's

27½"

⑤

FIG. 7

Finial

Block 1⅜"×2¼"×3¼"

⑨

15½"

⑥

Top ⅞"×18"×35"

④

Pediment Board ⅞"×12"×27½"

⑤

Rail 23½"

⑯

Glass ⅞"×9¼"

Glass ⅞"×9½"

Upper Section Birch Plywood ¼"×23⅜"×48"

Back Post ② 48" Long

Stile 42" Long ⑭

⑰

⑱

23"

9½"

⑳

⑲

7"×⅞"×9½"

Door Upper Section 24½"

Top·3 shelves· & Floor ⅞"×18"×35"

Birch Plywood Lower Section ¼"×24½"×23¾"

Ⓐ

Shelf

④

Shelves,Floor 3" Tops Gained ⅜" Into Posts

48"

Front Upper Sec·

Glass

Front Lower Sec·

Miter Joints

⑮ Door Rail

Floor Upper section

Door Stop Strip

Upper Post ①

Upper Stile ③

Ⓕ 3½"

Ⓒ

Post Lower Section

Ⓝ

Ⓗ

Ⓜ

Ⓓ

28½"

Shelf Ⓗ

Ⓘ

3"

Ⓙ

Panel Ⓚ ¾"×10⁷⁄₁₆"×18¹⁄₁₆"

Ⓘ

Ⓒ

Ⓐ

Door 24¾"

6⁷⁄₁₆"

20⅝"

Ⓛ 24"

Ⓗ

Rail ⅞"×2⅝"×28"

Ⓔ

Back Post 28½" Long

4"

Ⓑ

Floor ⅞"×18⅝"×36½" Shelf & Top·

FIG. 2

(5) 1 Pediment board ⅞″ x 12″ x 27½″

(6) 2 Curved moldings on pediment; make from pieces ⅞″ x 4½″ x 15½″

(7) Straight molding on pediment, 2 pieces ⅞″ x 1⅝″ x lengths as needed

(8) Carved molding under middle finial ¾″ x 2¼″ x 6″

(9) Block back of middle finial 1⅜″ x 2¼″ x 3¼″

(10) 3 Finial bases 1⅞″ x 1⅞″ x 2⅞″

(11) 3 Finial base caps ⅜″ x 2¼″ x 2¼″

(12) 3 Finials 1⅞″ diam. x 5⅜″

(13) 2 Carved rosettes for pediment ⅞″ x 3½″ diam.

(14) 2 Door stiles ⅞″ x 1¾″ x 42″

(15) Bottom door rail ⅞″ x 2⅜″ x 23½″

(16) Upper door rail ⅞″ x 4⅝″ x 23½″

(17) 3 Horizontal door muntins ⅞″ x ⅞″ x 23″

(18) 2 Vertical muntins ⅞″ x ⅞″ x 7″

(19) 6 Vertical muntins ⅞″ x ⅞″ x 9½″

Birch Plywood

(20) 2 Plywood backs ¼″ x 23⅝″ x 48″

FIG. 8

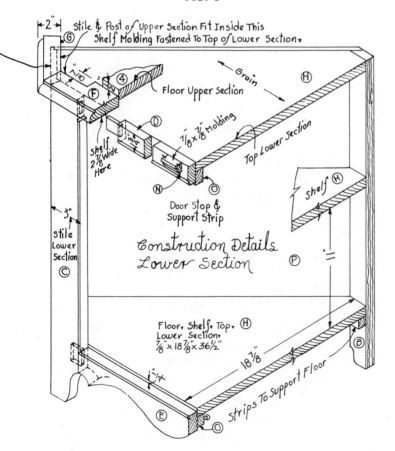

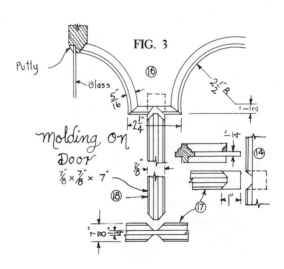

TWENTY-SIX

Walnut Corner Cupboard with Paneled Doors

THE DESIGN OF THE CORNER CUPBOARD SHOWN in Fig. 1 is somewhat unusual, since unlike those with glass doors used for the display of china, this one has paneled doors enclosing the top section as well as the lower section. More than likely it is a country-made piece, although there are elements of refinement lifting it well above many such innovative examples. It has a few shortcomings, which an accomplished designer would have avoided. The two upper doors are not alike in width, making the panels on the right-hand door an inch wider than those on the left-hand door. This incongruity has been corrected on my drawings of the cupboard. The shelves in the upper section of the cupboard are separated in an odd and seemingly haphazard manner, though the builder may have had some logical reason for separating them in this manner. He allowed only 7¾ inches between the top shelf and rail (F), and then only 5¾ inches between shelves in the space below. Such narrow openings so high up on the cupboard seems a strange way of spacing them, and so I have altered the spacing of shelves on my drawing, and put in one shelf less than I found on the cupboard shown in Fig. 1.

The cupboard is an object of some distinction in spite of these shortcomings which I have tried to correct. In most other respects the builder exhibits a sense of refinement and good taste, and a feeling for proportions that is pleasing.

To build the cupboard, first get out stock to make the two corner posts (A) and the back post (B). All three are 74½ inches long. Grooves ¼ inch deep are cut crosswise on the insides of posts (A) to help support shelves. This gaining in on the posts to support the shelf ends is shown in Figs. 3, 4, and 5. And although grooves were not cut into post (B) in the back, to which the shelves were only nailed, by doing this you can give that much more added support to the shelves, and even make assembling shelves and posts a little easier. If you do this, all shelves will have to be made ¼ inch wider than I show them in my drawings.

When these grooves have been cut into the posts, rabbet back edges of posts (A) for a place to nail on the ¼-inch plywood back so its edges do not show. Solid boards, thicker than the plywood back I substituted on my drawings, were used for the back of Fig. 1, but birch plywood makes a better back, and reduces weight.

All shelves, floor, and top (seven in all) may now be glued up, cut to size and shape, and fitted to the grooves in the posts. Then make stiles (C). Cut mortises into stiles (C) to fasten rails (D), (E), and (F). Then bevel the edges of posts (A) and stiles (C) to join them together as shown in Fig. 3. This joint will be held together with glue after rails (D), (E), and (F) have been glued to stiles (C) to make the front frame, and after the seven shelves have been glued to the posts.

Before shelves can be permanently fastened to the posts and stiles, openings for the two drawers and for the candle slide must be made in rail (E). Drawer guides and three supporting members to hold the candle slide must be fastened to the two shelves between which these three members are located. Details for doing this are shown in Figs. 2 and 6. When this has been done, glue the shelves to the posts. Several nails, or even wood screws, should be used to more securely fasten post (B) to every shelf, and a nail driven through post (A) into each shelf, where the vertical molding will subsequently hide it, will also help. Fasten the top shelf more securely to posts and stiles with several wood screws whose heads will be hidden once the horizontal molding at the top is in place.

Reinforcing strips, shown in Fig. 5, should be glued and screwed fast under the floor to fasten it to posts, stiles, and to rail (D). Do not nail the plywood backs to the cupboard until drawers and slide board have been made and fitted in place.

Doors for the cupboard may be made next. Panel edges are feathered and contoured on the inside to thin and shape them so they will fit into the grooves cut into door rails and stiles. (See Fig. 7.) Cut a molding on edges of rails (J) and (K), and on stiles (H) and (I) on the outside of the door bordering the panels.

To make the upper doors, cut grooves 1 inch deep into edges of stiles and rails to hold the 12"-x-14" panels. Then bandsaw rails and stiles to shape, as shown in Fig. 2. Smooth the bandsawed edges carefully with file and sandpaper, and shape the molding surrounding the panels. Cut mortises in stiles (O) and (P), and tenons on all six rails, and fit these joints. Reduce the thickness of panel edges, contouring and shaping the feathered edges as carefully as possible with carving gouges. (See Figs. 2 and 7.)

Make a pattern from Fig. 8 to saw the pediment to shape. Carefully smooth all edges. Fasten the pediment board to the front edge of the top with glue and wood screws. The carved rosettes, which on the cupboard shown in Fig. 1 are little more than ⅛ inch

thick, may be made thicker and about 3 inches in diameter, and glued to the pediment board either before or after carving them. A backup block is fastened with wood screws to the back of the pediment board to provide enough thickness to support the finial base.

FIG. 1

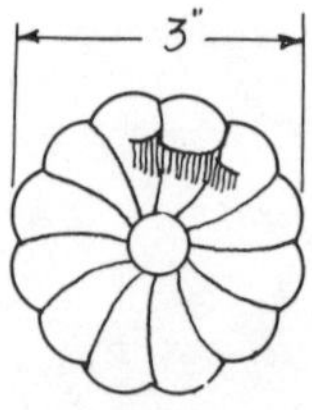

FIG. 12

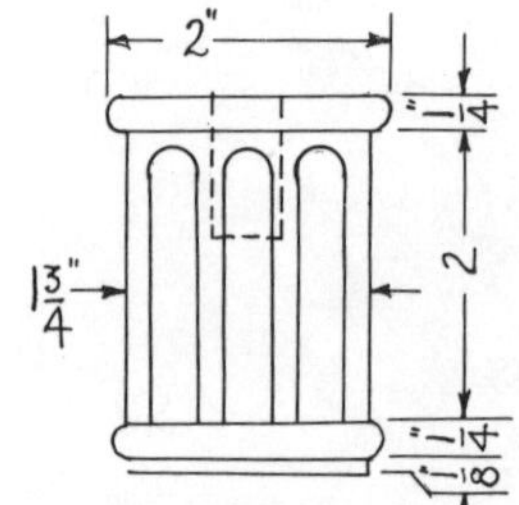

FIG. 10

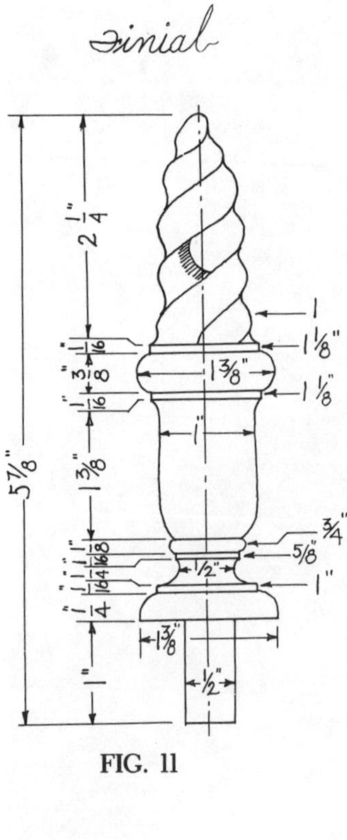

Finial

FIG. 11

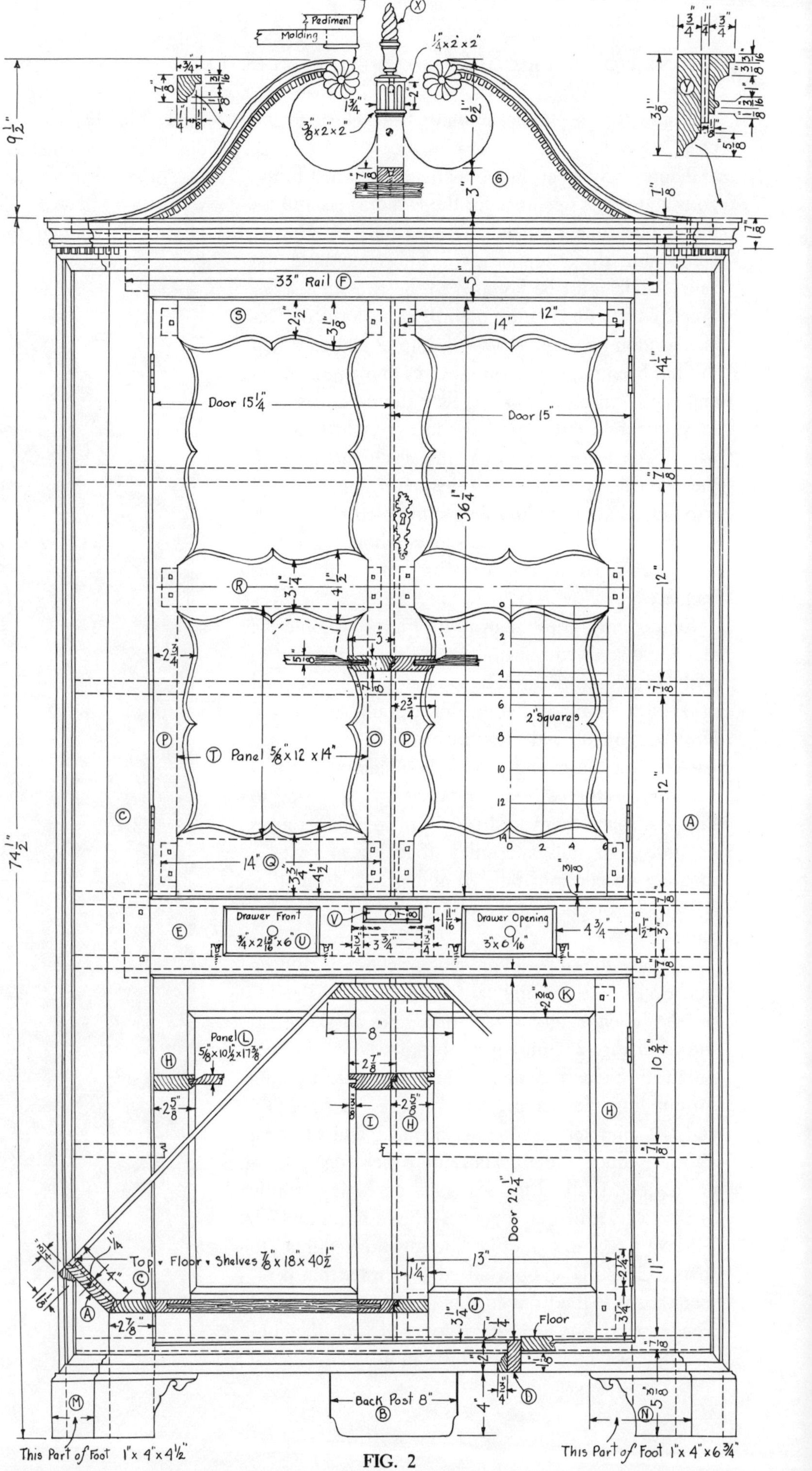

Pediment
Molding

$1\frac{1}{4} \times 2 \times 2$

$\frac{3}{8} \times 2 \times 2$

$6\frac{1}{2}$

G

Y

$9\frac{1}{2}$

33" Rail F

Door $15\frac{1}{4}$

Door 15

$36\frac{1}{4}$

2" Squares

Panel $\frac{5}{8} \times 12 \times 14$

T

14" Q

Drawer Front $\frac{3}{4} \times 2\frac{1}{2} \times 6$ U

Drawer Opening $3 \times 6\frac{1}{16}$

$4\frac{3}{4}$

Panel L $\frac{5}{8} \times 10\frac{1}{2} \times 17\frac{3}{8}$

$2\frac{5}{8}$

$2\frac{5}{8}$

$2\frac{5}{8}$

Door $22\frac{1}{4}$

13"

11"

$74\frac{1}{2}$

Top · Floor · Shelves $\frac{7}{8} \times 18 \times 40\frac{1}{2}$

$2\frac{7}{8}$

Back Post 8"

B

This Part of Foot $1" \times 4" \times 4\frac{1}{2}"$

This Part of Foot $1" \times 4" \times 6\frac{3}{4}"$

FIG. 2

$10\frac{3}{8}$

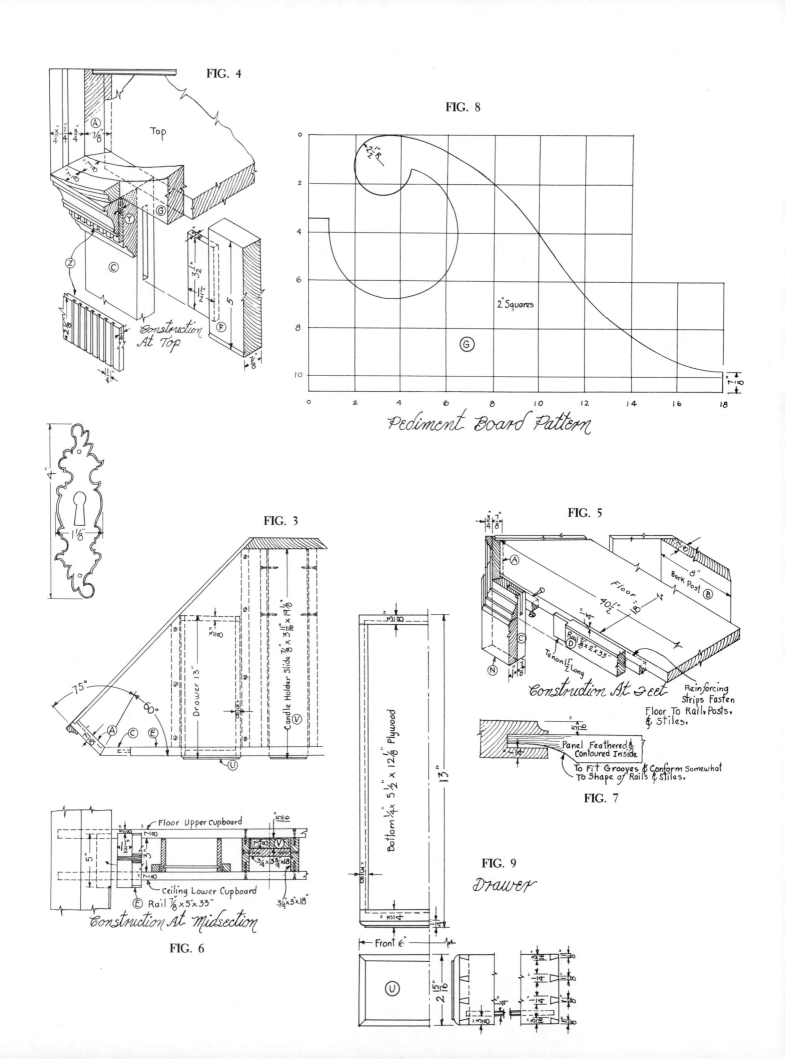

FIG. 4

Top

Ⓐ

Ⓖ

Y

Z

Ⓒ

Ⓕ

Construction At Top

FIG. 8

2" Squares

Ⓖ

Pediment Board Pattern

FIG. 3

75°

60°

Ⓐ Ⓒ Ⓔ

U

Drawer 13"

Candle Holder Slide ⅞" x 3⁷⁄₁₆" x 19½"

FIG. 5

Ⓐ

Floor ⅛"

Back Post Ⓑ

Ⓒ

Ⓝ

Ⓓ Rail ⅞" x 2" x 33"

Tenon 1½" Long

Construction At Feet

Reinforcing Strips Fasten Floor To Rail, Posts, & Stiles.

Panel Feathered & Contoured Inside

To Fit Grooves & Conform Somewhat To Shape of Rails & Stiles.

FIG. 7

Floor Upper Cupboard

Ⓔ Rail ⅞" x 5" x 33"

Ceiling Lower Cupboard

V

¾" x 3¾" x 18"

Construction At Midsection

FIG. 6

Bottom ¼" x 5½" x 12⅛" Plywood

13"

Front 6"

U

2¹⁵⁄₁₆"

FIG. 9

Drawer

In Fig. 4, I show the shape of the straight molding around the top, below the pediment, and how it is put on in three layers. Fig. 4 also shows how the dentils are formed by cutting grooves across a strip of wood (Z) on the table saw.

The curved molding at the very top may be formed on the shaper, or it may be hand-carved. The dentils cannot be formed in the manner shown at the bottom of Fig. 4, but the wood may be notched with hand tools. Saw the strip of wood on which the dentils are to be made to the shape of the curve on top of the pediment, making it wide enough to go to the top of the curved molding. Then carefully mark the spacing of the dentils on its bottom edge (they are ⅜ inch wide, ³⁄₁₆ inch high, and are spaced ¼ inch apart), and saw out the spaces, from the bottom edge to the height needed. Then true sawn edges with a file.

The molding fastened to rear edges of both end posts, and that which goes around the base above the feet, may now be made, and glued fast with a few small finish nails to help hold it in place.

Feet for the cupboard are made from a board 1 inch thick and 4 inches wide, and long enough to make the four pieces required. Weight of the cupboard is supported by posts (A) and (B), and stiles (C), and the feet (N) and (M) serve mostly as window dressing, being facings to give the appearance of feet, and shaped as such. After cutting these to shape, and mitering the corner joints, which should be glued together, the feet should be fastened to posts (A) and stiles (C) with wood screws from the inside.

Make and fit the two small drawers, and the slide board to hold the candle. Details and dimensions to make the drawers are given in Fig. 9. Once the drawers and candle slide have been been fitted in place, the plywood backs may be nailed fast to the shelves, and to posts (A) and (B).

Turn and carve the finial as shown in Fig. 11. Fit doors with hinges and locks to finish the job.

BILL OF MATERIAL

Walnut

2 End posts (A) ⅞″ x 4″ x 74½″
1 Back post (B) ⅞″ x 8″ x 74½″
2 Stiles (C) ⅞″ x 2⅞″ x 74½″
1 Bottom rail (D) ⅞″ x 2″ x 33″
1 Middle rail (E) ⅞″ x 5″ x 33″
1 Top rail (F) ⅞″ x 5″ x 33″
1 Pediment board (G) ⅞″ x 10⅜″ x 36″
3 Door stiles, bottom doors (H) ⅞″ x 2⅝″ x 22¼″
1 Door stile, bottom door (I) ⅞″ x 2⅞″ x 22¼″
2 Bottom rails, bottom doors (J) ⅞″ x 3¼″ x 13″
2 Top rails, bottom doors (K) ⅞″ x 2⅜″ x 13″
2 Panels, bottom doors (L) ⅝″ x 10½″ x 17⅜″
2 Boards for feet (M) 1″ x 4″ x 4½″
2 Boards for feet (N) 1″ x 4″ x 6¾″

1 Door stile, upper doors (O) ⅞″ x 3″ x 36¼″
3 Door stiles, upper doors (P) ⅞″ x 2¾″ x 36¼″
2 Door rails, upper doors (Q) ⅞″ x 4½″ x 14″
2 Door rails, upper doors (R) ⅞″ x 4½″ x 14″
2 Door rails, upper doors (S) ⅞″ x 3⅛″ x 14″
4 Door panels, upper doors (T) ⅝″ x 12″ x 14″
2 Drawer fronts (U) ¾″ x 2¹⁵⁄₁₆″ x 6″
1 Candle slide board (V) ⅞″ x 3¹¹⁄₁₆″ x 19⅛″
1 Base for finial (W) 1¾″ x 1¾″ x 2″
1 Finial (X) 1⅜″ diam. x 5⅞″
Board with molded edge below pediment (Y) ¾″ x 3⅛″ x 45″ (approx.)
Dentil board at top (Z) ¼″ x 2⅛″ x 45″ (approx.)
2 Carved rosettes, glued to tops of pediment ¼″ x 3″ diam.

Straight molding under pediment ¾″ x 1⅞″ x 50″ (approx.)

Straight vertical molding on ends, and above feet ¾″ x 1⅛″ x 190″ (approx.)

Curved molding around pediment top ¾″ x ⅞″ x length as needed

Poplar

Floor, shelves, and top 7 pieces ⅞″ x 18″ x 40½″

4 Drawer sides ⅜″ x 2¹⁵⁄₁₆″ x 12¾″

2 Drawer backs ⅜″ x 2¹⁵⁄₁₆″ x 6″

2 Guides on sides of candle slide ¾″ x 3″ x 18″

1 Board to support candle slide ¾″ x 3¾″ x 18″

2 Drawer guides ¾″ x ¾″ x 18″

2 Drawer guides ¾″ x ¾″ x 12″

1 Block under finial base ⅞″ x 1¾″ x 6¼″

Birch Plywood

2 Backs ¼″ x 24¼″ x 69⅛″

2 Drawer bottoms ¼″ x 5½″ x 12⅜″

TWENTY-SEVEN

Cherry Corner Cupboard

THE WELL-STOCKED CHERRY CORNER CUP-board shown here in Fig. 1, though reasonably plain and unpretentious so far as embellishment in the form of ornamentation is concerned, has the necessary appealing characteristics to command respectful attention in almost anyone's home. Though a product of rural handiwork, its rather plain, unsophisticated lines and proportions make it an outstanding piece of furniture well worth copying.

To build it, start by making the glazed doors for the upper section first. These are the most difficult members to make, and by making them first, the cabinetwork into which they must be fitted can more easily be adjusted to their finished size than the other way around.

UPPER SECTION

Plane and sand stock to make door stiles (M) and (N), rails (P), and enough to make muntin rails (R) and muntin stiles (S). Notice the overlapping of door stiles (M) and (N) in the center, necessitating rabbeting the overlapping edges. This is shown in Fig. 2. The left-hand door is held in place, when closed, by a slide bolt like the one shown in Fig. 15, fastened inside the door at the bottom of stile (M). Saw the curved members (Q) to shape, using a radius of 18⅛ inches for the outside curve. (Q) can be cut from stock 6 inches wide and 23¼ inches or more long.

Moldings on these door members are formed on a spindle shaper. My suggestion, if you have no shaper, is to have this work done at the nearest planing mill, but if you can do this in your own workshop, the detailed drawings shown in Figs. 3 and 12 will show you how these members are shaped and put together. Notice in Fig. 2 how the lower end of curved member (Q) makes a half-lap joint with door stile (O) where the upper muntin rail is joined to them with a mortise-and-tenon joint. Muntin stiles are joined with the V-shaped joints to the other members with glue, and merely slipped into place after the rest of the door frame has been glued together.

You will perceive that the molding used on this and other cupboard doors in this book is given a slightly different shape from that commonly found on doors of this kind. The more commonly used molding shape may, of course, be substituted for the shape shown in Fig. 12, should you wish to do this, since such substitutions would make no great difference.

Once the doors have been made, get out stock for side posts (A) and back post (B). Grooves ¼ inch deep are cut across the two side posts on the inside to hold the shelves, floor, and top in place. This could be done on the back post also, if the shelves were made ¼ inch wider, but is not deemed necessary there, since nailing the plywood sides and the back post to the shelves, floor, and top adequately supports the shelves and their contents. Make stiles (C), and plane the angles on the edges where (A) and (C) are joined together. Make shelves, top, and floor, and fit these into the grooves in posts (A). Cut mortises and grooves into edges of (C) at the top where they are joined to face boards (D) and (E).

Make face boards (D) and (E), as shown in Figs. 2 and 4, and join them to each other with glued tongue-and-groove joints. When the door frame, consisting of stiles (C) and face boards (D) and (E), have been joined and fitted to the doors, leaving the necessary clearance for the doors to open and close without binding, and when shelves, top, floor, and posts (A) are also properly joined and mated, the upper case comprising these members may be glued together.

Make the curved molding for the top, and also the carved, molded ornamental drop below the middle finial base. These may be fastened to the face board with glue, and reinforced with a few wood screws from the back. The two carved rosettes (F) are glued to the curved moldings.

Fig. 5 shows backup strip (U), which may be fastened with one or more wood screws to the back of face board (D) to help support the middle finial base.

Both doors are joined to stiles (C) with brass butt hinges, and these and the door latch, shown in Fig. 13, should be fitted to the doors before glass is put into the doors. Glazing compound is used to hold the glass in place. The doors need not be fastened to stiles (C) until later when the whole piece of furniture has been made. All hardware should be removed when finishing coats are applied, and the doors should be fitted with glass only when all finishes have dried and hardened.

LOWER SECTION

To make the lower section, proceed much as you did when making the upper section. Doors for the lower section are much more easily made than the glazed ones in the upper section. Beveling edges of panels, also called panel-raising, is done as shown in Fig. 16, by first cutting shallow saw kerfs around each side on the front of the panel, and then beveling

the border outside these on the table saw. This is done by tilting either the saw, or the saw table, depending upon the kind of table saw you have. The beveled surface is then smoothed down with a scraper blade and abrasive papers.

FIG. 1

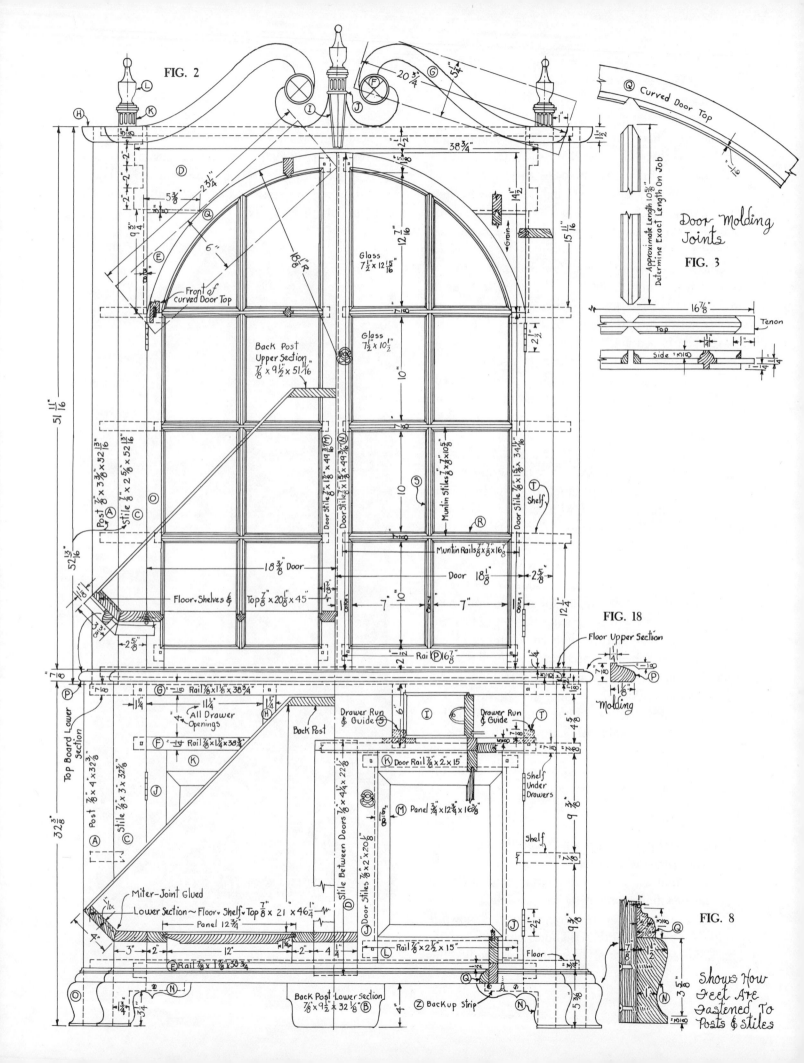

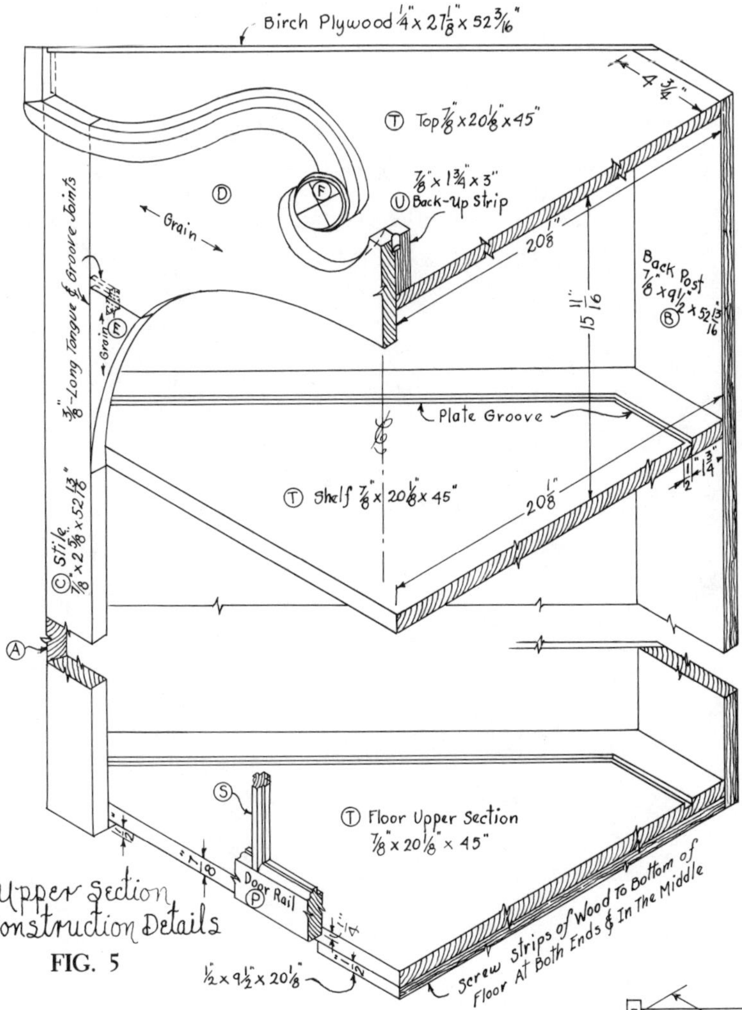

Birch Plywood $\frac{1}{4}$" x $27\frac{1}{8}$" x $52\frac{3}{16}$"

4 $\frac{3}{4}$

133

Ⓣ Top $\frac{7}{8}$" x $20\frac{1}{8}$" x 45"

$\frac{7}{8}$" x $1\frac{3}{4}$" x 3"
Ⓤ Back-Up Strip

Ⓓ
Ⓕ

← Grain →

$20\frac{1}{8}$

Back Post
$\frac{7}{8}$" x $9\frac{1}{2}$ x $52\frac{3}{16}$
Ⓑ

$15\frac{11}{16}$

$\frac{7}{8}$" Long Tongue & Groove Joints

Grain ↓

Plate Groove

$1\frac{3}{8}$
$\frac{1}{2}$ $1\frac{1}{4}$

Ⓣ Shelf $\frac{7}{8}$ x $20\frac{1}{8}$ x 45"

$20\frac{1}{8}$

Ⓒ Stile
$\frac{7}{8}$ x $2\frac{3}{8}$ x $52\frac{3}{16}$

Ⓐ

Ⓢ

Ⓣ Floor Upper Section
$\frac{7}{8}$" x $20\frac{1}{8}$" x 45"

Ⓟ Door Rail

Upper Section
Construction Details
FIG. 5

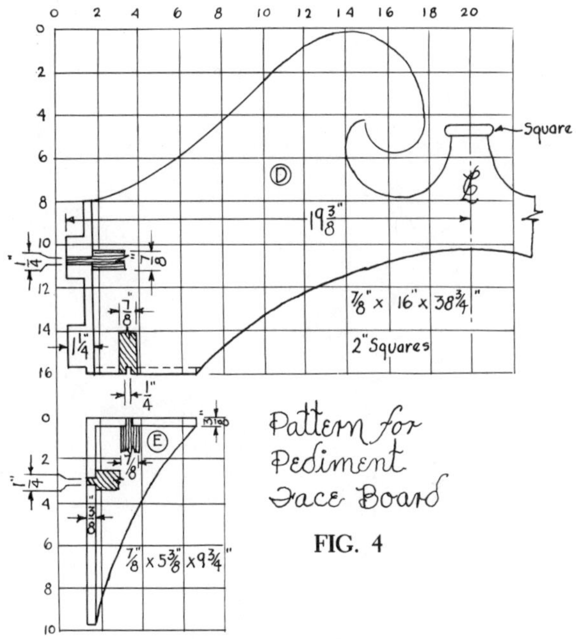

$\frac{1}{2}$ x $9\frac{1}{2}$ x $20\frac{1}{8}$

Screw strips of Wood To Bottom of
Floor At Both Ends & In The Middle

FIG. 6

Pattern for Pediment

0 2 4 6 8 10 12 14 16 18 20

Square

Ⓓ

$19\frac{3}{8}$

$\frac{1}{4}$
$\frac{7}{8}$

$\frac{7}{8}$
$1\frac{1}{4}$

$\frac{7}{8}$" x 16" x $38\frac{3}{4}$"

2" Squares

$1\frac{1}{4}$

Ⓔ
$\frac{7}{8}$

$1\frac{1}{4}$

$\frac{7}{8}$" x $5\frac{3}{8}$" x $9\frac{3}{4}$"

Pattern for
Pediment
Face Board
FIG. 4

Birch Plywood $\frac{1}{4}$" x $28\frac{3}{8}$ x $26\frac{7}{8}$"   FIG. 6

Ⓐ
Ⓑ

$9\frac{1}{2}$

Drawer Run & Guide
$1\frac{1}{2}$" x 2" x 7"

Top, Shelves & Bottom
$\frac{7}{8}$" x 21" x $46\frac{1}{4}$"

$46\frac{1}{4}$

Ⓟ

21

Ⓖ
Ⓗ

Ⓕ

Ⓒ Stile $\frac{7}{8}$ x 3 x $32\frac{3}{8}$

Drawer Run & Guide
$1\frac{1}{2}$ x $3\frac{3}{4}$ x $19\frac{1}{4}$

$4\frac{1}{4}$
$\frac{7}{8}$

$4\frac{9}{16}$

$9\frac{9}{16}$

Ⓓ

$22\frac{1}{8}$

Ⓑ

$6\frac{1}{16}$

Ⓩ

9"

Ⓠ   Ⓔ $8\frac{3}{4}$ Long

Lower Section
Construction
Details

$\frac{3}{4}$

$\frac{3}{8}$

$1\frac{1}{2}$
$1\frac{3}{4}$
$1\frac{3}{8}$

$4\frac{7}{8}$"

Ⓛ

$\frac{7}{8}$"
$1\frac{3}{16}$
$1\frac{1}{2}$

$\frac{1}{2}$

$2\frac{1}{4}$ Square
$2\frac{1}{8}$

Ⓚ

$1\frac{3}{4}$

$2\frac{3}{4}$

Round $\frac{1}{2}$"

Finial & Base

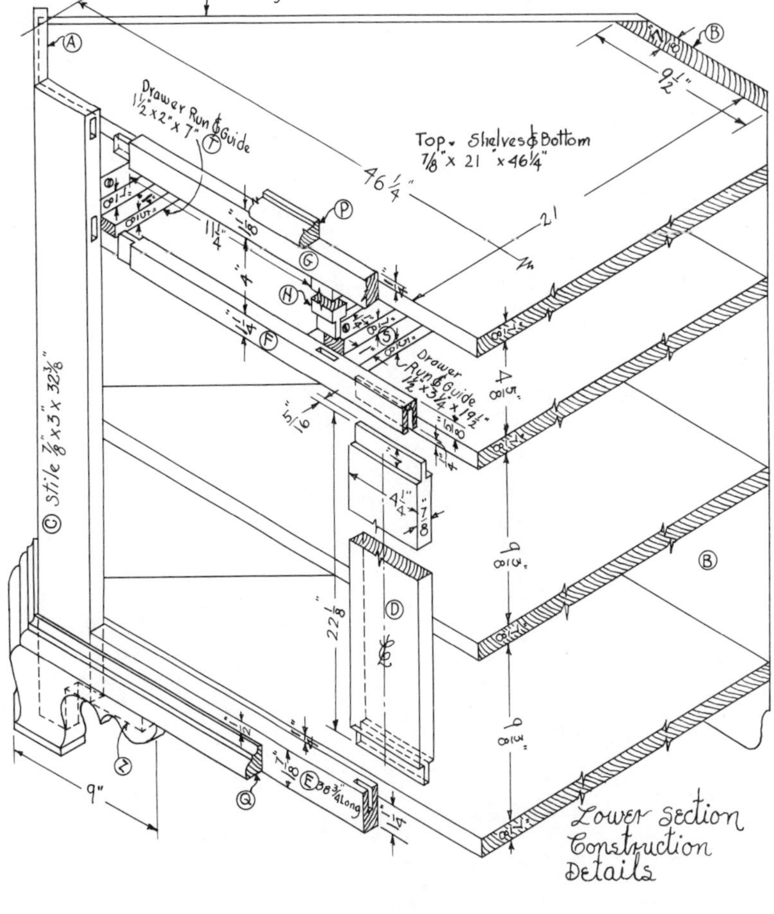

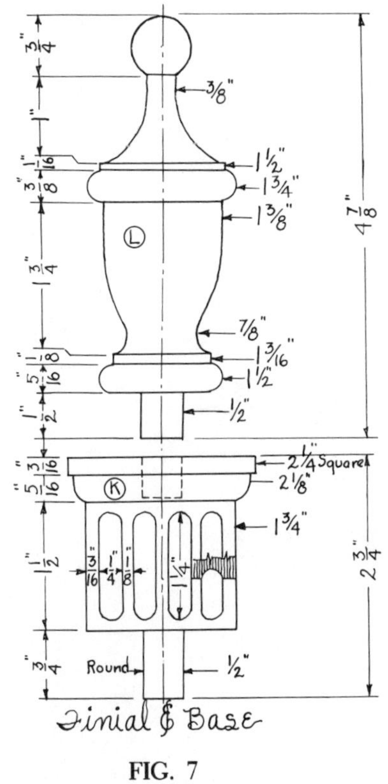

FIG. 7

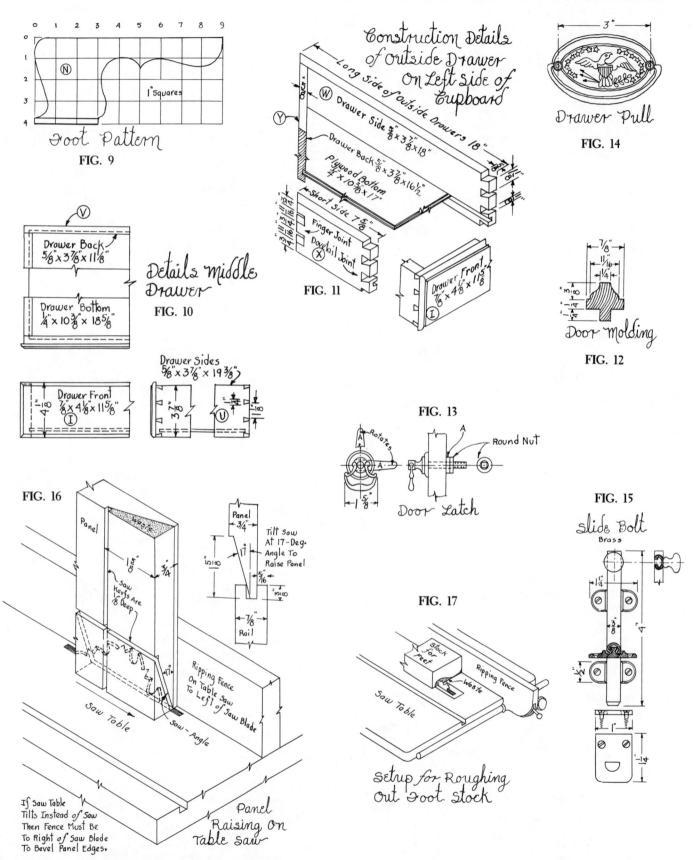

Foot Pattern
FIG. 9

Details Middle Drawer
FIG. 10

Construction Details of Outside Drawer On Left Side of Cupboard

FIG. 11

Drawer Pull
FIG. 14

Door Molding
FIG. 12

FIG. 13

Door Latch

FIG. 15

Slide Bolt
Brass

FIG. 16

Panel Raising On Table Saw

FIG. 17

Setup for Roughing Out Foot Stock

Facing boards (N) and (O) for the feet may be cut from a piece of stock 1½ inches thick and 4 inches wide, and long enough to make all four pieces. The way this molding can be formed is shown in Fig. 17. Since posts (A), (B), and stiles (C) go clear to the floor, most of the weight of both upper and lower sections is carried by them, and feet facings (N) and (O) are added more for appearance' sake than to support the weight of the cupboard and its contents.

Make posts (A) and (B) and stiles (C). Lay out and cut mortises in stiles (C) where rails (E), (F), and (G) are glued to them. Cut grooves across posts (A) to support shelves, floor, and top. Make shelves, floor, and top, and fit them into these grooves. Then plane the angles on the edges of (A) and (C) where they are to be glued together. Saw the lower ends of (C), as shown in Fig. 2. Before gluing the shelves to the posts, make drawer runs (S) and (T) which also serve as drawer guides. These should be fastened to the shelf which supports the drawers with wood screws, as shown in Figs. 2 and 6, before gluing this shelf to posts (A). When shelves, top, and bottom have been glued to posts (A) and nailed to post (B), rails (E), (F), (G), and stiles (D) and (H) should be made. Cut and fit the mortise-and-tenon joints; then assemble and glue stiles (C), (D), (H) and rails (E), (F), (G) together to make the front frame, being careful to see that this frame is properly aligned to all shelves, and so fitted to posts (A) that you have tight, good-fitting joints where (A) and (C) are glued together.

Doors should be made and fitted to the door open-ings so they open and close freely without binding. Hinges and latches may be fitted to the doors and assembled frame before the frame is glued to the posts, since it is easier to do it this way than it will be after the frame is fastened to the shelves and posts. When making the doors, glue the mortise-and-tenon joints, but use no glue to hold the panels in place. Actually, it is best to leave a narrow space between panel edges and the groove bottoms made in stiles (J). This precuation allows for the swelling when atmospheric conditions cause the panels to expand crosswise.

Make the drawers next. The middle drawer should give you no trouble, but the two on either side, because of the sharply angled backs, may prove a little more difficult to make, though if the finger joints are carefully made the job should not be too difficult. If the bottoms of these drawers are correctly laid out, the drawers should slide into their openings smoothly and drawer fronts should fit snugly against the frame.

Fasten feet (N) and (O) to posts and stiles, as shown in Fig. 8, and also make and fasten molding (Q) above the feet to the lower section. A wood screw through the bracket of (N) and some glue should be used to fasten (N) to molding (Q).

When upper and lower sections have been made and assembled, place the upper section on top of the lower section and fit the molding shown in Fig. 18 around the front and posts of the upper section. This molding may be glued and bradded to the top of the lower section.

BILL OF MATERIAL

LOWER SECTION

Cherry

2 Side posts (A) ⅞" x 4" x 32⅜"
1 Back post (B) ⅞" x 9½" x 32⅛"
2 Stiles (C) ⅞" x 3" x 32⅜"

1 Stile between doors (D) ⅞" x 4¼" x 22⅛"
1 Rail below doors (E) ⅞" x 1⅞" x 38¾"
1 Rail above doors (F) ⅞" x 1¼" x 38¾"
1 Rail above drawers (G) ⅞" x 1⅛" x 38¾"
2 Stiles between drawers (H) ⅞" x 1¼" x 6"
3 Drawer fronts (I) ⅞" x 4⅛" x 11⅝"
4 Door stiles (J) ⅞" x 2" x 20⅛"

2 Top door rails (K) ⅞″ x 2″ x 15″

2 Bottom door rails (L) ⅞″ x 2½″ x 15″

2 Door panels (M) ¾″ x 12¾″ x 16⅜″

2 Front feet (N) 1½″ x 4″ x 9″

2 End feet (O) 1½″ x 4″ x 5″

Molding at top of lower section (P) ⅞″ x 1⅛″ x 54″ (approx.)

Molding above feet (Q) ⅞″ x 1⅜″ x 54″ (approx.)

Poplar

Top, bottom, and shelves 4 pieces (R) ⅞″ x 21″ x 46¼″

2 Drawer runs and guides (S) 1½″ x 3¼″ x 19½″

2 Drawer runs and guides (T) 1½″ x 2″ x 7″

2 Drawer sides (U) ⅝″ x 3⅞″ x 19⅜″

1 Drawer back (V) ⅝″ x 3⅞″ x 11⅛″

2 Drawer sides (W) ⅝″ x 3⅞″ x 18″

2 Drawer sides (X) ⅝″ x 3⅞″ x 7⅝″

2 Drawer backs (Y) ⅝″ x 3⅞″ x 16½″

Backup strips for feet (Z) ¾″ x ¾″ x 3¾″

Birch Plywood

2 Drawer bottoms ¼″ x 10⅜″ x 17″

1 Drawer bottom ¼″ x 10⅜″ x 18⅝″

UPPER SECTION

Cherry

2 Side posts (A) ⅞″ x 3⅜″ x 52¹³⁄₁₆″

1 Back post (B) ⅞″ x 9½″ x 52¹³⁄₁₆″

2 Stiles (C) ⅞″ x 2⅝″ x 52¹³⁄₁₆″

1 Pediment face board (D) ⅞″ x 16″ x 38¾″

2 Extensions at bottom of face board (E) ⅞″ x 5⅜″ x 9¾″

2 Carved rosettes glued to face board molding (F) ¼″ x 2⅜″ diam.

2 Curved moldings for top of face board; make from stock (G) 1″ x 5¼″ (approx.) x 20¾″ (approx.)

2 End moldings, top of posts (H) 1″ x 1½″ x 4¼″ (approx.)

Carved molding glued to face board below middle finial (I) ⅜″ x 1¾″ x 5″

Small block under middle finial base (J) ¼″ x 2⅛″ x 2¼″

3 Finial bases (K) 2¼″ x 2¼″ x 2¾″

3 Finials (L) 1¾″ diam. x 4⅞″

1 Door stile, left-hand door (M) ⅞″ x 1⅞″ x 49³⁄₁₆″

1 Door stile, right-hand door (N) ⅞″ x 1⅝″ x 49³⁄₁₆″

2 Door stiles, right and left door (O) ⅞″ x 1⅝″ x 34¹¹⁄₁₆″

2 Bottom door rails (P) ⅞″ x 2½″ x 16⅞″

2 Curved door tops; make from stock (Q) ⅞″ x 6″ x 23¼″

6 Muntin rails (R) ⅞″ x ⅞″ x 16⅞″

8 Muntin stiles (S) ⅞″ x ⅞″ x 10⅝″. Check exact length needed for top muntin stiles when fitting door parts together.

Poplar

Floor, shelves, and top 5 pieces (T) ⅞″ x 20⅛″ x 45″

Backup strip to help support middle finial (U) ⅞″ x 1¾″ x 3″

TWENTY-EIGHT

Step-Down Windsor Chair

IN FIG. 1 WE HAVE A SOMEWHAT UNPRETEN-
tious-looking chair, but one whose seemingly unsophisticated and disarmingly simple clean-cut lines
serve to hide the difficulties to be overcome and re-
solved when one undertakes the job of reproducing
it. The offset on the splat atop the chair is the rather
ambiguous reason for the step-down appellation, but
naming it a Sheraton-type country Windsor would
more appropriately designate its roots. Be that as it
may, the simple, unpretentious lines of the bamboo-
shaped members, the scooped-out seat, the rake of
the members, all serve to make this a desirable piece
of furniture to copy.

Chair building, under the best of circumstances, is
seldom an easy task, and more often than not it re-
quires special skills and know-how. One reason for
this is that in many instances various members do not
join each other at right angles as they are more apt
to do in carcass furniture. Chair building often in-
volves working with curved members, joined to both
straight and other curved members, and in some instances at awkward angles. Then there is always the
problem of joining members that may be quite slen-
der for the stresses they must bear, and accomplish-
ing this without weakening the structure while at the
same time preserving good proportions.

So, while the chair shown here seems to fulfill
most of the criteria required to give it beauty, sturdi-

FIG. 1

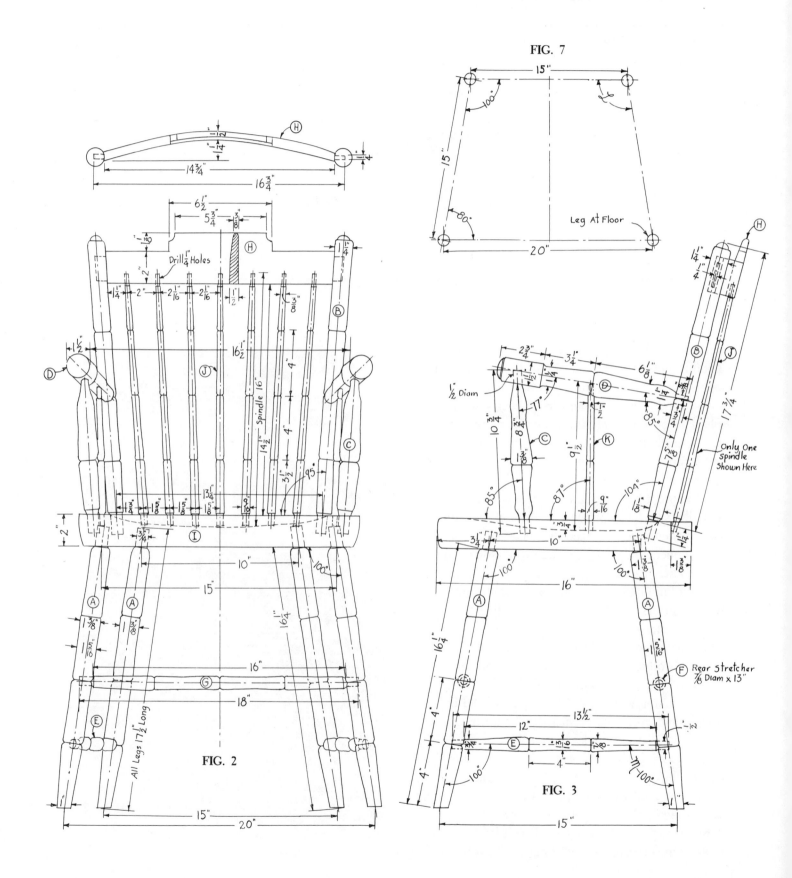

FIG. 7

FIG. 2

FIG. 3

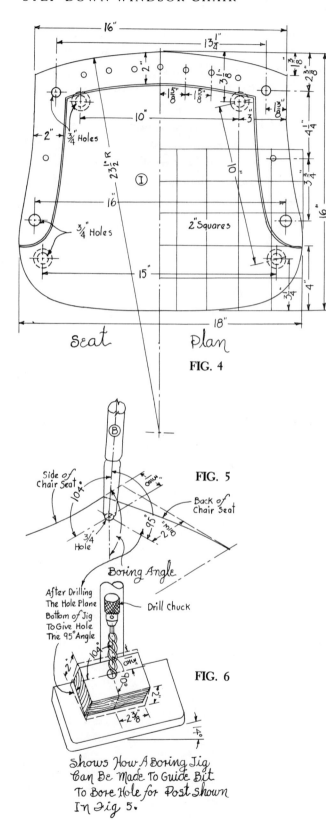

Seat   Plan

FIG. 4

FIG. 5

Side of
Chair Seat

Back of
Chair Seat

¾"
Hole

Boring Angle

After Drilling
The Hole Plane
Bottom of Jig
To Give Hole
The 95° Angle

Drill Chuck

FIG. 6

Shows How A Boring Jig
Can Be Made To Guide Bit
To Bore Hole for Post Shown
In Fig. 5.

ness, and comfort, thus making it a desirable piece to own, its construction presents something of a challenge.

With the possible exception of the long spindles (J) in the back, anyone who can do wood turning should have little difficulty turning the other members. To turn long thin spindles on the lathe, one should have a "back-rest," which is an attachment that can be fastened to the lathe bed, having two small wheels with smooth rims, which can be adjusted to bear against the back of thin spindles while turning them, so that vibration will be altogether eliminated or at least greatly minimized. Such an attachment does not usually come with a lathe when you buy one but must be specially ordered. The alternative to having such equipment is to round these members with hand tools like a spokeshave, after first turning the ends to the proper diameter on the lathe, to fit the holes, which is not too difficult to do. With care, the rings separating the sausagelike segments may also be started with the point of the skew chisel on the lathe, after the sticks have been rounded with spokeshave, files, and sandpaper.

Legs (A), posts (B) for the chair back, arm supports (C), arms (D), rungs (E), (F), and (G), and top (H) are all made of hard rock maple, which not only turns well on the lathe, but is a strong and sturdy wood. Thin spindles (J) for the back, and (K) under the arms, are made of hickory, which has great resilience and strength, and will bend without breaking. Poplar is used for the seat, because it is more easily scooped out than would be the case with a harder wood like maple. It also is not subject to checking as a piece of maple as thick as this would be.

In Fig. 5, I show the angles the chair post makes with the seat. The ideal way to get the correct boring angle to bore the holes for these in the seat is to have a drill press on which the drill press table can be tilted from side to side, and also from front to back. Such equipment is seldom available in a home workshop, but usually is to be found only in furniture factories where chairs are mass-produced. This being so, the home craftsman must improvise, and find some other way to achieve the proper boring angles, like the method I show in Fig. 6, to make a boring jig which can then be clamped to the top of the chair seat to act as a guide for the bit. If the drill press table cannot be tilted at all, then some other way must be found to drill the holes at the proper angle. One such method could be to adjust the seat with wooden wedges under the chair seat on top of a table, and hold it in the proper position with clamps so that the hole can be bored perpendicular to the tabletop.

To drill or bore holes to fasten rungs like (E) to both side legs, you need only tilt the leg 10 degrees to drill the holes; but when other holes are then drilled to join rear stretcher (F) to the back legs, and stretcher (G) to the front legs, the angles like those shown at (L) in Fig. 7 must also be considered.

While I have now pointed out some of the problems that will be encountered, and suggested some solutions, I also wish to make the point that success in building such a chair presents challenges to test your skill in overcoming difficulties, and arriving at solutions.

BILL OF MATERIAL

Maple

4 Legs (A) 1⅜″ diam. x 17½″
2 Back posts (B) 1¼″ diam. x 19″
2 Arm supports (C) 1⅜″ diam. x 10¾″
2 Arms (D) 1½″ diam. x 12⅛″
2 Side rungs (E) ⅞″ diam. x 13½″
1 Rear rung (F) ⅞″ diam. x 13″
1 Front rung (G) ⅞″ diam. x 18″
1 Top. Saw from piece (H) 1¾″ x 3⅛″ x 16¾″

Poplar

1 Seat (I) 2″ x 18″ x 16″

Hickory

7 Spindles for back (J) 9⁄16″ diam. x 16″
2 Spindles under arm (K) 9⁄16″ diam. x 9½″

TWENTY-NINE

Chippendale Upholstered Side Chair

THOUGH UNADORNED WITH CARVING, AS ARE many chairs in this style, this simpler example bears the unmistakable stamp of the eighteenth-century master who created this style of furniture. Relatively speaking, it is a simplified version of the more ornately carved chairs usually associated with this category. The example shown in Fig. 1, which I own, is made of mahogany.

Only genuine, top-grade South American mahogany, which is heavy and quite dense in structure, should be used on the chair parts exposed to view. Because tacks must be driven into stretchers covered by upholstering materials, seat stretchers may be made of less dense, softer wood, such as yellow poplar.

To build the chair, first saw out two back legs, which require stock 2 inches thick for the front of the leg, and 4 inches wide for the sides. A full-sized pattern for these may be drawn from details given in Figs. 3 and 13. Shape and smooth these; then make layouts for mortises, and cut these where rear seat rail and stretchers are to be joined to them. Lay out and cut tenons at the upper ends to join the back legs to the chair-top rail.

Make a full-sized pattern of chair-top rail (C) from Fig. 13, and after shaping the stock to conform to the shape shown above Fig. 2, bandsaw the top to shape, and file and sand all surfaces. Notice that a small

FIG. 1

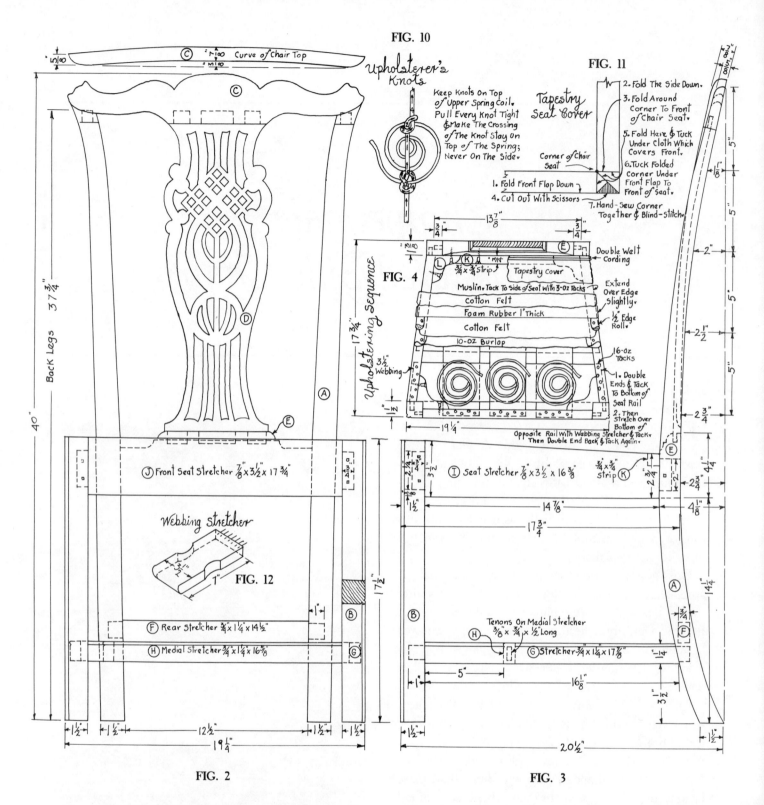

FIG. 10

Upholsterer's Knots

Keep Knots On Top of Upper Spring Coil. Pull Every Knot Tight & Make The Crossing of The Knot Stay On Top Of The Spring; Never On The Side.

FIG. 11

Tapestry Seat Cover

2. Fold The Side Down.
3. Fold Around Corner To Front of Chair Seat.
5. Fold Here & Tuck Under Cloth Which Covers Front.
6. Tuck Folded Corner Under Front Flap To Front of Seat.
7. Hand-Sew Corner Together & Blind-Stitch.

Corner of Chair Seat

1. Fold Front Flap Down
4. Cut Out With Scissors

Curve of Chair Top

Back Legs 37¾"
40"

FIG. 4

Upholstering Sequence
17¾"

13⅞"
¾" ¾"
Double Welt Cording
¾" x ¾" Strip
Tapestry Cover
Muslin. Tack To Side of Seat With 3-oz Tacks
Extend Over Edge Slightly.
Cotton Felt
Foam Rubber 1" Thick
½ Edge Roll.
Cotton Felt
10-oz Burlap
16-oz Tacks
3½" Webbing
1. Double Ends & Tack To Bottom of Seat Rail
2. Then Stretch Over Bottom of Opposite Rail with Webbing Stretcher & Tack. Then Double End Back & Tack Again.
1½"
19¼"

J Front Seat Stretcher ⅞" x 3½" x 17¾"

Webbing Stretcher

1" **FIG. 12**

F Rear Stretcher ¾" x 1¼" x 14½"
H Medial Stretcher ¾" x 1¼" x 16⅜"

17½"

B
G

I Seat Stretcher ⅞" x 3½" x 16⅜"
¾" x ¾" Strip K

14⅞"
17¾"

Tenons On Medial Stretcher ⅜" x ¾" x ½" Long

G Stretcher ¾" x 1¼" x 17⅞"

5"
16⅛"
20½"

14¼"

FIG. 2

FIG. 3

amount of shaping with carving tools must be done on the front at both ends of (C), which is clearly shown in Figs. 1 and 2.

Make seat rail (E) and stretcher (F) and then lay out and cut mortises into (C) and (E) where back legs and splat (D) must be joined to (C) and (E).

Make a full-sized pattern of the splat (D), from the layout shown in Fig. 13. This splat is curved in the middle from top to bottom, as shown in Fig. 13, but is flat crosswise. Stock ⅞ inch thick, 7 inches wide, and 21½ inches long must be used to make it, even though its thickness throughout is only ½ inch. The openings in it must be sawed out, either with a coping saw, or on a power jigsaw, and all sawed edges

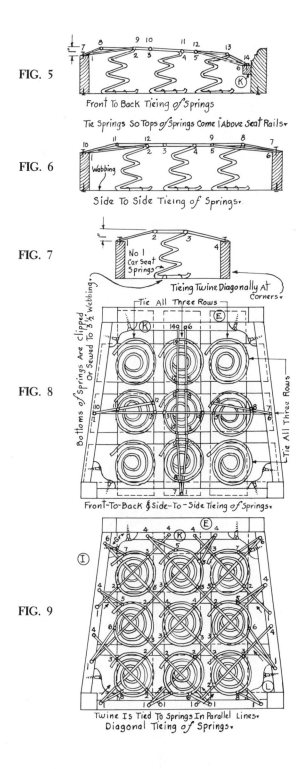

FIG. 5

Front To Back Tieing of Springs

Tie Springs So Tops of Springs Come ¼ Above Seat Rails.

FIG. 6

Side To Side Tieing of Springs.

FIG. 7

Tieing Twine Diagonally At Corners.

FIG. 8

Front-To-Back & Side-To-Side Tieing of Springs.

FIG. 9

Twine Is Tied To Springs In Parallel Lines.
Diagonal Tieing of Springs.

and the pieces properly fitted together, the chair back may be glued together.

Cut, square, and smooth stock for front legs (B), and for stretchers (G) and (H). Front legs and these stretchers have ¼-inch beads cut on one edge of each, as shown in Figs. 2 and 3. Notice the angle of the tenons cut on both ends of stretchers (I) and (G). They must be tilted at the angle shown in Fig. 4 so the chair front can be properly joined to the chair back. Seat stretchers (I) are made flush with outsides of front and back legs, while stretchers (G) are offset about ¼ inch where they are joined to the legs.

Strip (K) is fastened with wood screws to the inside of the rear seat rail, to hold tacks which are used to fasten spring twine there. (See Figs. 3, 5, 8, and 9.)

When the front legs, stretchers, and chair back have all been fitted together properly, the joints may be glued. Care must be taken when doing this to be sure the angles formed by side stretchers with chair back and chair front are exactly alike on both sides of the chair. Otherwise, gluing these together without carefully checking these angles could result in a lopsided chair frame. The four corner braces (L), inside the chair seat, if properly made, will help prevent this. They are put on so their upper sides come flush with the tops of the seat stretchers.

When glued up, and sanded smooth, the assembled chair should have its finish applied, after which the seat can be upholstered. Directions for upholstering the chair are given in Figs. 4, 5, 6, 7, 8, 9, 10, and 11.

To upholster the chair seat, use nine #1 car-seat springs, placing them upon the webbing, as shown in Figs. 8 and 9. Clip the bottoms of the springs to the webbing to hold them securely in place.

Using the best-grade spring twine obtainable, tie the springs first front-to-back, and then side-to-side, as shown in Fig. 8. Drive a 16-ounce tack partway into the front-seat stretcher at 1, Fig. 8. To this tack, tie the middle of a long piece of twine, and then tie it with an upholsterer's knot (Fig. 10) to the center of the top coil of the spring at 2. An upholsterer's knot is a square knot made by passing the twine over the top of the coiled spring, then looping it around the upper coil and back toward you under the wire.

carefully smoothed with files and abrasive papers. Chairs with openwork splats of this kind, if reproduced in furniture factories today, in all likelihood would be made of 3-ply laminated stock, but on the chair shown in Fig. 1 it is from a piece of ⅞-inch solid stock.

Once all joints on the chair back have been made,

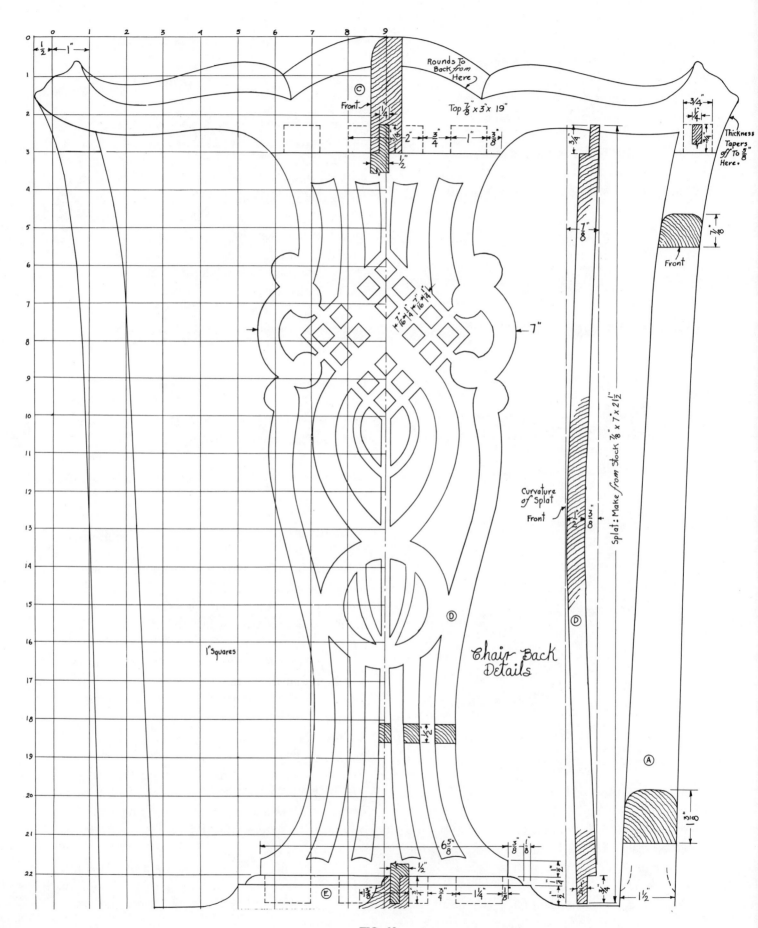

FIG. 13

From there loop it over the spring, then back under the string, thus forming a square knot. Pull this knot tight, being sure to keep loops of the knot on top of the wire, which increases the life of the twine, since the top of the knot will stand greater wear than would be the case if it were not done this way.

Proceed from 2 to 3, from 3 to 4, and so on to 6 at the rear where you drive another 16-ounce tack partly into the wood, and tie the end of the twine to it before driving the tack down all the way. Starting once more at 7 on the front stretcher with the other half of the twine, tie it from front to 14 in the back, in the same manner as you did the first half. Tie the two other rows of springs in the same manner. When tying the knot at 2 and 5, compress the spring so its top will be about 1 inch higher than the tops of the seat stretchers. Then when the spring is tied at 8, and from there back to 14, the upper coils of the springs can be pulled down so they too will be only 1 inch higher than the top of the seat frame.

Now tie the springs from side-to-side, as shown in Figs. 6 and 8. Start at 1 on the left seat-rail, and go from 1 to 6, where you tack it as you did the front-to-back twine. Then tie 7 to 9, and 10 to 12 in the same manner.

Next tie the springs diagonally, as shown in Fig. 9. Rows of twine should be kept parallel to each other, as in Fig. 9.

When the springs have been tied, tack a piece of 10-ounce burlap over them as shown in Fig. 4. When tacking burlap, muslin, upholstering material, or any other cloth to a seat, start tacking in the middle and tack from there to the ends on both sides. First slip-tack; that is, drive the tacks only partly into the wood so they can be moved if necessary to adjust the cloth to where it should go, and only then drive the tacks all the way into the wood.

Next tack strips of ½-inch edge-roll to the tops of front and side rails, as shown in Fig. 4. This helps keep filling material in place and prevents sharp edges of seat stretchers from wearing through the upholstering materials.

To fill and pad the seat, you can choose to use several different kinds of filling material. Curled hair was for many years considered best for this purpose,

but is now almost entirely replaced by rubberized hair, or by foam rubber, or by both. Certain advantages of using these as replacements should be noted here. The cost is usually a great deal less, and they may be held in place easily by gluing them to the burlap, wood, or other materials with rubberized spray glue which holds them in place more firmly. Afterward, edges of the filling material may be trimmed to shape, and corners trimmed to get good contour around the edges. Furthermore, since the filling material is glued fast, no holes or sunken areas will be left to be filled in with cotton, as would be the case where filling material like hair is held in place as it used to be with loops of twine.

Extend the foam rubber ¼ inch or more over the front and sides of the seat frame to form a well-rounded contour at the edges of the seat. Over the foam rubber put a layer or two of cotton felt, and hold this in place with a good grade of muslin tacked to the sides of the seat with 3-ounce tacks, as shown in Fig. 4.

Now fit and cut the upholstering material. Tapestry was used to upholster this chair, and it is a long-lasting appropriate material to use on this style chair.

Slip-tack the cover until corners are cut and fitted. Leave enough cloth on sides and front to tack it fast to the bottoms of the seat stretchers, and start tacking at the middle of each side. At the back of the chair the cloth is doubled under and tacked to strip (K), and then covered with double-welt cording covered with tapestry used on the seat. Such cording is made by using a special foot on an upholsterer's sewing machine. The cording is glued to the upholstering material to hold it in place.

At the front of the seat, some of the cloth should be trimmed off so it will not be too thick to tuck the side under the front. (See Fig. 11.) Such corners should be blind-stitched before the double-welt banding, shown on the chair, is put on around the bottom edges of the front and sides, and over the top of the seat at the back.

Finally, tack a piece of black cambric to the bottom of the chair seat to hide webbing, springs, etc., and to keep out dust and dirt.

BILL OF MATERIAL

Mahogany

2 Back legs (A) 2″ x 4″ x 37¾″
2 Front legs (B) 1½″ x 1½″ x 17½″
1 Chair top rail (C) 1¼″ x 3″ x 19″
1 Splat (D) ⅞″ x 7″ x 21½″
1 Rear seat rail (E) 1⅜″ x 4¼″ x 13⅞″
1 Rear stretcher at bottom (F) ¾″ x 1¼″ x 14½″
2 Side stretchers at bottom (G) ¾″ x 1¼″ x 17⅞″
1 Medial stretcher at bottom (H) ¾″ x 1¼″ x 16⅝″

Poplar, or some other Semihardwood like Soft Maple, which does not split easily

2 Side seat stretchers (I) ⅞″ x 3½″ x 16⅜″
1 Front seat stretcher (J) ⅞″ x 3½″ x 17¾″
1 Strip of wood inside back-seat stretcher (K) ¾″ x ¾″ x 10″
4 Corner braces inside seat (L) 1″ x 2″ x 4″

Index